Light for our Path
2010
A year of Bible reflections from around the world

IBRA
INTERNATIONAL BIBLE READING ASSOCIATION

Light for our path 2010

Edited by Kate Hughes

International Bible Reading Association

Light for our Path aims to build understanding and respect for a range of religious perspectives and approaches to living practised in the world today, and to help readers meet new challenges in their faith. Views expressed by contributors should not, however, be taken to reflect the views or policies of the Editor or the International Bible Reading Association.

The International Bible Reading Association's scheme of readings is listed monthly on the Christian Education website at www.christianeducation.org.uk/ibra_scheme.php and the full scheme for 2010 may be downloaded in English, Spanish and French.

Cover photograph by Alison Earey
Editor: Kate Hughes

Published by:
The International Bible Reading Association
1020 Bristol Road
Selly Oak
Birmingham B29 6LB
United Kingdom

Charity number 211542

ISBN 978-1-905893-16-4
ISSN 0140-8267

Designed and typeset by Christian Education
Printed and bound in the UK
by Mosaic Print Management: www.mosaicpm.com

Contents

Foreword

Dear Friends

Welcome to this year's *Light for our Path*. The readings are grouped into twenty-two themes, which are numbered and named in the Contents list on pages v and vi. Some of the themes concentrate on one book of the Bible, and the names of the books are also mentioned in the Contents list. Some readers value the continuous reading of a biblical book, others particularly value the insights provided by the wider themes which draw on both the Old and New Testaments; I hope that the group that prepares the readings has got the balance between the two types of theme about right this year.

In the last two years, for reasons of both economy and space, we have provided only six readings each week, with only one reading for the weekend, combining Saturday and Sunday. We have been listening to our readers' comments, and before next year's edition of *Light for our Path* will be rethinking this arrangement. However, for this year we suggest that you use the Introduction page for each week as your Sunday Bible study. Read the **Preparing for the week** section which introduces the theme, ponder the **Text for the week**, and think about the questions provided **For group discussion and personal thought**. You will then be well prepared to get the most out of your daily Bible study for the rest of the week.

This year *Light for our Path* has borrowed a feature from our sister publication, *Words for Today*, and provided a page of prayers you may like to use as you study the Word of God. Today's world has many problems: wars, climate change, financial difficulties, natural disasters. But by reading the Bible we can renew our relationship with God, discover more about him, and know that in any difficulty we can rely on his faithfulness and his promises. I hope that this year's *Light for our Path* will be a good companion for you as you negotiate the difficulties and opportunities of the days ahead.

Kate

Kate Hughes – Editor

Reading *Light for our Path*

Before reading, be quiet and remember that God is with you. Ask for his Holy Spirit to guide your reading.

If you do not have a Bible with you, you can work solely from *Light for our Path* by referring to the short Bible passage printed in bold type. (Only the editions printed in English have this.)

You can begin by reading just the short extract from the daily Bible passage that appears in the notes. Or you may prefer to read the full text of the daily passage from your Bible. The weekly notes use a variety of Bible translations, which are named at the beginning of each week. You may like to see how the extract in bold type compares with the same passage in your own Bible. And if your Bible mentions parallel passages in other places, comparing these passages can widen your thinking.

At the beginning of each week's notes there is a text for the week, which can be used as a focus for worship or reflection throughout the week.

When you finish each day's reading, spend a little time reflecting on it. What does it say to you about God? About yourself? About others? About the world in which we live? Has it changed your thinking? Does it suggest something that you should do? Then use the final prayer (marked with a cross), or any prayer of your own you need to make.

In the Introduction page for each week's notes there are questions and suggestions for group discussion or personal thought. These are only suggestions – your own reading and prayer may have drawn your attention to other aspects that you would like to explore further. The important thing is that you should let God speak to you through his Word, so that as you read steadily through the year you will be able to look back and see that you have got to know him better and have grown spiritually.

Prayers

Our Bibles before us, Lord, we ask you:
open our eyes to read your word,
open our ears to hear your word,
open our hearts to heed your word,
so that our lives may reflect the Living Word, Jesus Christ.

Ann Buckroyd

Leading God
you called Abraham out from his native land and sent him on a pilgrimage.
Liberating God,
you broke the tyrant's yoke and called Moses to deliver your people.
God of community,
you gave your people a new land and called David to create a nation.
Prophetic God,
you spoke to Amos in the market-place, calling his generation to justice;
> to Isaiah in the royal court, calling Israel to face the future;
> to Hosea at home, declaring your forgiving love.

Supporting God,
you comforted your people in exile and gave vision to Ezra and Nehemiah.
Suffering God,
you stood alongside Jesus in Gethsemene loss and Calvary desolation.
Boundless God,
you opened Paul's eyes and caused the infant Church to break barriers of race.
Travelling God,
you have ever walked with your Church to take us into your future.
God of every age and time,
for the Bible which offers us the story of your presence in every generation,
we give you grateful thanks.

Donald Hilton

Acknowledgements and abbreviations

We are grateful for permission to quote from the following Bible versions:

GNB   *Good News Bible*, 4th edition, published by The Bible Societies/HarperCollins, © American Bible Society, 1976.

NIV   *The Holy Bible, New International Version*, Hodder & Stoughton, © International Bible Society, 1980.

NLT   *Holy Bible, New Living Translation*, copyright 1996, 2004. Used by permission of Tyndale House Publishers, Inc., Wheaton, Illinois 60189. All rights reserved.

NJB   *The New Jerusalem Bible,* published by Darton, Longman & Todd, © Darton, Longman & Todd Ltd and Doubleday & Company, Inc., 1985.

NKJV *New King James Version,* © Thomas Nelson & Sons. Used by permission.

NRSV *New Revised Standard Version Bible*, published by HarperCollins, © Division of Christian Education of the National Council of the Churches of Christ in the United States of America, 1989.

IBRA would like to thank Ann Buckroyd and Donald Hilton for permission to include prayers on p.v.

Readings in Luke

1 The coming of the Messiah

Notes based on the *New International Version* by
Pedro Vieira Veiga

Pedro Vieira Veiga is a young pastor who lives in Rio de Janeiro with his family. He works at an independent Christian church in the neighbourhood of Ipanema, though his main responsibility lies with a small group from the nearby town of Petrópolis. He is also a psychology student.

Friday 1 January: Preparing for the week

The birth of a child is a moment that resonates profoundly within us all. No matter what, a child brings forth in all of us hope and wonderment. So it was with Jesus. As his father and mother stared at him, they could not help but be amazed. Yet as we read the story of how that baby came to be expected, of how he was born and of how he grew, we must consider the impact his life would come to have on our own.

Text for the week: *Luke 2:11*
'Today in the town of David a Saviour has been born to you; he is Christ the Lord.'

For group discussion and personal thought

• How can a great promise be both a blessing and a challenge? Have you experienced this in your life?
• To be thankful for unique blessings is one thing; to be thankful for the everyday, nearly invisible, miracles is quite another. How can we change our attitudes – and thus change our lives?
• Do you recall the day the Lord first came to you?

Saturday 2 January

Luke 1:1-25

A brand new opportunity

But the angel said to him: 'Do not be afraid, Zechariah; your prayer has been heard.'

(part of verse 13)

There is a feeling around New Year that fills our hearts with hope and great expectations – and prompts us to make all those New Year's resolutions. Resolutions are promises we make to ourselves, to be worked towards over time. In this narrative of the days that preceded our Lord's birth, we are told the story of a servant, Zechariah, who had been given the great honour of going into the Temple. That alone would have been enough to make that day special. However, when an angel tells him that his prayer has been heard – God's promise of a son would turn a long lost dream into reality – he doesn't know what to say or do. So he starts asking the angel for guarantees. Zechariah was being given a great and powerful dream – this unexpected son would be the one 'to make ready a people prepared for the Lord' yet he had trouble believing it. Sometimes we too are faced with new opportunities that may also seem a little too much to believe in or make happen. Still we keep setting higher goals for ourselves every year, most of which we end up forsaking. Why don't we try seeking God's plans and resolutions for our lives this year? Surely we can count on him should it become too great a challenge for us. The most valuable resolution is to believe.

† Lord, you are my brand new opportunity and your faithfulness lasts for ever. So I give myself up to you in this year and in the years to come. Help me to believe. Amen

Pedro Vieira Veiga

Readings in Luke

Sunday 3 January

Luke 1:26-45

Believing is receiving

'I am the Lord's servant', Mary answered. 'May it be to me as you have said.' Then the angel left her. . . . 'Blessed is she who has believed that what the Lord has said to her will be accomplished!'

(verses 38 and 45)

Have you ever looked back at your life and realised that most of it didn't actually happen as you had expected? Have you ever been taken aback by the surprises that come your way? Very often, we find ourselves trying to capture that turning point, that single moment when everything went upside down. Those were probably Mary's first thoughts on that day. Having a baby before getting married was already overwhelming, we might say, let alone giving birth to the Son of God. We can't really tell whether or not she hesitated at first, but we do know from this passage that she was surprised and a little – maybe a lot – scared. Nonetheless, after taking it all in – the angel, the greeting, the message and the promise – she acted on her faith and let God be God. And her faith changed not only the course of history, but our lives as well. Therefore, it's important that we acknowledge our feelings of surprise, fear, loneliness, anger, whichever they may be, so that we can fully surrender ourselves to God's power, act on our own faith and let him fulfil his promises in our lives. And he will. He always does.

† Dear Lord, even though sometimes I feel lost and confused, I need your help to believe at all costs. For I know you have never failed me. Amen

Readings in Luke   Pedro Vieira Veiga

Monday 4 January

Luke 1:46-56

A thankful heart

And Mary said:
'My soul praises the LORD
and my spirit rejoices in God my Saviour.'

(verses 46-47)

Do you remember the last time you thanked God for something? Not in a relieved 'thank God' kind of way, but really thanking him and rejoicing in him? We all need to revisit our hearts daily and find those moments in which we have nothing to say, but 'Thank you, Lord'. It is wonderful to realise that grateful thoughts can easily lead to a grateful life. In this passage, Mary praises the Lord for the blessing she had just been given, but she can't stop there. She goes on and on thinking of how the world would change, how her people would be eternally blessed through her own gift. She starts thanking God for the many blessings that will come from that. Her heart is filled with such gratitude that her words could only fall short of expressing such feelings. Sometimes we put so much effort into waiting for something big to happen in our lives that we take for granted the daily blessings we are given. We fail to see and recognise God's hand in the small miracles that keep us alive. We don't make time to just sit back, look out of the window and pray with a thankful heart. Even though sometimes it feels as if we have nothing to be thankful for, his constant love is guiding us at all times.

† Father, I thank you for my life, for rescuing me, for keeping me safe. You are God, my saviour, and my spirit rejoices in you.

Pedro Vieira Veiga

Readings in Luke

Tuesday 5 January

Luke 1:57-80

What are you going to be?

Everyone who heard this wondered about it, asking, 'What then is this child going to be?' For the Lord's hand was with him.

(verse 66)

This passage is beautiful and inspiring. The birth of a child always is. This story, however, contains a few peculiarities that make it even more amazing, such as the way Zechariah and Elizabeth decide on the name of the child, a name no one would expect, and how the father is given his voice back. It is a beautiful story.

But the question remains unanswered: 'What is this child going to be?' A question we have all asked or heard before. The future of a person is always intriguing, to say the least. As adults, we worry about our future and about the generations to come. Every single day we are faced with questions about what lies before us, especially during these first days of the year. However, the days go by and sometimes our answers about tomorrow become mere intentions or errands to be run some other time. We never stop worrying. But the answer to the question about John is unique: 'For the Lord's hand was with him.' It sounds like a promise, a covenant. That promise wasn't just for John. It extends to us as we accept Jesus as our Lord and Saviour. We can make as many plans as we like, as long as we never forget that his hand is with us. And that plans can be changed.

† God, my life is in your hands, and so are my plans for tomorrow and the days to come. Take my worries and concerns, for I believe in your love. Amen

Readings in Luke   Pedro Vieira Veiga

Wednesday 6 January

Luke 2:1-14

Epiphany

But the angel said to them, 'Do not be afraid. I bring you good news of great joy that will be for all the people. Today in the town of David a Saviour has been born to you; he is Christ the Lord. This will be a sign to you: You will find a baby wrapped in cloths and lying in a manger.'

(verses 10-12)

This is the day on which we celebrate the wise men finding Jesus by following that shining star. But what does Epiphany mean? It is the Greek word for 'to show, to manifest'. This day is celebrated as the day God manifested himself in human form.

If you had witnessed that moment, can you imagine your feelings? That little baby, sleeping in poor conditions, was the Son of God, God himself incarnate. What would it have meant to see God show himself in that manner? Would you have believed it was him? Can you remember the first day you believed? For that was the day God manifested himself to you. 'A Saviour has been born to you; he is Christ the Lord.' That man, who lived and suffered and died because of his decision to love above all else, to listen to those who weren't even allowed to speak, and to give himself to those who weren't even acknowledged as human beings, that man gave us life that day. Make this a day of celebration in your calendar, a day to revisit that moment when Jesus was born in you.

† Dear God, we thank you for making yourself known to us in so many different ways, and for always loving us first. Amen

Pedro Vieira Veiga

Readings in Luke

Thursday 7 January

Luke 2:15-24

Put your mouth where your heart is

When they had seen him, they spread the word concerning what had been told them about this child, and all who heard it were amazed at what the shepherds said to them.

(verses 17-18)

Talking about someone is what makes them famous. Be it good or bad, the more publicity people get, the bigger their fame. Every once in a while, we find ourselves 'commenting' on what they wore, where they ate, who they married, and so on. We might even know people who talk about nothing else except the lives of others.

This passage tells us of something similar – but not quite the same. The shepherds did talk about what they had heard and seen, but it wasn't out of curiosity. It was out of amazement and hope. How many people have amazed you so much that you couldn't stop talking about them? How many of them never failed you? We are not responsible for making people believe in how we feel about God, but we should let them know about what he feels for us. Isn't that what amazed us in the first place? There are many gifted people who have become famous for their gifts. But the giver of those gifts, the giver of love and life, how often do we get to talk about him? Let your mouth speak of what fills your heart.

† Dear God, help me to be the bearer of your great news through my words and actions. Let the world be filled with peace as my life has been. Amen

Readings in Luke   Pedro Vieira Veiga

Friday 8 January

Luke 2:25-40

Living and learning

And the child grew and became strong; he was filled with wisdom, and the grace of God was upon him.

(verse 40)

This week has been an opportunity to learn from Jesus' birth in the same way that we try to learn from his life. This passage takes us back to the day when Jesus was presented in the Temple, to his consecration. The rest of his early childhood is summarised in this last verse. What can we learn from it? Jesus grew. The child grew. The fears, the feelings, the life we experience as children change as we grow, and it was the same for him. He became strong both physically and intellectually, for he was filled with wisdom. As we become adults we are also expected to take care of our bodies, minds and souls.

Many people make the mistake of believing that God doesn't care about what we look like on the outside. That is true only to a certain point. Our bodies and minds are the temple of God. Although he doesn't ask us all to look like fashion models or speak like professors, it is important that we live healthy lives, taking care of what he has entrusted to us, for his grace will always be upon us. The better we live, the more open our spirits will be to see the perfection in God's creation.

† Heavenly Father, I praise your name for the life you have given me and all your creation. May I always honour you by caring for both. Amen

Pedro Vieira Veiga

Readings in Luke

Saturday 9 January

Luke 2:41-52

Become what you are

'Why were you searching for me?' he asked. 'Didn't you know I had to be in my Father's house?' But they did not understand what he was saying to them.'

(verses 49-50)

Many people spend a lot of time trying to figure out what they are going to do next; others keep wondering if they have already got everything they were supposed to get out of life; and some keep questioning themselves about their lives and plans, whether they have succeeded or not. Of course there are those who simply don't care. Where do you fit in? In one of these groups? In all of them? In none? Whenever a child is born, its future becomes one of its parents' great concerns. The child's success in life is, to some extent, its own. Mary and Joseph probably asked themselves many times about Jesus' future. Even though they had received the promise from the angel, they must still have worried in their hearts. Can you relate to those feelings? Sometimes being given a promise doesn't automatically make our faith stronger. It takes a lot of time, patience and effort. The same thing happens to us when we wonder about the future. God's plans and instructions are overshadowed by our fears, and we feel as if we can't understand what he's saying. Yet we must not forget that we are what God made us to be. Praying, believing, trying, failing and succeeding these are all necessary, but God's grace is with us no matter what.

† Dear Father, help me become what you made me to be and I'll serve you all my life. Amen

Readings in Luke   Pedro Vieira Veiga

The economy of God

1 The economy of grace

Notes based on the *New Revised Standard Version* by
Helen van Koevering

Helen has lived and worked in northern Mozambique for 14 years. In recent years she has worked as an ordained priest in training clergy and lay women for ministry; more recently she has also begun to work with a forestry company whose local partner is her church, the Anglican Church of the Diocese of Niassa.

Sunday 10 January: Preparing for the week

The English word 'economy' derives from the Greek word *oikonomia*, related to household, inhabited earth and ecology. *Oikonomia* is used in the New Testament epistles to refer to God's offer of salvation in Christ, which raises the question of the tension between the economy of God and that of the world. The latter may be materialistic, divisive, atheistic and idolatrous in its norms and behaviours, whereas the former meaning encompasses inclusion, unity, generosity, justice and gift. The ground rules for the economy of God are different, motivated by love, grace and overflowing generosity. As someone once said, the economy of the world asks, 'What have you done on earth to increase the GNP?', whilst the economy of God asks, 'What have you done to the least of these our sisters and brothers?'

Text for the week: *Ephesians 2:8-10*

By grace you have been saved through faith, and this is not your own doing; it is the gift of God . . . For we are what he has made us, created in Christ Jesus for good works, which God prepared beforehand to be our way of life.

For group discussion and personal thought

- Does your life balance? Does what you've done to increase the GNP balance what you've done to the least?
- Bonhoeffer said that grace is not earned, but it is costly. In your experience, what does he mean?

Monday 11 January

Ephesians 2:1-10

A liturgy of life

For by grace you have been saved through faith, and this is not your own doing; it is the gift of God . . . For we are what he has made us, created in Christ Jesus for good works, which God prepared before-hand to be our way of life.

(verses 8 and 10)

Here is laid out for us a liturgy of life in Christ Jesus. Paul had spoken of Christ being raised up and enthroned with God (Ephesians 1:20), and of faith versus works in Romans (3:28); here we read an extension of those thoughts. Paul brings us to an understanding of grace as the heart of the economy of God, grace being God's rich kindness towards us, God's gift to us. It is grace, in this reading, that has saved us, shifting from Paul's description of justification by faith apart from the works of the law, to this – salvation is the result of God's gift alone. It is this grace that has formed us for good works, works that God prepared for us to be our way of life. It is this grace that is at the centre of our being and works in this world. With this in mind, perhaps that buzz phrase, 'What would Jesus do?', which is used so often among Christian young people, should rather read 'What has Jesus prepared for me to be and do?' A bit more wordy, but perhaps a bit closer to the liturgy of life that Ephesians gives us.

† Lord, your grace is overwhelming, freely given and abundant. Remind me of that when I make decisions today, when I choose what I do and how I should respond. Your grace is all I need. Amen

The economy of God   Helen van Koevering

Tuesday 12 January
Philippians 4:4-9

Economics of thankfulness

Finally, beloved, whatever is true, whatever is honourable, whatever is just, whatever is pure, whatever is pleasing, whatever is commendable, if there is any excellence and if there is anything worthy of praise, think about these things . . . and the God of peace will be with you.

(verse 8 and part of verse 9)

I recently went to a wonderful party for a church member here in Mozambique! Señor Buanacaia celebrated his seventieth birthday, sur-rounded by his family and many friends. He and his family had clearly saved for this event, and there was an abundance of food and bottles of wine on each table. Everyone wore their best capulanas (wrap cloths), and a table was laden with gifts. Each gift was celebrated with dancing, singing and kisses, led by Señor Buanacaia and his eldest daughter. The best part was his speech: he listed all the events of his life, good and bad, the births of his children and the death of his wife, the past year of bad health and the health of today. All this was given with thanks to God. Even for the bad times, he thanked God for all he had learnt, for God's justice and care, for God's peace. He had us laughing and deeply moved, listening and reflecting on our own life's journey. Truly, a grateful heart, one that has learnt thankfulness, gives life. As we give out in thankfulness, the economics of God means that we receive back life abundantly for ourselves and for those around us.

† Jesus, we can learn so much from the poor, whose perspective of the world's economy is different because they are not included. Open my eyes and my heart to see and know you, and to be thankful that you love me so much that you give me your peace. Amen

Helen van Koevering   The economy of God

Wednesday 13 January

Philippians 2:5 11

Self-emptying economics

The economy of God is not about self-aggrandisement, satisfying all our wants, or keeping up with the neighbours. It is not about giving us more leisure time, making sure we have the best in life, or getting us the best deals. It is not about spending our savings at Christmas on loved ones, nor about giving some money to a charity. It is all about having the mind of Christ. . .

> *who, though he was in the form of God,*
> *did not regard equality with God*
> *as something to be exploited,*
> *but emptied himself,*
> *taking the form of a slave,*
> *being born in human likeness.*
> *And being found in human form,*
> *he humbled himself*
> *and became obedient to the point of death –*
> *even death on a cross.*

(verses 6-8)

The economy of God has the self-emptying quality of Christ's life. The building up of others, helping the least (or even our neighbours), choosing to buy and eat what is good for the earth and the poorest, giving your best, knowing when enough is plenty, seeking to serve rather than be served – these are qualities coming from Christ's lived example, as relevant and radical today as then. These are signs of the kingdom of God that surrounds us, but whose standards and norms we choose daily.

† Father, may your kingdom come and your will be done here on earth as it is in heaven. May the life that Jesus showed us be the life that we choose and live, by your grace and in your love. Amen

The economy of God   Helen van Koevering

Thursday 14 January

2 Corinthians 8:1-15

Generous economics

[T]hey voluntarily gave according to their means, and even beyond their means, begging us earnestly for the privilege of sharing in this ministry to the saints – and this, not merely as we expected; they gave themselves first to the Lord and, by the will of God, to us.

(part of verse 3, and verses 4-5)

The grace of God granted to the churches of Macedonia is offered today around the world. Padre Luis has a real gift for teaching that stewardship is vital in the evangelistic witness of the church here in Mozambique. He teaches this generosity to some of the poorest congregations in our diocese, and his own church represents the reality of God's generosity in God's people. Where there was strife and dissension, the generosity that Padre Luis has shown and taught has turned them into a community generous in their speech, actions and hospitality. When Padre Luis ran a week-long stewardship workshop, the last service was remarkable – he encouraged people to be generous in their love of God and in their care for the poorest in the community, and they gave their second shirt, or their second pair of shoes, along with money, right there in the service! A visitor from a development organisation in Angola turned to me and said, with tears running down his face, 'The same spirit that is at work in Angola is at work here!' What is the key to this generosity that grows the church? Padre Luis teaches that abundant generosity comes from first giving ourselves to the Lord, and allowing God's grace to multiply that generosity to others. Just as today's reading tells us.

† Lord, open my heart to give myself more and more to you, that I may know your abundant generosity towards me, and show it to the world. Amen

Helen van Koevering

The economy of God

Friday 15 January

1 John 3:16-24

Economics of love

How does God's love abide in anyone who has the world's goods and sees a brother or sister in need and yet refuses help? Little children, let us love, not in word or speech, but in truth and action.

(verses 17-18)

Love, in God's economy, is a verb. The author of 1 John insists that belief in Jesus means showing love to fellow believers – that's what it means to love in truth. When we help another, respond to a need, serve another, share peace with another, we are doing God's work of love. The truth has been given freely to us, by grace, and we have that grace to call on in order to live the life to which Jesus calls us, and which pleases him. There is no excuse not to love others when the power to love is given to us. It comes down to choice: choosing to live either within God's economy of love in action, a love given so that we might give, or within a love that comes only with fine sounding words. Note that this message is addressed to 'little children' (verse 18). This is not a condescending adult or demanding teacher, but a disciple of Christ addressing newer disciples who still have much to learn and who need to hear the message clearly and deliberately: believe in Jesus Christ and love one another. Believing and loving allows space for the Spirit of Jesus to abide in us, to do Christ's work and to know God. That is the exchange which is the economy of God.

† Lord Jesus, I am still a child in the ways of God, and need to learn. Be my patient companion, my loving friend, and show me how to love others as you would love. Amen

The economy of God   Helen van Koevering

Saturday 16 January

1 Peter 3:13 – 4:6

Timeless economy

For Christ also suffered for sins once for all, the righteous for the unrighteous, in order to bring you to God . . . You have already spent enough time in doing what the Gentiles like to do ... But they will have to give an accounting to him who stands ready to judge the living and the dead.

(chapter 3, part of verse 18, and chapter 4, part of verse 3, and verse 5)

The economy of the world is focused on present gratification, today's news, and lives of finite time. In God's economy all life is timeless. The message of salvation, and the grace that saves, came at a pivotal point in the history of the world, when the Son of God was born as a man. Christ's love in action, his death and resurrection, were for all people in all times and places, and baptism now speaks sacramentally of that same timeless grace that is God's economy. Baptism marks the beginning of a journey through life and beyond it, even to the time when all of us will stand before God. How our earthly time is used within this timelessness reveals who we truly are: followers of Christ, living within the economy of God, with a vision of the future glory of heaven; or followers of the world's economy, the present age around us. Today's reading says that we have wasted enough time not focusing on the goodness of God, so let's not waste any more. Be ready, don't fear and know you are blessed!

† Lord, teach me about your economy – about generosity, giving, thankfulness and love – as I go about my life this weekend and look towards the new week. Thank you that you are with us always to show us your way, even to the end of the age. Amen

Helen van Koevering

The economy of God

The economy of God

2 The economy of fools

Notes based on the *New International Version* by
Peter Ibison

Married with two children, Peter is a member of the Anglican Church in Buckinghamshire, where he lives. He is studying with the Open Theological College and works in the telecommunications industry.

Sunday 17 January: Preparing for the week

Life can be hectic at times and anxiety can take its grip on our lives. It is at such times that we easily lose sight of eternity as the demands of the present absorb all our energies. Our passages this week serve to give us fresh perspectives when life is tough.

Text for the week: *1 Corinthians 7:31*
This world in its present form is passing away.

For group discussion and personal thought

• What hinders you from having an eternal perspective as you go about everyday activities?

• Jesus warns about our hearts being weighed down with dissipation and the anxieties of life. What is most likely to cause your heart to be pulled in different directions?

• What practical measures can you take to enable change to occur in such cases?

Monday 18 January

1 Corinthians 1:18-25

Worldly wisdom, godly wisdom

The apostle Paul wrote his letter to the Corinthians from Ephesus, addressing specific abuses in the church, including immorality and litigation amongst believers. However, his first concern was for disunity, a failing in the church that grieves the heart of God deeply.

As we begin the week, there are two observations about the Early Church that will help us to avoid the pitfalls of disunity. First, the church in Corinth struggled with unity because it was engaged in spiritual 'one-upmanship' – one group followed Paul, another Apollos, another Cephas and yet another Christ. Taken captive by the cult of personality, they sought to elevate those who offered wisdom, oratory skill or philosophical insights. Whenever the church cares more about the medium than the message, disunity will result.

Second, the church in Corinth saw its own human strivings as a means of reaching God. The Greeks were particularly proud of their heritage of wisdom and learning. But

Has not God made foolish the wisdom of the world?

(part of verse 20)

A foolishness that included using simple fishermen with an uncomplicated message to confound the authorities.

For the Greeks the issue was that of wisdom: our source of pride may lie elsewhere. Beware of the temptation to lean on such sources of confidence in our own standing before God, for where we lean on the things of this world, comparisons result and disunity quickly follows.

---

† Lord, you say that if anybody lacks wisdom, they should ask. Lord, give me wisdom today that I may know the route to take and have the courage and determination to take it. Amen

Peter Ibison   The economy of God

Tuesday 19 January

Philippians 3:4b-14

Worldly confidence, godly confidence

The apostle Paul wrote this letter to the Philippians while he was in prison in Rome, around 12 years after he had first visited Philippi. He warns the church to be on its guard against Jewish persecutors. These men may have been tempted to say of Paul, 'You follow Christ and do not know what it means to be a Jew.' Paul, in response, sets out his CV and it looks very impressive. He cites seven sources of confidence that he could, if he chose, draw from in his standing before God (verses 5-6): everything from being circumcised to persecuting the church. But in our relationship with God our earthly credentials do not help us, in fact reliance on them actually hinders us in our standing before God. Paul says,

I consider them rubbish, that I may gain Christ and be found in him, not having a righteousness of my own that comes from the law, but that which is through faith in Christ – the righteousness that comes from God and is by faith.

(part of verse 8, and verse 9)

It is as if Paul is saying, 'If I relied on my credentials I would not be relying on Christ – I needed to make a choice between the two.' If we examine our hearts and ask God to show us our own sources of confidence, what will be revealed? Is our confidence in our denominational membership, our service in the community, our wealth, education or intellect – or in God? This is the first step in growth. The second is to place our trust fully in Christ.

---

† Lord, help me to understand where my confidence lies. Forgive me when I place my confidence in earthly things – and help me to look instead to you as my rock, my shelter and my saviour.

The economy of God   Peter Ibison

Wednesday 20 January
James 5:13-20

The power of prayer to bring change

Today's passage talks about prayer and raises a number of questions:

- Why do we confess our sins? Sin erects two barriers: between human beings, and between human beings and God. Confession's primary concern must always be the benefit of the person wronged – and, if possible, the restoration of relationship.

- To whom do we confess our sins? James does not imply any hierarchy:

Confess your sins to each other and pray for each other so that you may be healed. The prayer of the righteous is powerful and effective.

(verse 16)

We are all sinners and in need of restorative grace: parents need to ask forgiveness from their children as well as children from parents, managers from their workers as well as workers from managers.

- What was Elijah's prayer? The text of 1 Kings 17-18 does not record it, only that Elijah proclaimed a drought to King Ahab, which lasted over two years, and later appeared again to Ahab and proclaimed that heavy rain was on its way. But his prayer is implicit in the text – he stood before the Lord and proclaimed a drought and bowed low to the ground as he waited on the Lord for rain.

- What makes our prayer powerful and effective? Speaking aloud? Praying in the heart? Standing? Bowing low? Our earnestness? Scripture talks more of the grace of a loving heavenly Father in answering prayer – that is where our reliance should be.

† Father, thank you for prayer, for being a God who answers our prayer, a God to whom we can bring our failings and ask for forgiveness. Stir within me a desire for worthy things as I pray to you and ask you to act. Amen

Peter Ibison

The economy of God

Thursday 21 January

Romans 8:22-27

Creation's decay, creation's liberation

From the moment sin entered the world, the whole of creation has been subject to decay – but only for a season. The apostle Paul speaks of creation groaning like a woman in childbirth, waiting to be freed from the decay that first became a reality in the Garden of Eden. Creation itself seems eager for liberation and waits for the redemption of those who follow Christ as a sign of the dawning of a new age:

The creation waits in eager expectation for the sons of God to be revealed.

(verse 19)

Creation can serve as a reminder that the best is yet to come. In spite of the many beautiful things in the world, the inescapable reality is that 'all is not as it ought to be'. Creation is subject to decay; we are subject to sinful desires. Creation waits and groans; so do we. Creation will be renewed; we will be redeemed. Our futures are entwined. We also need to raise our gaze from the finite to the eternal. Like someone walking a long distance, we need to focus on a point on the horizon, perhaps a distant mountain, by which to navigate. If we focus on our ultimate destination – the promise of heaven and life with our Saviour – we will get life's difficulties and sufferings into perspective and not be overwhelmed by them. Fixing our gaze on the eternal, we hope for what we do not yet have and, as Paul reminds us, 'we wait for it patiently' (verse 25).

† Lord, thank you for the beauty and gift of creation. Help me to appreciate all you have given but not to think that this is all there is. Thank you for today's reminder that the best is yet to come.

The economy of God

Peter Ibison

Friday 22 January
Luke 16:19-31

Wealth and poverty

Today's reading describes two men: an unnamed rich one and a poor one called Lazarus. The rich man was clothed in purple (a costly dye extracted from shellfish) and fine linen, and feasted happily every day. He lived a life of extravagance and self-indulgence and failed to 'do good, be rich in good deeds and be generous and willing to share' (1 Timothy 6:18). He was not deliberately cruel to Lazarus – he simply failed to notice him. Lazarus on the other hand was a hungry man who lived in abject poverty and extreme physical discomfort. Helpless, he didn't even have the strength to ward off the dogs that pestered him. One man had all he wanted; the other had nothing. In the economy of God, their fate was equally different:

'Son, remember that in your lifetime you received your good things, while Lazarus received bad things, but now he is comforted here and you are in agony.'

(verse 25)

There is a beautiful contrast here: a man who was once laid at the gate to beg was now carried by angels to sit at Abraham's side. The rich man pleads for pity and asks for Lazarus to bring him relief – still expecting Lazarus to serve his needs. Earthly realities no longer apply, however, and a great chasm is fixed between the two men. Today's is a sobering passage; as one of its many lessons, let us be people who notice the needs of others. Let us not be seduced by wealth (in the 'here and now') but instead be people who are generous and willing to share.

† Lord, open my eyes to see the needs around me. Open my ears to hear the cries of the needy. Open my heart to respond with love and compassion. Amen

Peter Ibison   The economy of God

Saturday 23 January

1 Corinthians 7:29-31

Perspectives on time

The church in Corinth faced both pressures and temptations from an immoral world. The city was renowned for its immorality – the Greek verb 'to Corinthianise' meant to practise sexual immorality. The church was in crisis – and persecution lay around the corner. In times of crisis, our true values are brought into sharp focus and it is for this reason that Paul talks about the need to accept new attitudes towards marriage, human emotions and material possessions. His message is that we ought not to be preoccupied with this world, which 'in its present form is passing away' (verse 31).

> [T]he time is short. From now on those who have wives should live as though they had none; those who mourn as if they did not; those who are happy, as if they were not.

> (part of verses 29-30)

Why did Paul give such extreme commands, especially as elsewhere he holds marriage in great honour? Some have argued that Paul gave this instruction because he believed the second coming was imminent. Others have pointed to the fact that Corinth was facing an extreme crisis that called for drastic measures. However, there is a third possibility. Paul may have deliberately over-emphasised his point in order to grab the people's attention. He is not saying that we should not express emotions such as grief and happiness, but that we need to be mindful of the transience of this life in all we do. 'Live for eternity's values' is Paul's message. We need to remind ourselves that this world will pass, and that a new world will come.

---

† Lord, I offer the prayer that Moses prayed: 'Teach us to number our days aright that we may gain a heart of wisdom'. Amen

(Psalm 90:12)

The economy of God   Peter Ibison

Readings in Luke

2 Beginnings

Notes based on the *New Revised Standard Version* by
John Holder

John Holder was born in Barbados and for several years was Deputy
Principal of Codrington College, the Anglican theological college for the
province of the West Indies. He is now Anglican Bishop of Barbados,
and is married with one son.

Sunday 24 January : Preparing for the week

The words running through this week's readings from Luke's Gospel are the
text for the week: Prepare the way of the Lord! The week starts with John
the Baptist, the forerunner, the one who goes before to alert people to the
important person following behind. But Jesus is also preparing himself for
his future ministry, with his time alone in the wilderness and his declaration
in the Nazareth synagogue.

Text for the week: *Luke 3:4*
Prepare the way of the Lord.

For group discussion and personal thought

• How can you prepare the way of the Lord for those you meet, to make
it easier for them to come into contact with him?
• How can you prepare yourself to do the Lord's work more effectively?

Monday 25 January

Luke 3:1-14

The ministry of John the Baptist

In today's reading we are introduced to the ministry of John the Baptist. Luke places his ministry in the historical context of the Roman conquest and occupation of Palestine, which was supported by Herod and the house of the High Priest. It is into this land controlled by a seemingly invincible military power that the message of John bursts forth. Luke uses the words of Second Isaiah to describe the atmosphere of excitement and great anticipation. It is the time of

The voice of one crying out in the wilderness
'Prepare the way of the Lord.'

(part of verse 4)

According to Luke, the oppressive power of Rome could not in any way halt or hinder the awesome power of God that was at work in the ministry of John the Baptist. God's intervention will initiate a dramatic reversal. The ultimate purpose of it all is the salvation of God's people. Luke portrays the ministry of John the Baptist, and that of Jesus, as one of hope for the people of God in a situation where hope was desperately needed. They affirmed that God was still present, at work and in charge of his people and his world. The scourge of HIV/AIDS, war, poverty, and natural disasters may all lead us to ask the same sorts of question that were probably asked by those who heard Isaiah, and by those who listened to John the Baptist and Jesus. The response now is still the same: In spite of adverse conditions, it is still possible to experience the salvation of God.

† O God, give us hope in conditions that deny and destroy hope.

John Holder

Tuesday 26 January

Luke 3:15-22

Preparing for the ministry of Jesus

The question about identity that surfaces in this passage comes amid great expectations. The Messiah, it was believed, was on his way to relieve the plight of the Jewish people. Could John the Baptist be this long-expected agent of God's salvation? John makes his identity clear:

John answered all of them by saying, 'I baptize you with water; but one who is more powerful than I is coming; I am not worthy to untie the thong of his sandals. He will baptize you with the Holy Spirit and fire.

(verse 16)

There is no secret about the identity of John the Baptist. He shifts the focus away from himself and points to the one who will correct all that is going wrong. John uses a farming image to emphasise the radical nature of this act of purification (verse 17). Present conditions are incompatible with the presence of the Messiah. The belief that God corrects what is wrong is one of the most fundamental convictions of the Bible. We may not always know God's time, or how he will achieve it, but we live with the hope of Jesus, John the Baptist, Luke and the church, that conditions that do not reflect the love, care and compassion of God are still under God's watch and control. We are called to work to remove these conditions, and the reference to Herod in verse 19 reminds us that there were obstacles even for the Messiah's forerunner. But the Christian hope is that God's power is never diminished by the obstacles. Herod is simply a name in history; Jesus is our living Saviour.

† O God, strengthen our faith to withstand the obstacles we meet in life.

John Holder

Readings in Luke

Wednesday 27 January

Luke 3:23-38

Jesus' pedigree

Jesus was about thirty years old when he began his ministry. He was the son (as was thought) of Joseph son of Heli.

(verse 23)

This passage is seldom read in church – just a boring collection of names. But there is more to it than meets the eye. Luke uses it to support the conviction that Jesus had a direct link to God that passed through his ancestors to his first ancestor Adam. It reflects the church's conviction that Jesus is both human and divine. He was not a 'bolt out of the blue'. As the culmination of God's plan, Jesus possessed lineage and ancestry, he had a history, a history that led back to God. God was therefore at work at every point of this history, preparing for the entry of his son, Jesus, the Messiah, into the world. Those listed are the links in the chain that leads from God through Adam to Jesus. This list is more than a collection of historic names; it is the story of how God uses ordinary human beings to carry out his work in the world. The long list of Jesus' ancestors is not impressive: they were ordinary people through whom God worked to achieve an extraordinary event. Like them, we can hope that God will also use us for his purpose. Class, race and gender will not impede him in his work of bringing salvation through ordinary people. It is this message, brim-full of hope for my own condition, that allows me to see myself as an instrument of God's grace in his world. It says that God can use whosoever he wills, even me, to carry out his acts of grace and salvation.

† O God, make me an instrument of your salvation.

Readings in Luke

John Holder

Thursday 28 January
Luke 4:1-15

Jesus prepares himself for ministry

The story of Jesus' temptations leads us into the heart of another struggle about identity – this time, the identity of Jesus. If he is the Son of God, what does this mean for his ministry and his future? In today's episode, he wrestles with some of the options for his ministry. Should he fulfil his own need for food, or even use it to win the crowds? But his response is:

'It is written, "One does not live by bread alone".'

(part of verse 4)

Food remains the basic commodity for survival, and we must ensure in our own day that we do not exploit other people through our control of food. Jesus could also acquire power by the wrong means, by worshipping the devil and so embracing and supporting evil, but he insists that this was not his way to go:

'Worship the Lord your God,
and serve only him.'

(part of verse 8)

He could perform spectacular feats like leaping from the temple and so hold the crowd in the palm of his hands. But this is not the way to go:

Do not put the Lord your God to the test.'

(part of verse 12)

Jesus comes through this wrestling match unscathed. He returns to his home in Galilee 'in the power of the Spirit', equipped to perform his ministry. Like Jesus, we can be bombarded with temptations. Like him, we may be desperate to satisfy our physical needs – but this story reminds us that we must never compromise our spiritual well-being for short-term personal gain.

---

† O God, give us the courage to deal with our temptations and conquer them.

John Holder

Readings in Luke

Friday 29 January

Luke 4:16-30

An uncomfortable sermon

This passage places Jesus at the religious heart of his people. He is in a synagogue and has an important role in the worship, reading and expounding the scriptures. He is portrayed as a devout Jew and an educated rabbi. His text is from the prophet known as Third Isaiah, and is a mandate to liberate the oppressed and downtrodden. Jesus here adopts the mandate. His ministry is presented as one of liberation, reflecting Luke's special interest in Jesus' concern for the poor and oppressed. Isaiah identifies three categories of people: the poor, the captives and the oppressed represent those who were pushed to the fringes of society and depend on others for their survival. However, in this passage they are the ones who will experience God's special work of salvation in Jesus. The high point of the liberation mandate adopted by Jesus comes at the end·

'He has sent me . . .
to proclaim the year of the Lord's favour.'

(part of verse 18, and verse 19)

The 'year of the Lord' is the Jubilee year of the Old Testament, when the Jews were called upon to intervene in the lives of the poor in order to restore them to a position in the community that would ensure their survival. Here Jesus is initiating this type of intervention. His task is to address the condition of the marginalised in order to assure them of their place in the kingdom of God. The mandate of Jesus is that of the Church, and indeed of every Christian. We still need to hear the call to work for the poor and marginalised. How can you respond to this call in your community?

† O God, help us to be like our Lord, a voice for the poor and marginalised.

Saturday 30 January

Luke 4:31-44

An encounter with evil

In this passage Jesus is confronted with a number of conditions that make us less than what God wants us to be. We believe that God wants each of us to enjoy the best health. We also know, however, that sickness and other conditions can rob us of this great experience. The story in verses 31-37 is of a man who is described as having 'the spirit of an unclean demon' – probably a mental condition. However, he was able to see in Jesus what others probably could not see, even if at first he saw Jesus as a threat:

'I know who you are, the Holy One of God.'

(part of verse 34)

Did he think that Jesus would chase him out of the synagogue? His encounter with Jesus returns him to a normal life as a member of his community, to whom others could easily relate. He does not have to hide away or be scared. The story portrays Jesus as a source of life and wholeness, and this picture is repeated in the healing of Simon's mother-in-law (verses 38-39) and in the description of the many who were brought to Jesus and healed (verses 40-41). At the very heart of the message of Jesus are these powerful acts of healing and the restoration of wholeness. This should also be our experience as Christians, and we should bring this experience to others, as God's instruments. Be an experience of healing and wholeness for someone today.

† O God, make me an instrument of your healing and wholeness.

John Holder

Readings in Luke

Clothing

1 Clothing our nakedness

Notes based on the *New Revised Standard Version* by
Marian Strachan, with Eileen Talbot

Marian Strachan is the wife of a Baptist minister, working in both city
centre and village churches in Devon, England. Previously they have
worked in Leicester; Samoa; in a university chaplaincy; and have also
served the United Reformed Church. Marian has taught in Papua New
Guinea, Samoa and England.
Eileen Talbot, writing for Thursday 4 February, was a missionary in Nepal, supporting hospital and community health work. She is a member
of the Bible study group mentioned on page 111.

Sunday 31 January : Preparing for the week

Clothes are essential for our well-being and dignity. In affluent societies, they
often become too important. Where people are poor, clothes sometimes
have to be pawned or sacrificed in exchange for food or money. To be
stripped of our clothing is humiliating and degrading. Providing clothes for
others can be an expression of love, generosity or mercy.

Text for the week: *Matthew 25: 36*
'I was naked and you gave me clothing.'

For group discussion and personal thought

- What can clothes tell us about people? Do we sometimes make
  judgements about people based on the clothes they wear?
- In affluent societies huge sums of money are sometimes spent on
  clothes. Can this be justified?

Monday 1 February
1 Samuel 2:18-21

A mother's provision

Most of us have been fortunate enough to have at least one adult who has guided and provided for us during our childhood. It may have been a parent, relative or friend. One of those caring for Samuel was, of course, his mother Hannah, though she gave him up when he was just a small child. After many years of failing to conceive, Hannah had promised God that, if he would bless her with a child, she would give the child into his service. She did this and saw Samuel only once each year, but it was an opportunity to provide for him and show her love for him.

> *Samuel was ministering before the LORD, a boy wearing a linen ephod. His mother used to make for him a little robe and take it to him each year, when she went up with her husband to offer the yearly sacrifice.*

(verses 18-19)

The little robe that Hannah made for Samuel was a sleeveless garment reaching to the knees. It went over his undergarment, but under the ephod, perhaps to keep him warm. The ephod, a linen waist cloth, was worn while Samuel assisted in the Temple. Samuel served in the Temple faithfully until, in adulthood, he became one of Israel's greatest priests. Hannah trusted God and was generous with what he gave her. The costly gift of her son (verse 20) resulted in further blessing both for Hannah and the nation.

---

† Thank you, Lord, for all who provided for us and influenced us during childhood. Help those who care for children to make wise and loving decisions.

Marian Strachan, with Eileen Talbot

Clothing

Tuesday 2 February

Exodus 22:21-27

A cloak taken in pledge

Fairness, compassion, generosity and justice are essential in every society. The challenge for Christians today is the same as it was for the people of God in biblical times. Caring for the weak, the underprivileged and the voiceless has to be our concern, because God is compassionate. In today's reading, laws protecting vulnerable and weaker members of society come together. There was to be protection for aliens or strangers, frequently homeless in foreign lands, for widows, orphans, the poor, and destitute borrowers. Garments are valuable items, especially for poor people. When these had to be pawned, Jewish law required mercy.

If you take your neighbour's cloak in pawn, you shall restore it before the sun goes down; for it may be your neighbour's only clothing to use as cover, in what else shall that person sleep? And if your neighbour cries out to me, I will listen, for I am compassionate.

(verses 26-27)

There is a warning and a challenge here for us all not to close our hearts to those in need or take advantage of vulnerable people and societies. Financial exploitation of the needy is to be condemned. Rich nations must not impoverish poor nations. Child labour for the production of inexpensive clothing has been one issue in our own time, as has the exploitation of immigrants for cheap labour. There are many wrongs and abuses that we can help to change.

† Compassionate God, help us never to grow weary of caring and working for vulnerable and needy people.

Clothing   Marian Strachan, with Eileen Talbot

Wednesday 3 February
Isaiah 3:18 – 4:1

Stripping as humiliation

On that day the LORD will take away the finery of the anklets,
the headbands, and the crescents . . .
Instead of perfume there will be a stench . . .
and instead of a rich robe, a binding of sackcloth;
instead of beauty, shame.

(verse 18 and part of verse 24)

These words from the prophet Isaiah were meant to shock and offend. They were a judgement on the arrogance and haughtiness of Judah's high society women, who flaunted and revelled in their affluence. In their society the rich prospered, while others were crushed by poverty and injustice. Today, as in Isaiah's time, this message is uncomfortable to hear. Affluence and grinding poverty exist side by side in many countries, and a world where the rich prosper while the poor starve is a judgement on many of our societies. It is sometimes difficult for us to imagine things differently. We have become so used to inequalities. And it is hard to live for God in a sacrificial way in a world where complacency, greed, competition, self-indulgence and self-seeking are accepted by many. But the prophetic voice calling for justice needs to be encouraged and supported by the people of God, by all of us, who know the blessings of food, clothes, medicines and education in our daily lives.

† Merciful God, help us all, and our leaders, to live with open ears and hands. May we hear the cries of the poor and downtrodden, share what we have, and strive to change injustices.

Marian Strachan, with Eileen Talbot

Clothing

Thursday 4 February

Matthew 25:31-40

Acts of mercy

Picture this scene in Nepal. A boy in rags had been found wandering at the bus station. He had no home, so a policeman brought him to the nurse at the mission clinic. 'Can you provide him with clean clothes, before we make arrangements for him?' he asked. While the nurse looked for clothes, the policeman began questioning the motives of those working in the mission hospital. He questioned whether their good deeds were aimed at encouraging people to become Christians, since proselytising was forbidden. 'But why did you bring the boy here if you were worried about our motives?' asked the nurse. Soon the boy was looking very different in the clean clothes he was now wearing. One of the mission workers smiled at the policeman, 'Do you think we should take the clothes back in case he becomes a Christian?' she teased! Today, in Nepal and around the world, churches, individual Christians, and people of good will can be seen to be involved in many acts of mercy.

'Lord, when was it that we saw you hungry and gave you food, or thirsty and gave you something to drink? And when was it that we saw you a stranger and welcomed you, or naked and gave you cloth-ing? And when was it that we saw you sick or in prison and visited you? And the king will answer . . . 'Truly I tell you, just as you did it for one of the least of these . . . you did it to me'.

(part of verse 37, verses 38-39, and part of verse 40)

† Each day, Lord, use my hands, eyes and feet, to serve others.

Clothing   Marian Strachan, with Eileen Talbot

John 19:23-24

Jesus stripped and humiliated

Our clothes are part of our identity as individual human beings, and they are certainly very important for our sense of dignity. Because of this, being stripped of clothing in public is sometimes used to punish, humiliate and degrade people. Inside prisons in various parts of the world, men and women are 'strip searched' to humiliate and shame them, and are then made to wear identical, shapeless clothing to try to remove their sense of individuality and identity. Jesus was mocked, tortured, and then suffered the indignity and humiliation of being stripped of his clothes. His public stripping meant that Jesus was seen as a criminal and an outcast.

When the soldiers had crucified Jesus, they took his clothes and divided them into four parts, one for each soldier. They also took his tunic; now the tunic was seamless, woven in one piece from the top. So they said to one another, 'Let us not tear it, but cast lots for it to see who will get it.'

(verse 23 and part of verse 24)

Time and time again during his earthly life, Jesus placed himself alongside the outcasts of his society. There was, and is, no place where God is not present, and no situation that he will not enter to show his love for us and his oneness with us.

† Such love for us, Lord . . . we thank you.

Marian Strachan, with Eileen Talbot

Clothing

Be generous – like God

Generosity usually requires a sense of thankfulness within our own life, and a good measure of practical common sense.

Followers of Christ are called to be people who give their lives, time, talents and treasure to others. It isn't necessary to be a Christian to be a generous person. But if we are Christians, generosity is not an option: it is part and parcel of our lives, because the driving force of our lives is to be like God.

In our reading today, about generosity, Jesus takes the old laws of revenge and retaliation to suggest that we need to take care not to hurt and exploit others. Jesus' words have to be understood as they apply in our own time and situation. For example, 'being forced to go a mile' referred to a Roman soldier's right to ask for his pack to be carried. If someone forced us to go with them today, we would be shouting for help!

[I]f anyone wants to sue you and take your coat, give your cloak as well . . . Give to everyone who begs from you, and do not refuse anyone who wants to borrow from you.

(verses 40 and 42)

At our city centre church, we try to apply Jesus' words in our ministry, but we do not give money to everyone who begs from us. Many would use it to buy drugs. But we provide food, or vouchers for a meal, or give other appropriate practical help. As Christians we respond to the needs of others out of thankfulness for all that God does for us.

† Lord, may my life be rich in thankfulness, common sense and generosity.

Clothing   Marian Strachan, with Eileen Talbot

Clothing

2 Robed in honour and glory

Notes based on the *New Jerusalem Bible* by
Anthea Dove

Anthea Dove is a great-grandmother, a retired teacher, retreat-giver and a writer. She was married in Kerala, South India, where she lived for six years. She is a Roman Catholic with a strong commitment to social justice and ecumenism.

Sunday 7 February: Preparing for the week

Clothing can have many different significances. An English bride wears white as a sign of purity; an Indian bride wears red as a sign of happiness. For some people (the prophets Elijah and John the Baptist among them), clothing is completely unimportant. For others, being seen in the right style and colour of dress is thought absolutely essential. At the same time, in the Western world, many people, especially the old, keep warm in the winter by wrapping themselves in layers of clothing because they cannot afford to heat their homes. This week we look at the symbolism of clothes, as signs of cleansing, honour, bereavement, integrity, mockery and holiness.

Text for the week: *Zechariah 3:3-5*

Now Joshua was dressed in dirty clothes as he stood before the angel. The latter then spoke as follows to those who were standing before him. 'Take off his dirty clothes and dress him in splendid robes and put a clean turban on his head.' So they put a clean turban on his head and dressed him in clean clothes, while the angel of Yahweh stood by and said, 'You see, I have taken your guilt away.'

For group discussion and personal thought

• How important are clothes in your life? Do some clothes have symbolic importance for you?

• Jesus said, 'I was naked and you clothed me.' What steps have you taken to help those who suffer from inadequate warmth and/or inappropriate clothing?

Monday 8 February

Zechariah 3:1-5

Cleansing

[Note that the order of verses in this passage is uncertain and varies between translations.]

There is a saying, 'Cleanliness is next to godliness.' I don't agree with this. If godliness means closeness to God, then it is far more important than being clean. I like to be clean, I like my house to be clean, but I can think of many brighter virtues than cleanliness, such as generosity, courage, humility, compassion . . . the list is very long. However, I do agree that Zechariah's image, where dirt is a metaphor for sin, is a powerful one. In Zechariah's vision, when Joshua was dressed in his clean clothes, the angel of Yahweh said to him,

'Look, I have taken your guilt away.'

(verse 5)

If we have been involved in hard exercise that makes us sweat and gets our hands, and possibly most of us, filthy, then it's a relief and a much greater happiness to be able to throw off the soiled clothes and step into a refreshing shower. And when we emerge and put on clean garments, we sometimes say, 'I feel like a new person.' We feel much greater relief and a much greater happiness when we have confessed our sins to God and know the wonderful blessing of forgiveness. When we are sincerely sorry, our guilt is washed away. Truly, we are now different people, ready and willing to walk in God's ways. It is pleasant to think of Joshua, dressed in his splendid robes and turban; it is pleasant to feel clean clothes against our skins and catch the scent of soap or moisturiser. But these things are as nothing compared to the joy we feel when our sins are forgiven.

† Dear God, may we never doubt your everlasting mercy, and always come to you when we are burdened by our sins.

Clothing

Anthea Dove

Tuesday 9 February

Daniel 5:1-7

Fine clothes

Belshazzar said,

'Anyone who can read this writing and tell me what it means shall be dressed in purple, and have a chain of gold put round his neck.'

(part of verse 7)

When Daniel was promised this reward, he told the king to keep his gifts for himself. Daniel the prophet was a true servant of God; he was not interested in fine clothes or the trappings of royalty. The chief purpose of clothing is to keep us warm, and those who are dreadfully cold are grateful for any kind of covering and not interested in their appearance. However, I think it is natural for most people to want to 'look nice', and in the different tribes and countries of the world people have always tried to adorn themselves with jewellery and brightly coloured clothes. This is good; it makes for variety and beauty that we can enjoy. But the pursuit of beauty can go too far, and in Western countries it has already reached ridiculous proportions. People are judged by their appearance, and so fashion becomes, for some people, of paramount importance. 'I wouldn't be seen dead in that!' you might hear someone say, referring to a garment of the style or colour that was the height of fashion only months earlier.

† Lord, help us to choose our priorities wisely, and never to judge people by their appearance.

Anthea Dove

Clothing

Bereavement

This passage gives us one of the most dramatic stories in the Bible and it is also proof of Elisha's faithful love for Elijah. The great prophet's cloak is a symbol of the divine power and spirit within him, and when he disappears from sight into the heavens, Elisha believes that if he inherits the cloak he will also inherit the spirit of his master. Perhaps it is from this incident that the phrase 'taking on the mantle' originates. Yet before he takes the mantle of Elijah's greatness, which means everything to him, Elisha first responds to his sudden loss like many people suddenly bereft of someone they love. Elisha saw Elijah being carried up to heaven in the whirlwind. He shouted:

'My father! My father! Chariot of Israel and its chargers!' Then he lost sight of him, and taking hold of his clothes he tore them in half.

(part of verse 12)

I think Elisha's reaction of tearing his garments was natural and human. It is as though he felt he had to do something drastic to let out his grief. Sometimes those with a Western mindset think they must not show their sorrow but must control it with dignity. Yet perhaps there are circumstances where dignity should not be the first consideration, and if people feel like weeping we should let them weep, as Jesus wept for Lazarus.

† Dear Lord, we ask you to console the bereaved with your presence.

Clothing   Anthea Dove

Thursday 11 February
Matthew 22:1-14

Integrity

This parable is one in which Matthew's language and style can puzzle and dismay us. He uses the hyperbole or exaggeration common in his day in order to emphasise the point Jesus is making, and he succeeds, because the story is vivid and memorable. But reading it today, we cannot help a reaction of startled dismay, because it seems an exceptionally harsh punishment that the man is given simply for turning up in the wrong dress. When we read of such dire penalties meted out to sinners, it helps us to remember Paul's consoling words in his letter to the Romans (11: 31), where he says that 'those who are disobedient now will also enjoy mercy eventually'. In this part of the parable, God does not seem like our loving Father, but when he says,

> 'Go to the main crossroads and invite everyone you can find to come to the wedding.'

(verse 9)

we have a picture of our inclusive God who loves everyone without exception. We are still left with the question: why was the king so angry? Perhaps it was because the man was not someone of truth and integrity; he was a sham, pretending to be something that he wasn't, and so dishonouring the king.

† Dear Lord, help us to beware of pretending to be other than we are, but to be truthful and transparent at all times.

Anthea Dove

Clothing

Friday 12 February

John 19:1-7

Mockery

Jesus was, and is, a king, but the soldiers who mocked him can have had no notion of who he really was. Their savagery was twofold: the physical pain they inflicted on him when they pierced his skin with the crown of thorns so that blood ran down his face, and the mental cruelty of their taunts as they draped the purple robe around him, continually slapping his face and addressing him as king. These were brutish, ignorant men, presumably egging one another on, like bullies in a school playground. But Pilate was not like these. He was educated and a man of authority. Clearly he had his misgivings. But even the chief priests joined in, shouting, 'Crucify him! Crucify him!' Pilate said,

'Take him yourselves and crucify him: I find no case against him.'

(verse 7)

We may wonder why Jesus seems to have been singled out for this treatment, different in so many ways from the common criminals they normally dealt with. Being different is the reason why so many people, including children, are bullied and mocked today. We mistreat people who are foreign, especially refugees; we mistreat fat people and those who are mentally or physically disabled in some way. Rather than welcoming strangers, we are afraid of them because they are different and too often we become aggressive towards them.

† Lord, help us to welcome and learn from those who are different from us.

Clothing   Anthea Dove

Saturday 13 February
Revelation 3:1-6

Holiness

When I hear the phrase, 'dressed in white robes' (verse 5), I immediately think of children in a nativity play: angels with cardboard haloes and shepherds with tea towels askew on their heads. But the Book of Revelation is one of the most solemn in the Bible and is to be taken very seriously. John is describing his tremendous vision of what is to happen, and sending messages to the different churches in Asia, in this instance to Sardis. He writes,

'So far I have failed to notice anything in your behaviour that my God could possibly call perfect.'

(part of verse 2)

For me, and I guess for most of us, this comment hits home. I am well aware that I am not perfect, far from it. Nor do I ever expect to *be* perfect, however hard I try. I cannot see myself entitled to wear those white robes, which are a symbol not only of purity but of victory and joy. But I will continue to persevere, because the alternative is to give in to laziness, greed, envy and pride. And whether or not I succeed in my struggles, I am sure that God loves me just as I am, and indeed, whatever I wear!

† Dear God, save us from discouragement. Help us to follow the teachings of your son with a cheerful heart.

Anthea Dove

Clothing

44

Readings in Genesis 1–35

1 In the beginning

Notes based on the *New Revised Standard Version* by
Tim Brooke

Tim Brooke previously worked as a teacher for the Anglican Church of Tanzania and as a social worker in London. He was then ordained priest in the Church of England, served as a parish priest, and is now retired but still active in ministry.

Sunday 14 February: Preparing for the week

The first part of Genesis (chapters 1–11) seeks to show how our world came into being through the creative power of God and how it all went so wrong. The turning point of the book comes in chapter 12 when God decides to call one man, Abraham, and his family to change the world, and Abraham responds to that call. The remainder of the book goes on to tell the story of the patriarchs, Abraham, Isaac and Jacob – the three great ancestors of Jews, Christians and Muslims. Because of the length of Genesis, the final part, the story of Joseph, will be dealt with in another year.

Text for the week: *Genesis 1:31*
God saw everything that he had made, and indeed, it was very good.

For group discussion and personal thought

- Why did God create the world?
- God saw that the world he had created was good. Is it still good?
- What does 'made in God's image' mean in practice? What difference does it make to our attitude towards people we do not like?

Monday 15 February

Genesis 1:1-19

God creates the universe

When I lived in Tanzania I never failed to be amazed by the night sky. The stars that make up the Milky Way were especially breathtaking. They are now so often invisible in Britain either because of moisture in the air or light pollution. Gazing up at the Milky Way arching overhead, I knew I was looking towards the centre of our galaxy with its two hundred thousand million stars – but only seeing a tiny proportion of them. Astronomers tell us that the light of even our nearest star takes four years to reach us. The light of the stars on the furthest edge of the galaxy takes 100 000 years to cross to the opposite edge. And that is just our home galaxy, one of the billions of other galaxies that make up the universe! The scale is awesome and we have no words to describe who or what is behind creation. When we are tempted to pin God down to anything smaller or to make 'him' in our own image, we need to remember how the Lord answered Job out of the whirlwind: 'Where were you when I laid the foundation of the world?' (Job 38:4). In face of the marvels of nature our response must be silence and humility.

Then God said, 'Let there be light', and there was light.

(verse 3)

† When I look at the heavens, the work of your fingers, the moon and the stars that you have established, what are human beings that you are mindful of them? O Lord, our Sovereign, how majestic is your name in all the earth!

(Psalm 8:3,4,9)

Tim Brooke

Readings in Genesis 1–35

Tuesday 16 February

Genesis 1:20 – 2:3

God creates life

Both accounts of creation (we will read the second one tomorrow) show that God saw the world as incomplete without living beings. There needed to be birds and fish and sea monsters and insects and animals. But above all there should be human beings who would join in God's work of creation, multiply, fill the earth and subdue it. The exciting thing was that God wanted to team up with human beings in this work of creation. God was not personally going to create each of us separately, one by one. God made it possible for me to exist by 'creating male and female', who were then able to create other human beings. If my father and mother had never met, I would never have come into being as the person I am. Incredibly, we not only have the capacity to create other human beings, we also have an innate ability throughout our lives to be creative and we have an innate ability to love unselfishly. That means we share some of the attributes of God. The consequence is that each individual is uniquely valuable not because of his or her successes. Human success or failure does not matter to God. What gives us value is that there is something of God in each of us.

So God created humankind in his image,
in the image of God he created them;
male and female he created them.

(verse 27)

† Lord, help us to discover new ways of using your gifts of love and creativity in our lives.

Readings in Genesis 1–35   Tim Brooke

Wednesday 17 February (Ash Wednesday)

Genesis 2:4-25

God lets go

This second account of the creation of the world is also about the creation of life – first a man, then trees and other food plants and, crucially, plenty of water. The man is put in the Garden of Eden to till it and to look after it for God. God limits his own power by handing over part of his world in trust to the man. Then out of the blue God says it is not good for the man to be alone (verse 18) and he creates the animals and birds to keep him company. But God does not name them. He brings them to the man and asks him to give them names. 'Monkey', the man says, or 'Blackbird', or 'Giraffe'. It is great fun. But still God is not satisfied. Man needs a creature more similar to himself. And so he creates woman to be man's companion, with a closeness that can only be described as becoming one flesh. There are two great truths here. One is that God demonstrates how he is a God of love. True love is about empowering the object of one's love, bringing out all the potential they have. Tilling the ground and naming the animals are part of God's power-sharing arrangement with human beings. Having language means no longer just living for the present moment but having power to plan for the future, even to change the world. The second equally important truth is that human beings are created to be social and that anything that isolates them cannot be part of God's will.

The LORD God took the man and put him in the garden of Eden to till it and keep it.

(verse 15)

† Lord, show us how we should look after your creation.

Tim Brooke

Readings in Genesis 1–35

Thursday 18 February

Genesis 3:1-24

The end of a perfect friendship?

Our dog Sam was sick on the carpet while we were out. When we came back there was no wag of the tail or excited welcome in his eye. Instead he looked down and his tail was between his legs. If a dog can feel guilt, a human being can feel it a thousand times more – at least since the Garden of Eden. Having been made in the image of God, Adam and Eve now become even more like a god through knowing that evil is possible as well as good. They no longer live in a state of perfect innocence, meeting up for a chat with the Lord God at the end of the day as he takes a stroll through the garden. Now they are able to stand back and judge themselves. They can see themselves from outside and they know they have done wrong. Embarrassed with guilt they decide on a cover-up, literally with fig leaves but figuratively too by passing on the blame. They know they have betrayed the trust the Lord God put in them. There is no place for sin in the Garden of Eden and so they are expelled. Is that the end of their relationship with the Lord God? No. Before they go, God touchingly replaces the fig leaves with more substantial garments made of skins, a token of mercies to come. Then he sends the man out still to cultivate the ground, still to be his partner in the world.

Therefore the LORD God sent him forth from the garden of Eden to till the ground from which he was taken.

(verse 23)

† Lord, we thank you that you continue to put your trust in us, however unworthy we may be. Give us grace not to betray that trust.

Readings in Genesis 1–35   Tim Brooke

Friday 19 February

Genesis 4:1-16

Who is my brother?

Climate change, care for the earth, feeding the world are all issues that do not go away. Interestingly, the command to look after the environment and make it fruitful – 'to till the ground and keep it' – comes in the Bible before the command to look after other people. On Wednesday we saw how Adam was to be keeper of the Garden of Eden. Now Cain refuses to accept that he is his brother's keeper. In what sense can we be anyone's keeper? If being a keeper means keeping track of a person's every movement or preventing them having any sort of independence, then Cain is right to question whether he should be his brother's keeper. But we know that Cain is justifying himself only to get out of an uncomfortable situation. If being someone's keeper means having that person's interests at heart, putting their well-being before our own, caring about what is best for them, then we are all required to be our brother's or our sister's keeper. So the two commands in fact converge. Looking after the environment, making it productive, trying to slow down climate change are all ways of being my brother's keeper.

Then the LORD said to Cain, 'Where is your brother Abel?' He said, 'I do not know; am I my brother's keeper?'

(verse 9)

† Lord, help me to understand who are my brothers and sisters and how I can put their interests before mine.

Tim Brooke

Readings in Genesis 1–35

Saturday 20 February

Genesis 6:5-22

Walking with God

I like walking. My longest walk was 70 miles over three days. A friend and I were making a pilgrimage, carrying a tent and sleeping bags and walking in a straight line across the mountains of South Wales from the border with England to the cathedral of St David, the great patron saint of Wales. We enjoyed talking on the way, commenting on the beautiful scenery, sharing ideas and funny moments and a near-disaster when my friend fell part-way down a steep mountainside.

We were relaxed, clearly aware of one another's presence but not needing to look at one another face to face. We found too that we did not have to talk all the time. We were comfortable simply being silent together, perhaps the best sign of a good friendship.

Noah walked with God. Was it a bit like walking with any good friend? Is God still looking for walking partners? Is walking with God what Christian life should be all about – not just formal prayers but chatting with God as we go along in life, talking with him, listening to him, picking up suggestions about how we can share in his work in the world? It could also be walking in silence, wondering maybe what God is thinking. The earth remains full of violence – does it still grieve him to his heart (verse 6)? If we walk with God, we may begin to see the world, and the people we meet on the way, more and more through his eyes. And that is surely what he wants for us.

Noah walked with God.

(verse 9)

† Lord, help me to understand what it means to walk with you. Give me the vision to see the world through your eyes.

Readings in Genesis 1–35
2 The great flood

Notes based on the *Good News Bible* by
Iain Roy

Iain Roy is a retired minister of the Church of Scotland and former Moderator and Clerk of the Presbytery of Ardrossan, still active in preaching and pastoral care. He was for many years industrial chaplain to the ICI Nobel Explosives Company at Ardeer.

Sunday 21 February: Preparing for the week
Global warming has brought home to many of us today the distress widespread flooding can cause. That this is something others have known over the centuries is confirmed by the story of the flood, which appears not only in Genesis but in other ancient literature. What makes the Genesis version of the story unique is the personal and individual story of salvation it depicts through the relationship of God to Noah.

Text for the week: *Genesis 8:22*
'As long as the world exists, there will be a time for planting and a time for harvest. There will always be cold and heat, summer and winter, day and night.'

For group discussion and personal thought
• What things in life cause you to feel overwhelmed and therefore tempted to think God has forgotten you? Stevie Smith's poem, 'Not Waving but Drowning', could get your thinking started.

• Thanksgiving itself can be an aid to overcoming the things that get us down; for example, thankfulness for the life of a loved one can be a comfort in bereavement; gratitude for years of good health can help us come to terms with a period of illness. What can you use in this way?

• In what ways is the idea of the 'Covenant' still relevant today as an approach to responsible living in relation to each other, to animal life, to the world's resources, and towards God the giver of it all?

Monday 22 February

Genesis 7:1-16

The faithful one

I wonder if Noah felt the burden of God's word to him?

The LORD said to Noah, 'Go into the boat with your whole family; I have found that you are the only one in all the world who does what is right.'

(verse 1)

It was a lot to live up to! The reality for most of us is rather different. Our experience is more like Paul's: 'I don't do the good that I want to do; instead I do the evil that I do not want to do' (Romans 7:19).

What we have in this story is really a continuing theme of the Old Testament, the idea of the 'remnant', the faithful few who go on witnessing while others lose their way. It is always necessary, however, for us to read the Old Testament with a New Testament eye. When we do this here, it leads us to Christ, our Saviour, the only one who truly did what was right through his mighty act of grace and love on the cross.

But the Noah story too is a story of salvation as the final words of our passage beautifully and simply express:

'Then the Lord shut the door behind Noah'

(verse 16)

† Lord God, give us the humility to see our faults, and the wisdom to seek your forgiveness and a fresh start.

Readings in Genesis 1–35

Iain Roy

Tuesday 23 February

Genesis 7:17-24, 8:1-5

The one who remembers

The devastating nature of the flood echoes throughout this passage: the loss of life, human and animal; by implication, the loss of and damage to human habitation; the consequent need, when the waters recede, for a fresh start. It would have been easy, therefore, for Noah to think God had forgotten him. The truth was different.

God had not forgotten Noah and all the animals with him in the boat; he caused a wind to blow, and the waters started going down.

(chapter 8 verse 1)

What was true for Noah is also often true for us. Overcome sometimes by the things that happen to us or ours, we not only feel we are drowning, we feel forgotten. The phrase, 'Things are getting on top of me' sums it up. It is then we need most of all to remember that God has not forgotten us, that his whole purpose in sending Christ into the world, and Christ's own purpose in going to the cross, was to show that he stands beside us in everything that happens to us. This is the truth we ourselves have also to witness to every day, by being there for others when they need us.

† O Lord! Thou knowest how busy I must be this day: if I forget thee, do not thou forget me.

(Sir Jacob Astley's prayer before the battle of Edgehill, 1642)

Iain Roy

Readings in Genesis 1–35

Wednesday 24 February

Genesis 8:6 22

One man's gratitude

If God did not forget Noah, certainly Noah did not forget God. Unlike many of us, when ordeals are over and burdens lifted, Noah did not forget who had saved him. He showed his gratitude tangibly.

Noah built an altar to the LORD.

(part of verse 20)

Before he could make this response, the flood had asked two things of Noah: courage and patience. Courage to entrust himself, his family, and the animals to that frail craft on such turbulent waters; patience, as the waters receded, to wait until they finally did so, sending out first the raven, then the dove again and again.

It is the same qualities of courage and patience that are often asked of us as we struggle against serious illness, or try to overcome bereavement, or face adversity, tragedy, setback or need. But we only really begin to triumph over these things when we see our way to thank God for carrying us safely through them.

---

† Grant us courage and patience in the face of our troubles, and give us a thankful heart when, with your help and the help of others, we overcome them.

Readings in Genesis 1–35 Iain Roy

Thursday 25 February

Genesis 9:1-17

God's gift, our responsibility

The Bible is a God-centred book, but in this passage it seems to describe a human-centred universe.

God blessed Noah and his sons and said, 'Have many children, so that your descendants will live all over the earth. All the animals, birds, and fish will live in fear of you. They are all placed under your power.'

(verses 1-2)

The truth is different. God was creating a covenant, a two-sided agreement. On the one side he gives us the world for our enjoyment and provision; on the other side, he asks us to live responsibly, using this gift, not abusing it. However old this idea of the covenant may be, it is entirely modern, making this passage one of the most relevant passages in Genesis for our life today. Our relationship to the environment and to animal life is a crucial issue today. We may have power but we also have great responsibility, especially to future generations, for how we exercise it. To see the world as God's world, not ours, is a good beginning to the proper stewardship of the world's resources.

† Gracious God, remind us of your covenant with us: the bounty of your provision, but the corresponding obligation to use wisely and live responsibly.

Iain Roy

Readings in Genesis 1–35

Genesis 11:1-9

Except the Lord builds

The idea of the skyscraper is not new. Humanity has always had an urge to build high to express commercial success, political power, or even spiritual aspirations.

They said to one another, 'Come on! Let's make bricks and bake them hard . . . let's build a city with a tower which reaches the sky, so that we can make a name for ourselves.'

(part of verses 3-4)

The covenant God had made with his people was not very old before it was being broken.

The ostensible reason for this grandiose building was to avoid dispersion. The idea of dispersion is a recurring theme in Jewish literature. Indeed, it has been the context for so much of Jewish history. 'My ancestor was a wandering Aramean, a homeless refugee, who took his family to Egypt to live' (Deuteronomy 26:5). The penalties the Jews have paid for dispersion have included purges, persecution and, finally, the Holocaust. Other races too have paid a price for being strangers in a strange land.

The real name God calls us to make for ourselves is the building of stable and harmonious communities with sound relationships between peoples of diverse ethnic origins and different cultural, religious and political backgrounds. The love of Christ embraces us all.

† Lord Jesus Christ, whose arms were stretched out upon the cross that all might be embraced by them, help us to build our nations and communities on the sound basis of your love for us all.

Readings in Genesis 1–35   Iain Roy

Saturday 27 February

Genesis 12:1-20

Another obedient man

God spoke and Abram responded. Would that it were always so!

The LORD said to Abram, 'Leave your country, your relatives, and your father's home, and go to a land that I am going to show you.'

(verse 1)

Many emigrants could testify to the price they have paid for leaving their native land to make a new life elsewhere. It is in this context that we must see Abram's response to God's request. Nevertheless, he did not shirk the demand on him and his family. Yet he did not go blindly. Even if he had, his experiences on the journey would soon have opened his eyes to the cost. Dietrich Bonhoeffer, the German theologian and martyr of the Second World War, wrote an important little book called *The Cost of Discipleship*. It is a title to keep in mind for, as in so many things, so also in Christian discipleship, there is often no gain without pain. God *does* make demands on us, but never beyond what we, who receive so much from him, can give.

---

† Help us, Lord, to follow in the way of the faithful – Noah, Abram, and so many others – to serve you faithfully, not counting the cost.

Iain Roy

Readings in Genesis 1–35

Readings in Genesis 1–35

3 God's covenant with Abraham

Notes based on the *Good News Bible* by
John Oldershaw

John Oldershaw is a Minister of the United Reformed Church. He works with churches in the north-west of England helping them discover new ways of serving and worshipping God. As part of this work he is minister of a church set in a farming community.

Sunday 28 February: Preparing for the week

The book of Genesis is not history in a straightforward sense, but tells the dramatic story of God's dealing with the world and with the people who inhabit it. This week we are reminded of how he chose Israel to have a special role in his purpose, and in particular of the threefold promise he made to Sarah and Abraham. This was that their descendants would increase in number, have a land of their own and have a relationship with God that would benefit other people as well as themselves. Genesis shows how, despite setbacks, the promise is kept.

Text for the week: *Genesis 18:15*

Because Sarah was afraid, she denied it. 'I didn't laugh,' she said. 'Yes, you did,' he replied. 'You laughed.'

For group discussion and personal thought

The text for the week reflects Sarah's response to the promise of God. The notes for Saturday give you more background, but here are some talking and thinking points.

- Have you been aware of a promise God has made that you just could not believe? How was the promise fulfilled?
- Have you ever tried to tell someone about the promises that God makes, and the other person has just laughed at you? What was your response?
- Has there been a time when you felt that God had not honoured his promise, causing you to cry rather than laugh? How did you react?

Monday 1 March
Genesis 13:1-18

The land is divided

In today's reading are the roots of much of world history: holy land is torn apart and fought over: a situation that continues today.

[Q]uarrels broke out between the men who took care of Abram's animals and those who took care of Lot's animals . . . Then Abram said to Lot, 'We are relatives, and your men and my men shouldn't be quarrelling. So let's separate. Choose any part of the land you want. You go one way, and I'll go the other.'

(part of verse 7, and verses 8-9)

Lot chooses the rich land of the Jordan plain. It is a place of alluring prosperity, but the temptations of the city of Sodom, a place of wickedness, are close by. Anyway, Lot, his family, herdsmen and flocks move there.

It is interesting that in the cause of peace Abram gives Lot first choice. Perhaps he knew his relative well and so could predict the decision he would make, because it is after the choice is made that God reaffirms his promise to Abram (made in chapter 12) that the land he now inhabits, stretching as far as he can see, will belong to him and his descendants, and they will be more numerous than all the specks of dust in the earth. Abram explores the land and settles near the sacred trees of Mamre, a place where there will be a very significant encounter with God.

† Lord, some decisions are forced upon me, and on other occasions I decide that the time has come to make a choice. As I select my options may I be obedient to your will. Amen

John Oldershaw

Readings in Genesis 1–35

Tuesday 2 March

Genesis 14:13-24

Tithe, bread and wine

It does not take long before Abram's nephew, Lot, regrets his choice of land near Sodom in which to live. He is caught up in tribal warfare and taken away along with the other captives and their possessions. Abram comes to his rescue, and in the aftermath, as the spoils of war are divided, we are introduced to Melchizedek, described as king of Salem and priest of the Most High God. (There is more about him in Psalm 110 and Hebrews 7.)

Here is another clue that this tale of the wandering patriarch, Abram, has significance greater than his own story. Salem, as the Bible story unfolds, is identified as Jerusalem, and Melchizedek, in this chapter, offers Abram bread and wine, which makes connections with the Last Supper and the inauguration of the covenant Jesus effected between God and his people. The concept of tithe is also introduced when a tenth of the loot from the rescue mission is offered to the priest as God's portion.

And Melchizedek, who was king of Salem and also a priest of the Most High God, brought bread and wine to Abram, blessed him, and said 'May the Most High God, who made heaven and earth, bless Abram! May the Most High God, who gave you victory over your enemies, be praised!'

(verses 18-19, and part of verse 20)

† Dear God, your blessing was given to Abram as leader of your people: I pray that all those who are leaders of your people today may know your blessing. Amen

Readings in Genesis 1–35

John Oldershaw

Wednesday 3 March

Genesis 15:1-16

It's in a dream

Dreams are important. In our busy lives, with little space for silence, it is often only when we are asleep that God can break through and reveal truth to us. Abram has a dream (vision) and a nightmare. The dream has the amazing statement that his descendants will be more numerous than the stars in the sky. On a cloudless night, away from the light pollution of street lamps, the stars are beyond counting.

Abram put his trust in the LORD, and because of this the LORD was pleased with him and accepted him. Then the LORD said to him, 'I am the LORD, who led you out of Ur in Babylonia, to give you this land as your own.'

(verses 6-7)

Abram still cannot take it in and so a covenant is set up. Animals are sacrificed and divided. This is the way people of the time made pacts with each other, symbolising them by walking between the halves of the animals.

In effect God is saying 'You can trust me'. Abram is clearly still unsure and his worries result in a nightmare of his descendants being tortured. God does not say that this will not happen, but does promise that he will, in his own time, deal with the perpetrators. Abram is also promised that he will live a full life and die in peace.

† O God of Abram, you are my God too. Forgive me for those times when my trust in you falters. May I always remember those moments in my life when I have felt assured that even when times are hard you are a faithful God, more than worthy of my trust. Amen

John Oldershaw

Readings in Genesis 1–35

Thursday 4 March

Genesis 16:1-16

Jealousy

Sarai has a plan. Although she herself seems unable to have children, if Abram sleeps with her slave then, through her, she can build a family. This was a not uncommon suggestion in its day. The slave was the possession of the owner and so any offspring would be counted not only as the children of the father, but also of the original wife. There may have been a variety of reasons why Abram agreed to this plan, not least that it seemed the only way to ensure that God's promise was fulfilled. (At this point in the story it is not at all clear that Sarai is aware of what Abram knows.)

There is partial success, but the plan backfires. Abram may have shown too much affection to Hagar, the slave, because Sarai complains that, although it was her idea,

> 'It's your fault that Hagar despises me. I myself gave her to you, and ever since she found out that she was pregnant, she has despised me. May the LORD judge which of us is right, you or me!'

> (part of verse 5)

And it gets worse, because Hagar runs off and all could be lost, except that God finds her. In fact Hagar sees him, and is amazed that she survives the encounter. Although she returns, it is not by her son that Abram's descendants will be God's chosen ones, even though they also will be countless in number.

† Lord, there are times when we are tempted to force your hand or persuade you that our way is the best one to achieve your purpose. Forgive us and may we for ever rejoice that you are 'a God who sees'. Amen

Readings in Genesis 1–35

John Oldershaw

Friday 5 March

Genesis 17:1-22

The sign that's for ever

Three things happen in this chapter: first, Abram and Sarai receive God's spirit, his breath is within them, and a 'huh' is added to their names so that they become Abraham and Sarah. There is added significance for Sarah, as the meaning of her name changes from Sarai (mockery) to Sarah (princess). Instead of being ridiculed because she has no children, she is now to be honoured; indeed, twice in verse 16 God says 'I will bless her'.

Ironically, at this big moment in her life Sarah is not even present. Abraham is given the responsibility of passing on the news. Second, throughout the story God re-emphasises:

> *'I will keep my promise to you and to your descendants in future gen-erations as an everlasting covenant. I will be your God and the God of your descendants. I will give to you and your descendants this land in which you are now a foreigner.'*

(verse 7 and part of verse 8)

This time the covenant is marked in circumcision. All males will for ever, every day, be reminded that they belong to God in a mutual relationship of trust and belonging, by a sign that is both more intimate and more permanent than a tattoo. Third, Abraham laughs. God is promising that the future is secured in a child born through an aged woman. It is ridiculous.

---

† God, I live in a different world to Sarah. Being childless is not a source of mockery, but people do face ridicule for the way they dress, talk or look. As my sign of the covenant may I be accepting of others and acknowledge that in Jesus your promise now extends to all people. Amen

John Oldershaw

Readings in Genesis 1–35

Saturday 6 March

Genesis 18:1-15

And Sarah laughs

Sitting outside his tent at Mamre, Abraham sees three visitors. Although he does not know who they are, they know who Abraham is, and the name of his wife.

Then they asked him, 'Where is your wife Sarah?'
'She is in the tent', he answered.
One of them said, 'Nine months from now I will come back, and your wife Sarah will have a son.'

(verse 9 and part of verse 10)

The story is wonderfully domestic. Guests arrive, the man of the house sends his wife into the kitchen to make some bread (some translations say 'cakes'), the servant gets the meat ready, and the menfolk talk.

Abraham hears the same message about having a child and this time Sarah, who has been eavesdropping on the conversation, hears what is said and it is her turn to laugh. Now the visitors challenge her, through Abraham, about her laughing. Having become 'princess' she realises that she has turned the 'mockery' onto God, and she is the one who understands that, although Abraham had seen three men, it actually is, as verse 1 tells us, the Lord who had visited them. Of course, she does not want to challenge the word of the Lord, so she denies her laughter.

The men leave and the story moves on beyond today's text, but in due time the promise is fulfilled, Isaac is born, and in Hebrew the child's name means 'he laughs'.

---

† Lord, help me to enjoy laughter but help me never to laugh at the expense of other people. In knowing you I pray that I may have great joy in my heart. Amen

Readings in Genesis 1–35   John Oldershaw

Readings in Genesis 1–35

4   Abraham, Lot and Isaac

Notes based on the *New Living Translation* by
Anthony Loke

Revd Anthony Loke is an ordained minister with the TRAC Methodist Church in Malaysia and a lecturer in Old Testament in the Seminari Theoloji Malaysia, the largest ecumenical seminary in the country. His wife, King Lang, holds an MTheol in Christian Education. They have two teenage children, Charis and Markus.

Sunday 7 March: Preparing for the week

In this section of readings from Genesis, we read about the stories of two of the four ancient patriarchs of Israel, namely, Abraham and Isaac. This section also includes the story of Abraham's intercession for Sodom and Gomorrah, Abraham's nephew Lot, the birth of Isaac, and the births of Esau and Jacob.

Text for the week: *Genesis 22:16-18*

This is what the Lord says: Because you have obeyed me and have not withheld even your son, your only son, I swear by my own name that I will certainly bless you. I will multiply your descendants beyond number, like the stars in the sky and the sand on the seashore. Your descendants will conquer the cities of their enemies. And through your descendants all the nations of the earth will be blessed – all because you have obeyed me.

For group discussion and personal thought

• Was God's promise to Abraham conditional upon Abraham's obedience or was it an unrestricted promise?

• Is God's twin promise of land and children to Abraham still effective today?

Monday 8 March

Genesis 18:16-33

Intercession for evil

Should not the Judge of all the earth do what is right?

(part of verse 25)

The story of Abraham interceding for the fate of Sodom and Gomorrah is often used to illustrate the importance and need for intercession. While the story in Genesis 18 is quite straightforward, it raises many theological issues that are still relevant today.

First, why should God need to inform Abraham of what he was about to do to Sodom and Gomorrah (verse 17)? Was the sharing of intimate knowledge a part of the blessing given to Abraham?

Second, who exactly were the three men who came to visit Abraham in his tent (verse 22)? One is explicitly identified as 'the Lord' but who were the other two men? Christians have been quick to see the Trinity present here but the narrator does not tell us so, preferring to keep us in the dark.

Third, why did Abraham stop interceding when he reached ten men (verse 32)? The twin cities were destroyed because ten good men could not be found in Sodom and Gomorrah. Noah and his family constituted four persons. If and only if Abraham had dared asked one more time for just four persons, would the two cities still be destroyed?

One key lesson we can learn is that Abraham, the father of faith, dared to 'bargain' with God for the deliverance of two cities that deserved God's punishment. Should not even evil people be given a chance to be saved? If God's people will not intercede for them, what little hope do they have in finding salvation?

† O God, teach me also to intercede for those who are evil lest there may still be some good within them.

Readings in Genesis 1–35

Anthony Loke

Tuesday 9 March

Genesis 19:1-14

The depths of depravity

The outcry against this place is so great it has reached the LORD, and he has sent us to destroy it.

(part of verse 13)

Two of the visitors who stopped by at Abraham's tent proceeded to Sodom. Where is the third person, the one called 'the Lord'? Why did he leave the other two who proceeded to Sodom? The other two are now specially called 'angels', which in Hebrew is also 'messengers' (verse 1).

They arrived at Sodom and were met by Lot, Abraham's nephew. In extending hospitality, as is the custom in the Middle East, Lot invited the two men to stay in his house for the night. That night, the men folk of Sodom surrounded the house and demanded the two strangers. This story is reminiscent of a similar story in Judges 19:22-26.

Lot's offer of his two virgin daughters is difficult for many of us to comprehend. How could Lot offer his own flesh and blood to save the dignity and honour of two complete strangers he hardly knew? The point the storyteller is making is that Lot is still righteous and different from the rest of the people in the city. In this part of the story, Lot did not know that his uncle Abraham had already interceded for him earlier. He was in a sense already 'blessed' and he sought to 'bless' others, especially his prospective sons-in-law. However, Lot's standing in the city was already compromised (verse 9) and they rejected his offer. Even his future sons-in-law did not believe him when he told them of the imminent destruction of the city.

† Has someone already blessed me so that I can become a blessing to others?

Anthony Loke

Readings in Genesis 1–35

Genesis 19:15-29

No turning back

But Lot's wife looked back as she was following behind him, and she turned into a pillar of salt.

(verse 26)

The story of Lot's wife turning into a pillar of salt is a tragic one. Lot's family was saved because the Lord was merciful to him (verse 16). Yet Lot had lived in Sodom for a long time and, as the biblical scholar Joyce Baldwin once said, 'familiar things seem indispensable and doubly precious'. Lot lingered on, not wanting to leave, and the two angels had to seize and compel him to do so. Yet again, Lot did not want to flee to the hills and bargained with the two angels to run to a nearby small village instead. This was only a small request, so he thought. The village is later called Zoar, which means 'a little' (verse 21), a pun obviously intended to refer to Lot's 'little' request.

As the Lord rained fire and brimstone upon Sodom and Gomorrah, Lot's wife looked back and was caught up in the molten lava (verse 26). We can only surmise why she turned back, perhaps out of hesitation at whether she was doing the right thing, or being overcome by nostalgia for the city. Her example of turning back to the old ways and the old life with which she was familiar has become a paradigm for those who lack the commitment to go forward with God and keep looking back. Even Jesus gave the warning, 'Remember Lot's wife' (Luke 17:32).

---

† Teach me, O Lord, to lay my hands on the plough and look forward to what you have promised and not look back to what I have left behind.

Readings in Genesis 1–35

Anthony Loke

Thursday 11 March

Genesis 21:1-20

Jealousy and grace

'Do not be afraid! God has heard the boy crying as he lies there. Go to him and comfort him, for I will make a great nation from his descendants.'

(part of verse 17, and verse 18)

Our story moves forward to the time when God's promise of a legitimate son to Abraham and Sarah came true. Sarah, in her old age, conceived a son whom they named Isaac. Now Abraham had two sons, the firstborn being Ishmael, through Sarah's handmaid Hagar. Clearly a rift would be likely to develop between the two sons or the two mothers who bore them.

By this time, Ishmael was about 14 years old. Verse 9 tells us that Sarah was displeased when she saw Ishmael 'playing' (RSV) with her son Isaac. Some scholars think the verb in Hebrew means 'mocking', which is a pun on Isaac's name. As a result, Sarah demanded that Abraham should send Hagar and Ishmael away. Abraham was reluctant because he knew he would not be able to see them again.

God comes into the picture and tells Abraham to go ahead and do it, because he will take care of both mother and lad. God indeed protect Hagar and Ishmael in the desert. Many people argue that God had little or no purpose for Ishmael as he was not chosen by God. Ishmael was a result of Abraham and Sarah trying to 'help' God speed up the promise. However, we are told that 'God was with the lad' (verse 20). Ishmael may not have had a large role to play in God's purposes but neither was he completely outside the scope of God's grace and protection.

---

† Help me to see the larger purposes that you have for the whole world, including people who are not in your kingdom now.

Anthony Loke   Readings in Genesis 1–35

The binding of Isaac

[F]or now I know that you truly fear God. You have not withheld from me even your son, your only son.

(part of verse 12)

The story of the binding of Isaac is very well known in Jewish circles. It has been told and retold and subjected to much study. The story is about a test, the real test, of Abraham's faith in God. For the first time, Abraham is told to do something contrary to human reason or logic – sacrifice his only son, whom he loved. Wasn't Isaac the living promise that through him there would be descendants for Abraham (Genesis 21:12)? How can God then ask Abraham to sacrifice him?

To make matters worse, Abraham did not tell his wife about God's command. He bears the brunt of the responsibility alone. Even his son does not know the reason for the journey to Mount Moriah.

Once they reached there, Abraham did exactly as God told him. At the point when Abraham raised his knife, the angel of the Lord intervened. The story ended well – a sacrifice is provided by a ram caught in the thicket by its horns. Isaac is the passive character in this story. At that point, he is too young to comprehend the enormity of his father's act of obedience. In his older life, how did Isaac understand this event? Did his father ever speak and remind him of this incident? Did the incident change his life for ever, reminding him that he was indeed the son of God's promise?

† There will be times when God demands obedience from us and we do not know why but, like Abraham, we nevertheless need to obey him. Lord, help us when those times come.

Saturday 13 March

Genesis 25:19-34

Two nations in the womb

'The sons in your womb will become two nations. From the very beginning, the two nations will be rivals. One nation will be stronger than the other; and your older son will serve your younger son.'

(verse 23)

The story fast forwards to the time when Isaac himself becomes a father. His barren wife Rebekah conceived not one but two sons. Initially, she couldn't understand why there was violent movement inside her womb. Asking the Lord for an answer, she was told that there were two nations in her womb (verse 23). She would be the proud mother of twins. But these two boys would be very different. Given a glimpse into the future destiny of her boys, she was told that they would be the 'fathers' of two nations and would be divided. Even now, inside her womb, the brothers were fighting for supremacy. The younger son would eventually prevail over the elder.

When they were born, the boys were called Esau and Jacob. They were completely different in their physical appearance. At birth, Jacob already showed signs of wanting to get the better of his brother. Although his brother was born first, Jacob stretched his hand out to grab his brother's heel (verse 26). Another time, Jacob got Esau to sell his birthright for a bowl of pottage (verse 33).

Christians often explain that Esau was disregarded by God because he disqualified himself through his careless attitude towards his birthright. But we also forget that Jacob was true to his name – 'supplanter'. The third patriarch of the Israelites was no role model in his early life.

---

† It is an amazing thing that God can take anyone whom he chooses to be transformed and used for his greater purposes – Lord, use me too.

Anthony Loke   Readings in Genesis 1–35

Readings in Genesis 1–35

5 Jacob

Notes based on the *New Revised Standard Version* by
Emmanuel Borlabi Bortey

After 23 years in book publishing, Emmanuel Borlabi Bortey now serves as a Superintendent Minister of the Methodist Church in Ghana. He currently serves the Adabraka Circuit near the city centre of Accra, Ghana's capital city.

Sunday 14 March: Preparing for the week

This week's readings focus on Jacob, the third of the three founding fathers of the nation of Israel. The family life of these founding fathers clearly shows that they were mere mortals like you and me, with surprising moral weaknesses. That God used them to fulfil his purposes in spite of their sinfulness, should encourage us to know that God can be merciful and gracious to us as well, and that we also can be instruments for fulfilling God's purposes in our world.

Text for the week: *Genesis 32:26*

Then he said, 'Let me go, for the day is breaking.' But Jacob said 'I will not let you go, unless you bless me.'

For group discussion and personal thought

• Why did God choose to make Jacob the father of the chosen race? What lessons can we learn from the choice of Jacob?

• *'And a man wrestled with Jacob until daybreak'* (Genesis 32:24). How should we understand this encounter? Could it be a dream? If not, what really happened to Jacob in this incident? What lessons does this story teach us?

Monday 15 March

Genesis 27:1-17

Favouritism and family feuds

When Isaac grew old he decided to bless his elder son, Esau, before he died. His wife, Rebekah, overheard the conversation between Isaac and Esau in which Isaac requested Esau to go hunting and prepare him his favourite meal from the game hunted and then he would bless Esau before his death. While Esau was away hunting, Rebekah urged Jacob to take a meal she had hurriedly prepared and to deceive the blind Isaac so as to receive the blessing intended for Esau.

Then Rebekah took the best garments of her elder son Esau, which were with her in the house, and put them on her younger son Jacob; and she put the skins of the kids on his hands and on the smooth part of his neck. Then she handed the savoury food, and the bread that she had prepared, to her son Jacob.

(verses 15-17)

Genesis 25:28 provides the clue to why Rebekah went to such lengths to secure Isaac's blessing for her son Jacob: he was her favourite child, whilst Isaac favoured Esau. In this story, we see a family torn apart by favouritism. Family cohesion was sacrificed on the altar of favouritism, producing manoeuvering and scheming to outdo one another. Favouritism is a dangerous and destructive canker and parents must learn to avoid it. Even in the wider society (e.g. in work places) favouritism can be very disruptive and is counterproductive.

† Lord, save us from the danger of favouritism in our families and grant us grace to live in peace with one another in the home and in the wider society. Amen

Emmanuel Borlabi Bortey

Readings in Genesis 1–35

Agony inflicted by a well crafted deception

It took a really great deal of effort to hoodwink the blind Isaac into believing that it was Esau who had come to be blessed: the voice was Jacob's but all the other features had been successfully disguised. Jacob's hands had been made hairy to feel like Esau's, and the smell of the clothes was Esau's. So Isaac went ahead, ate the food and blessed Jacob, only for the real Esau to appear:

> His father Isaac said to him, 'Who are you?' He answered, 'I am your firstborn son, Esau.' Then Isaac trembled violently, and said, 'Who was it then that hunted game and brought it to me, and I ate it all before you came, and I have blessed him? – yes, and blessed he shall be!'
> When Esau heard his father's words, he cried out with an exceedingly great and bitter cry, and said to his father, 'Bless me, me also, father!'

(verses 32-34)

You can well imagine Esau's agony and the bewilderment of Isaac, the blind old man! Deceit can be painful and can leave us all dejected and dumbfounded. It is the more devastating when it is inflicted on us by a close acquaintance – a friend, brother, or sister. It leaves cherished relationships in ruins. This grand deception broke Isaac's family apart: Jacob had to flee from Esau's anger.

The temptation to deceive can come in various circumstances, especially when it seems to promise some advantage. We need to pray for grace to resist such temptations at all times.

† Father, banish from us the spirit of deception and grant us grace to be truthful under all circumstances.

Readings in Genesis 1–35   Emmanuel Borlabi Bortey

Wednesday 17 March

Genesis 29:16-30

Paid back in his own coin?

After fleeing from the anger of his brother Esau, Jacob settled with the family of his uncle Laban. He fell in love with Laban's second daughter, Rachel, and offered to serve Laban for seven years in exchange for the hand of Rachel in marriage.

Jacob said to Laban, 'What is this you have done to me? Did I not serve with you for Rachel? Why then have you deceived me?'

(part of verse 25)

Jacob was given a dose of his own medicine – deception – and how he loathed it! He had laboured expecting to receive Rachel, instead he was given Leah and he had to serve for an additional seven years to compensate for being given Rachel as well. Was he being paid back in his own coin?

We may not always be able to verify that 'the evil that men do lives after them', but we should heed Moses' admonition to the Israelites not to sin against the Lord for 'you may be sure that your sin will find you out' (Numbers 32:23). Did Jacob ever learn his lesson? Yes, but not until much later. Mutual self-deception dogged much of the relationship between Jacob and his uncle Laban. Old habits die hard, so beware! Avoid sinful habits lest you face the bitter consequences of sin.

---

† Heavenly Father, keep us in the paths of righteousness and save us from the perils and dangers of sinful habits. Amen

Emmanuel Borlabi Bortey

Readings in Genesis 1–35

Never give up!

After spending some 20 years in Haran with his uncle Laban, Jacob set out to return home to Canaan with his family, servants and all the wealth he had acquired. But the prospects of a meeting with his elder brother, Esau, deeply worried him. The night before the expected meeting,

> *Jacob was left alone; and a man wrestled with him until daybreak. When the man saw that he did not prevail against Jacob, he struck him on the hip socket; and Jacob's hip was put out of joint as he wrestled with him. Then he said, 'Let me go, for the day is breaking.' But Jacob said, 'I will not let you go, unless you bless me.'*

(verses 24-26)

The desperation with which Jacob held on to the man with whom he wrestled was linked to his deep apprehension about the imminent meeting with Esau. He needed a supernatural intervention to avert Esau's possible anger. Jacob had prayed fervently, asking God to deliver him from Esau's anger (Genesis 32:9-12); his journey was in obedience to God's directive (Genesis 31:3); and he had met with angels (Genesis 32:1). And when Jacob was given the opportunity (through the visitation of an angel – 'a man', verse 24) to get the assurance he badly needed, he held on to it with all his strength.

Jacob prayed to be blessed and he would not give up until he was assured of an answer. Jacob's persistence paid off: he was given a new name, Israel, symbolising a new character. The divine encounter resulted in a much-needed inner transformation, adequate for the daunting task of a meeting with Esau.

† Heavenly Father, grant us grace to hold on to you firmly in all circumstances. Amen!

Readings in Genesis 1–35   Emmanuel Borlabi Bortey

Friday 19 March

Genesis 33:1-11

Forgiveness and reconciliation

Jacob was deeply apprehensive about meeting his brother. As a precautionary measure, therefore, he sent his animals and servants ahead in three groups, with the offer of his animals as a gift to Esau (Genesis 32:13-21). Similarly, he divided his wives and children into three groups and went ahead of them himself, bowing to the ground, to meet Esau.

> *But Esau ran to meet him, and embraced him, and fell on his neck and kissed him, and they wept.*

(verse 4)

What a surprise! What an emotional meeting! Esau warmly embraced his brother Jacob and it took a great deal of persuasion for Esau to accept Jacob's gifts because it was evident he was no longer angry with Jacob. The two brothers were wonderfully reconciled.

Obviously it was Esau's readiness to forgive Jacob that made this reconciliation possible. When we are annoyed and deeply hurt, we need to pray for grace to be able to forgive whoever it is, no matter why, when or how we are wronged. Forgiveness heals broken relationships and indeed is vital for keeping the harmony in all relationships. We need to recognise the crucial role of prayer in all this. Certainly, the God who directed Jacob to return home had gone ahead to prepare the heart of Esau for a joyous reconciliation. And God indeed answered Jacob's prayer.

† Dear Lord, grant us the grace of forgiveness in our relationships; and wherever relationships have turned sour, grant us your reconciling spirit. Amen

Emmanuel Borlabi Bortey

Readings in Genesis 1–35

Saturday 20 March

Genesis 35:1-14

God blesses graciously

After being reconciled to his brother Esau, Jacob settled down in Canaan. God instructed him to settle in Bethel, where God had first revealed himself to him during his flight from Esau, and to set up an altar to worship God. After he had set up the altar at Bethel,

> *God appeared to Jacob again when he came from Paddan-aram, and he blessed him. God said to him, 'Your name is Jacob; no longer shall you be called Jacob but Israel shall be your name.' So he was called Israel. God said to him, 'I am God Almighty; be fruitful and multiply; a nation and a company of nations shall come from you, and kings shall spring from you.'*

(verses 9-11)

A careful reading of the story of Jacob clearly shows that God did not bless him because of any worthiness or special qualities in him. When God first revealed himself to Jacob, he had done nothing to deserve the promise of God's protection he was given. In today's reading God reveals himself again to Jacob and blesses him, promising to make him into a nation.

The story of Jacob is one of grace, not of merit. No one is ever worthy or deserving to receive God's mercy. God can choose to use anyone to fulfil his purposes, for 'I will have mercy on whom I will have mercy, and I will have compassion on whom I will have compassion' (Exodus 33:19). Our response? Humility, always and in all things, and thankfulness to our God who so graciously blesses us.

---

† Father, we are not worthy to receive your numerous mercies. Grant us grace to be humble and thankful to you always. Amen

Readings in Genesis 1–35   Emmanuel Borlabi Bortey

Readings in Luke

3 Confrontation in Jerusalem

Notes based on the *New Revised Standard Version* by
David Huggett

David Huggett is a Baptist minister. After pastoral experience in the north of England and London, he worked with the Bible Society, the Leprosy Mission and in adult Christian education. Now retired, he lives with his wife in Somerset and continues to be involved in preaching, writing and local church life.

Sunday 21 March: Preparing for the week

Confrontation is seldom comfortable, whether it is learning to confront ourselves, our weaknesses and failures, or confronting some situation, person, or political structure that challenges our sense of right and wrong. I read recently of a woman who confronted two young men who were acting unlawfully. They turned on her, knocking her on to a railway line and almost killing her. Jesus confronted evil in its many shapes and guises. By the last week of his life his confrontation was approaching a critical phase. His whole ministry had been leading up to this point, when he finally confronted the political, social and religious evil of his day and paid the ultimate price.

Text for the week: *Luke 22:26-27*
'[T]he greatest among you must become like the youngest, and the leader like one who serves. For who is greater, the one who is at the table or the one who serves? Is it not the one at the table? But I am among you as one who serves.'

For group discussion and personal thought

• What do you understand by 'the kingdom of God'? How might it influence the community where you live?
• What is meant by 'servant leadership'? How does it affect you?

Monday 22 March

A prophetic act

Recently, John Sentamu, the Archbishop of York, cut his clerical collar to pieces on a television programme. He did it, he said, to express his solidarity with the suffering people of Zimbabwe. It was described as a 'prophetic act' and was not unlike Jesus' action in entering Jerusalem on Palm Sunday.

No surprise that Jesus wanted to be in Jerusalem for the greatest Jewish festival of the year. But the way he entered the city appears to have been taken by the religious leaders of his day as a direct challenge. Jesus seems quite deliberately to be acting out the words of the prophet Zechariah (9:9). But what really worried the Pharisees was the bad publicity:

> *[T]he whole multitude of the disciples began to praise God joyfully with a loud voice for all the deeds of power that they had seen, saying, 'Blessed is the king who comes in the name of the Lord!'*

(part of verses 37 and 38)

On the other side of town, Pilate, the Roman Governor, would be making his dramatic entrance with all possible military pomp and ceremony – just to impress the Jews with his power and authority. And the religious leaders, whose own power and authority depended entirely on Rome's goodwill, were anxious that Jesus' action should not compromise their position.

Of course there is no virtue in being unnecessarily provocative, but Christ's call is still, 'Follow me', and if at times that involves upsetting the status quo for the sake of doing or saying what is right, then so be it.

† Gracious Lord, may all that I do be governed by your wisdom, so that every action I take may speak powerfully and yet graciously of your love for all.

Readings in Luke   David Huggett

Tuesday 23 March

Luke 19:41-48; 22:1-6

Warning to leaders

Finding a room for the night in Jerusalem during a major festival must have been a nightmare. However, the fact that each night during that final week Jesus withdrew and camped out with hundreds of ordinary people on the hillsides around the city said something powerful. He would not be a part of a religious system opposed to all he had said and done. With great sadness he sums it up:

> *'[Y]ou did not recognize the time of your visitation from God.'*
>
> (part of verse 44)

The irony was that it was those same Romans, who at all costs must not be offended, who were in the end the instruments of judgement, not only on their rejected Messiah, but upon the religious leaders themselves. Jesus' dramatic actions (verses 41-46) were a clear warning, but it was perhaps his daily teaching (verse 47), probably carried on in the very space he had cleared for himself in the Temple, that gave the leaders the opportunity to change their attitude.

There were good, faithful, sincere men among the Jewish religious leaders – men like Nicodemus. But Jesus was confronting the attitude of those with closed minds who believed that they and they alone were right. Ordinary people, and that was supposed to include this peasant rabbi from Galilee called Jesus, were not expected to challenge their teaching or their example. The next couple of chapters give some illustrations of the content of Jesus' teaching that was a clear challenge to them.

---

† Lord God, we pray for all who have the responsibility of leadership. Help them to be wise in the decisions they make, and humble enough to admit when they are mistaken. Above all help them always to seek the good of those they lead rather than their own advantage.

David Huggett

Readings in Luke

Wednesday 24 March

Luke 22:7-23

The final meal with his friends

Maybe you have enjoyed reading about Defoe's hero, Robinson Crusoe, as he grappled with the problems of being marooned on a desert island. Or you have marvelled at reports of the courage, skill and sheer determination of someone who has survived weeks alone in a jungle, or being cast adrift in a boat, or wandering lost in a desert.

Scientists study the potential psychological damage caused by isolation, but we do not need them to tell us what social creatures we human beings are, nor what a terrible experience loneliness can be. Jesus was no different. He chose twelve men with all their varied weaknesses because he needed company. Now, as he faces the greatest challenge of all, he expresses that deep human need:

> He said to them, 'I have eagerly desired to eat this Passover with you before I suffer.'

(verse 15)

Christians, too, need the support of human companionship. Family, friends, our local community, are all important for our well-being. So is the church. We should make it a priority to ensure that these relationships are kept in good repair.

Jesus expressed his own need as he sat down to this last meal with his closest friends, but at the same time he showed that he understood *their* deep need. The fellowship of the church not only blesses us, but also provides us with the opportunity to contribute to the well-being of other Christians. Even the simple hospitality of a meal can bring healing.

† We pray today for those who have recently become very lonely, perhaps through a bereavement, or a broken marriage or other relationship. Strengthen them, Lord, with your own presence, and give us the insight into their need that will show us how we can best support them.

Readings in Luke   David Huggett

Thursday 25 March

Luke 22:24-38

Facing up to failure

Confronting failure is never easy, yet it must be done. Society generally expects, even demands, success. In the West at least we do everything possible to avoid failure. We are encouraged to emulate the entrepreneur, the politician, the sportsman or sportswoman, the pop star – those who have made it to the top. Yet right from the beginning of his ministry Jesus had made it clear that he had time for the kind of people we class as failures: the poor, the hungry, the sad (Luke 6:20ff). Now, facing the greatest crisis of all and after all he had taught them, Jesus' friends fail him. They get into a pointless argument about rank and status (verse 24).

Peter, aware that a dangerous crisis is looming, boasts that he won't let Jesus down even if the others do. He will stick with him through thick and thin (verse 33). They all make the common mistake of believing that violence can best be overcome by more violence (verse 38). Soon their failures will be compounded as they fall asleep just when Jesus most wants their support.

They are not alone, of course. Even the best of us fails. From time to time we fail those closest to us who depend on us. Through things like stupidity, pride, selfishness, ignorance, we fail ourselves. Worst of all we fail God. Good then to know that he never gives up on failures. His promise is still:

> *'I have prayed for you that your own faith may not fail; and you, when once you have turned back, strengthen your brothers.'*

(verse 32)

† Thank you, Lord, that you never give up on us. Help us not to give up on one another. Help us also to learn from our failures.

David Huggett

Readings in Luke

Friday 26 March

Luke 22:39-53

Making choices

'Give us more choice', demand Western consumers. Choice is important but it can be risky and lead to unwelcome results. The choices Jesus made put him inevitably on a collision course with both religious and political authorities.

Mark tells us at the beginning of his Gospel (1:15) that Jesus chose as the subject for his preaching 'the kingdom of God'. From that moment he was committed to a course of action and teaching that would bring him into direct conflict with both the Jewish and the Roman authorities. His kingdom stood for truth, non-violence and, above all, love. That is why he prayed,

> 'Father, if you are willing, remove this cup from me; yet, not my will but yours be done.'

(verse 42)

This was not a question of bringing himself to the point of accepting the wrath of an angry God against a sinful humankind. Rather it was a prayer that, in spite of the cost that he would naturally prefer to avoid, he longed above all that the Father's purpose of establishing the kingdom with its unique values should be fulfilled.

Make no mistake. When we consciously choose to follow Christ, we too are committed to the same collision course. Hopefully it won't lead to the dramatic end to which it led Jesus, but certainly there will be times when living by the principles of the kingdom will leads us into opposition of one sort or another.

---

† Lord, we pray today for those who, having chosen to follow you, find themselves opposed, tortured, imprisoned, and even put to death for their faith. Give them strength to remain loyal, and vision to see beyond the sufferings and losses they endure to that joyful day when your kingdom will finally come in all its glory.

Readings in Luke   David Huggett

Luke 22:54-71

Betrayal

Trust is an essential ingredient in any human relationship. When trust is broken we feel betrayed. Such betrayal comes in many shapes and forms. Parents who abuse their children betray their trust. Brutus who stabs Julius Caesar betrays his friend. Even the state may betray the trust of its citizens – perhaps the worst modern example is the Holocaust.

Jesus trusted twelve men, but each in his own way betrayed that trust. The very least that Jesus could have expected from the political and religious authorities was to be treated fairly. Instead he received cruel mockery, physical torture and cynical questioning. The natural human response to such treatment is bitterness and anger. Psychiatrists call it 'betrayal trauma' and recognise that it can cause deep psychological damage and even long-lasting mental illness. But Jesus shows us that there is more than one way of dealing with it. He responded to Peter's betrayal with a simple yet profoundly eloquent look (verse 61). The guards who wantonly abused their power merited nothing but silence (verse 65). The insinuations and accusations of the leaders were answered with quiet dignity (verses 67-70). Yet right to the end what Jesus has to say to them is full of challenge. He refuses to be drawn into a fruitless discussion about who he is, but tells them bluntly that in the end it is the rule of God's kingdom that will prevail, not theirs.

> '[F]rom now on the Son of Man will be seated at the right hand of the power of God.'
>
> (verse 69)

† Thank you, Lord, for trusting me enough to call me to follow you. Make me worthy of that trust, and also the trust of others, and help me to support those who feel that they have been betrayed by others.

David Huggett

Readings in Luke

Readings in Luke

4 The way of the cross

Notes based on the *New International Version* by
Meeli Tankler

Meeli Tankler lives in Pärnu, Estonia. She is a psychologist, and teaches part-time in the theological seminaries of the Methodist and Lutheran Churches of Estonia. Married to a Methodist pastor, she is a local preacher, Sunday school teacher, choir director, Bible study leader, mother and grandmother.

Sunday 28 March: Preparing for the week

This week is called holy – and our thoughts this week are focused on the cross, for this is the cornerstone of our salvation and hope. We believe, as Paul wrote, 'the message of the cross . . . the power of God to us who are being saved' (1 Corinthians 1:18). As we follow the way of the cross together with Jesus, and stop here and there to contemplate some people or events, we can think about our possible reactions if we were there. The holiness of this week is reflected in the person of Jesus, and in the holy influence he has, even on his way to the cross.

Text for the week: *Luke 23:47*
'Surely this was a righteous man.'

For group discussion and personal thought

- How would you read each day's passage differently if you didn't know how the story would end?
- What does the story unfolding during this week mean for you personally – where are you in this? Would you rather stay away, and come back when all is well again? Or would you stay there, right at the cross, struggling with despair and unbelief, seeing the Son of God dying before your very eyes? How would your faith be different after this experience?

March

King of the Jews

The way of the cross begins on a royal note: Jesus is taken to the authorities accused of claiming to be a king. As the chief priests and law teachers cannot bring up religious issues before the Roman authorities, they have to find something else serious enough to warrant the death penalty.

Pilate asked Jesus, 'Are you the king of the Jews?'
'Yes, it is as you say,' Jesus replied.

(verse 3)

Pilate does not seem to be annoyed when Jesus gives an interesting but ambiguous answer to his direct question. Perhaps he recognises the difference between a potential rebel and a peaceful man. Perhaps he realises that Jesus is the king indeed, but not in the usual meaning of the word. For his kingdom is not of this world. Pilate must feel his royal dignity in a special way because he is really trying to rebut the charge against Jesus. But his accusers are not backing down.

Pilate finally tries to solve the problem by sending Jesus on to another authority, in hope that he will not have to make any final decision. And it is interesting that, by doing so, he wins himself a true friend in Herod that day! But the king is still waiting for the verdict.

---

† Our Saviour, help us to remember that you are a king indeed, king of the whole universe. Hallowed be your name, your kingdom come, and your will be done on earth as it is in heaven. Amen

Meeli Tankler

Readings in Luke

Tuesday 30 March

Luke 23:13-25

Jesus is surrendered to the crowd

Today's reading speaks about 'the crowd' that made the final decision to crucify Jesus. Pilate himself had called this crowd together, and it was quite diverse: it consisted of 'the chief priests, the rulers and the people' (verse 13). However, this crowd seemed very united in their common request to release Barabbas and to crucify Jesus. Three times Pilate tried unsuccessfully to release Jesus – and finally

Pilate decided to grant their demand . . . and surrendered Jesus to their will.

(verse 24 and part of verse 25)

Think about the power of similar 'crowds' in our time and circumstances. Are we aware of the danger of surrendering our sense of responsibility to the will of the crowd around us, be it a physical or a virtual crowd? Are we attentive enough to discern between truth and non-truth offered us as truth? Are we bold enough to refuse to make decisions 'according to the crowd's will' when we have reasons to question these decisions?

The way of cross from this point on is dictated by agitated, shouting people. Perhaps Jesus could say as he once said to James and John: 'You don't know what you are asking' (Mark 10:28). Salvation history is made, but the people making it have no idea of what is happening.

---

† Lord, we thank you for your willingness to be surrendered to the will of people who did not actually know you, and blindly followed the lead of false accusers. Help us to act in a responsible way whenever we are 'in the crowd'. Amen

Readings in Luke   Meeli Tankler

Wednesday 31 March

Luke 23:26-31

Simon from Cyrene on the way of the cross

Things happen. People may have their own plans but suddenly their path crosses that of someone else, and they find themselves sharing his or her destiny. Simon from Cyrene is 'on his way in from the country' (verse 26) at exactly the same time as Jesus is on his way out, to the place of crucifixion. They meet and become fellow travellers on a journey neither of them would have chosen of his own free will – the journey towards the cross.

They seized Simon from Cyrene . . . and put the cross on him and made him carry it behind Jesus.

(part of verse 26)

We are all called to join Jesus on this journey. Much as we would like to live in the bliss of his resurrection, the pathway towards that glorious day goes first to the cross. And, like Simon, we may be asked to carry the heavy cross on our shoulders for a while, following Jesus on his way to the cross where he carries our iniquities. There is no other way to salvation but the way of the cross.

But there is life on the other side of the cross. As Paul puts it, 'I have been crucified with Christ and I no longer live, but Christ lives in me. The life I live in the body, I live by faith in the Son of God, who loved me and gave himself for me' (Galatians 2:20).

† Lord Jesus, you once told us to take up our cross daily and follow you. Help us to understand the way of the cross for us personally, and to follow you. Amen

Meeli Tankler

Readings in Luke

Together in paradise

The way of the cross is drawing to an end. There are three crosses erected at the place called the Skull. And people are gathering in the expectation of a great show of painful death. Those nearest to the cross are shouting insults while watching the three men dying.

In the midst of mockery and humiliation, in the midst of suffering, Jesus still has an open heart for other people's pain. There is much hostility and contempt in the air. And suddenly, there is one very different voice saying these simple words in great reverence:

'Jesus, remember me, when you come into your kingdom.'

(part of verse 42)

There are two criminals crucified together with Jesus. And we are told that one of them, hanging on the cross, opens his heart to him in repentance right there, and receives the most hopeful response: 'Today you will be with me in paradise' (verse 43). We should pray for more people with such a strong faith – for people who are able to recognise the king even when he is hanging on the cross.

The way of the cross reveals unusual characters in the salvation story – criminals repenting and seeking God's grace in the last minute of their lives. Jesus did not reject this man. He told him they would meet each other again in paradise, this very day!

† Lord Jesus, we pray for people who are far from you and who have deep problems. We pray that they may meet you, the crucified, and find your grace and forgiveness. Amen

Readings in Luke   Meeli Tankler

Friday 2 April (Good Friday)
Luke 23:44-49

An unexpected testimony

The way of the cross is not finished yet. Today we meet another interesting person at the cross. He is fulfilling his duty as a Roman centurion. Crucifixions are common events for him, and he has grown indifferent to them. This day there is something unusual in the air, however – a really tense atmosphere between the mockers as a majority, and the few others who seem to be surprisingly sympathetic towards one of the three crucified criminals. Even one of the dying criminals is speaking to his neighbour on the cross in a most extraordinary way. And there is a sign saying something about the man in the middle being a king . . . Suddenly the sun stops shining, the curtain of the temple is torn, the man named Jesus calls for his Father and dies. Without fully understanding what is happening, the centurion feels he has to praise God right here and now.

The centurion, seeing what had happened, praised God and said, 'Surely this was a righteous man.'

(verse 47)

His open testimony about Jesus being 'a righteous man' bears a much deeper meaning than he probably intended. He is not simply saying 'not guilty', but dimly recognising that this man on the cross was far more than a mere human being. Matthew and Mark quote the centurion as saying, 'this man was the Son of God' (Matthew 27:54, Mark 15:39).

---

† Lord, we pray for apathetic, indifferent people doing their routine jobs day in and day out. We ask you to step into their dull lives with your majesty, to surprise and stir them, and wake them up to recognise you as Son of God. Amen

Meeli Tankler

Readings in Luke

A new tomb for Jesus

It is finished. Jesus is dead and all his body still needs is a tomb. And here is a man offering his own new tomb – a tomb cut into rock. Most probably this noble tomb was waiting for this good and upright man himself. But he offers it for Jesus' burial. Actually, he also conducts some kind of hurried funeral service for Jesus:

[H]e took it down, wrapped it in linen cloth and placed it in a tomb cut in the rock.

(part of verse 53)

Isn't this amazing? We can understand acts of goodwill for the living Jesus but now he is dead, and everything seems to be finished, Joseph is doing his best even for the dead body of Jesus. We are told that he has been 'waiting for the kingdom of God' (verse 51), and he still seems to be waiting. Even when the king is dead.

Everything is ready for the Sabbath rest. Closer friends of Jesus may be silently remembering him and grieving for him, but they are obedient to the commandment to keep the Sabbath in a certain way. Then the new day is dawning. Is Jesus' dead body still resting in this new tomb? Has the way of the cross ended here? Perhaps it is time to rise from the Sabbath rest and continue the journey in order to meet the king after death . . .

† Thank you, God, for sending your Son. Thank you for reconciling all things to yourself, whether things on earth or things in heaven, by making peace through his blood, shed on the cross. Amen

Readings in Luke

5 The risen Lord

Notes based on the *New Revised Standard Version* by
Catherine Williams

Catherine Williams is an Anglican priest working as Vocations Officer and
Assistant Diocesan Director of Ordinands for the Diocese of Gloucester,
England. Her role is to enable individuals and churches to discern God's
call. Catherine is married to the Vicar of Tewkesbury Abbey and they
have two teenage daughters.

April

Sunday 4 April (Easter Day) : Preparing for the week

What a day! In Luke's Gospel the disciples' experiences of the resurrected
and ascending Christ happen on a single day. It's a day filled with confusion,
terror, surprise, joy and challenge. It's a day that changes the world for
ever. From the discovery of the empty tomb at deep dawn, through the
journey to and from Emmaus, to the final blessing at Bethany, we travel
with the followers and friends of Jesus as they experience the risen Christ
and his call into a new and exciting future.

Text for the week: *Luke 24:5*

*'Why do you look for the living among the dead? He is not here, but has
risen.'*

For group discussion and personal thought

• Which is your favourite resurrection appearance of Jesus and why?
• This week, tell someone about your experiences of the risen Christ.
• Practise waiting on God.

Luke 24:1-12

At early dawn

Alleluia! Christ is risen.
He is risen indeed. Alleluia!

In the Church of England we use these responses at most services during the Easter season. We are encouraged to say them with passion and joy as we declare the resurrection of Jesus Christ, our 'good news'. We are used to the idea of resurrection – it's a central part of the Christian faith. Those caught up in the events of the original day of resurrection were far from sure what was happening. The women found an open, empty tomb and strange characters in dazzling clothes. The apostles were confronted by their womenfolk talking nonsense, and all Peter could find were linen cloths. Mixed emotions were displayed: confusion, terror and amazement. Running throughout the events echoed the words of the strangers:

> *'Why do you look for the living among the dead? He is not here, but has risen. Remember how he told you, while he was still in Galilee, that the Son of Man must be handed over to sinners, and be crucified, and on the third day rise again.'*

(part of verse 5, and verse 6)

Luke tells us the events of this incredible day began at 'early dawn'. The resurrection of Jesus heralds a new beginning unlike anything that has gone before. No wonder the first disciples took some time to work out what was going on. In our familiarity with the resurrection account it's important that we don't lose the wonder and mystery of God's unique and astonishing way of working.

† Lord God, thank you that in Christ you make all things new.

Readings in Luke   Catherine Williams

Luke 24:13-27

On the road

April

Two of the followers of Jesus, perhaps close friends or maybe even husband and wife, are travelling towards Emmaus. They are putting as great a distance as they can between themselves and the terrible events in Jerusalem. They are downcast, confused and miserable about the death of Jesus. Everything has gone horribly wrong and the imminent redemption of Israel seems an impossible dream. A stranger comes alongside and walks with the two. He asks them about their discussion and they, surprised at his ignorance of events, fill him in on recent happenings. Though the stranger doesn't seem to know about the death of Jesus in Jerusalem, he does have a prodigious knowledge of the scriptures. As the three walk together, the stranger, who is the risen Christ, unfolds the mystery of the crucifixion:

'Was it not necessary that the Messiah should suffer these things and then enter into his glory?' Then beginning with Moses and all the prophets, he interpreted to them the things about himself in all the scriptures.

(verses 26-27)

What an incredible Bible study it must have been: the Word of God incarnate explaining the Word of God in scripture – revealing God's saving plan for all. When we feel let down by God or our faith is confusing or lacks sense or direction, the risen Christ may come to us in surprising or hidden ways and reveal again for us God's truth. May we always be open to Christ revealing himself to us in surprising and unexpected ways.

† Lord, thank you for walking alongside those who are downcast or faltering in their faith. Help me to reveal you to those who are struggling.

Catherine Williams

Readings in Luke

Luke 24:28-35

Bread broken – eyes opened

The stranger on the road to Emmaus has a magnetic personality and the two travellers don't want to lose his company. They urge him to stay with them, to rest and eat. It's in the simple act of breaking bread at the table that the risen Jesus is revealed. The two have seen Jesus break bread many times before, not least at the Last Supper, when he gave bread and wine special and holy significance. The disciples were commanded to break bread in order to remember Jesus and to celebrate his presence with them.

Then their eyes were opened, and they recognised him; and he vanished from their sight.

(verse 31)

Once Jesus is revealed, the two make no delay in returning to Jerusalem, no longer wanting to run away from events, but ready to engage with the present reality of Christ in a new way. They are eager to tell their story to the others, and to hear the accounts of Jesus' appearances that day.

Every celebration of the Eucharist should be for us, as Christians, a meeting with the risen Christ. We remember his death and resurrection. We are fed with his body and blood, and we go out into the world renewed in hope and filled with the desire to tell others what we have discovered of the Lord of life. Whenever bread is blessed and broken our eyes should be opened to Christ who is alive and active amongst us.

† Lord, at every celebration of Holy Communion, keep my eyes open to your surprising presence.

Readings in Luke

Catherine Williams

A ghost?

The disciples were the first people to see a resurrected body. Though Lazarus and others had been brought back to life from the dead, they would die again. The resurrected Christ models a new way of being. His body is at home both in heaven and on earth and heralds the time prophesied in the book of Revelation when there will be a new heaven and a new earth.

The disciples are confused and frightened, and think they are seeing a ghost. Jesus introduces them to the qualities of resurrection. He has flesh and blood, and can eat and drink. Yet he can also appear and disappear at will, and is sometimes recognisable and sometimes not. Jesus reassures the disciples by bringing his peace and by showing them the marks of crucifixion:

'Why are you frightened and why do doubts arise in your hearts? Look at my hands and feet; see that it is I myself. Touch me and see; for a ghost does not have flesh and bones as you see that I have.'

(verses 38-39)

It is almost impossible to imagine what will happen to us and those we love after death. This episode with the resurrected Christ reassures us that we will be both changed and similar. Life will be lived in a new way but we will still be 'ourselves'. Alongside Christ we will remain inhabitants of earth and citizens of the kingdom of heaven; at ease in God's eternity.

† Give thanks for the promise of resurrection and God's gift of eternal life.

Catherine Williams

Readings in Luke

Friday 9 April

Luke 24:44 53

Seize the day!

Luke records the resurrection appearances, the great commission, the promise of the Holy Spirit and Jesus' ascension to heaven as occurring in a single day, in and around the city of Jerusalem. What an incredible day for the disciples – a day like no other, when their beliefs, imaginations and emotions are stretched to breaking point. Throughout, Jesus instructs them using words of scripture, giving root and validity to their experiences.

> Then he opened their minds to understand the scriptures, and he said to them, 'Thus is it written, that the Messiah is to suffer and to rise from the dead on the third day, and that repentance and forgiveness of sins is to be proclaimed in his name to all nations, beginning from Jerusalem.'

(verses 45- 47)

As they are the witnesses to the resurrection they have a great responsibility: to tell everyone what they have seen and heard. We believe today because of the faithful witness of those first disciples who were not afraid to tell their incredible story.

From the moment of his ascension Jesus is worshipped and his message goes out into the world. Standing in the shoes of those first witnesses we are called to proclaim Christ to our generation and share our experiences of Jesus with those around us. The message that through Jesus Christ God forgives his people and longs for them to return to him is still a message for all the nations – and we are the messengers.

† Lord, as your modern-day disciple, make me a worthy witness of the resurrection.

Readings in Luke   Catherine Williams

Saturday 10 April

Acts 1:1-14

Waiting

Luke continues his story of the disciples and their faith adventures in his second book, The Acts of the Apostles. Here again we have the account of the ascension and Jesus' promise of the Holy Spirit. This will be God's power sent down on the disciples to fill them with courage and boldness to tell their story. However, they have to wait, and as in the period following the crucifixion, they have no idea what will happen next or when it will be.

> '[I]t is not for you to know the times or periods that the Father has set by his own authority. But you will receive power when the Holy Spirit has come upon you; and you will be my witnesses . . . to the ends of the earth.'

(verse 7, and part of verse 8)

They pass the time together, supporting one another and praying constantly.

Waiting can be difficult and demanding. In the UK, people like to be busy and in control. We are not good at waiting for things. Instant food, running hot and cold water, goods bought on credit, the internet, and instant entertainment, mean that we can have what we need, and more, whenever we want it. Having to wait teaches us to rely on God and his provision and reminds us that it is God who is control of our lives and his timing is not always the same as ours. God's gifts will always exceed what we long for or what we imagine we need. Waiting patiently for a renewing of the Holy Spirit in our lives may be exactly what we need at this time.

---

† Lord, teach me to wait and to trust in your timing and provision.

Catherine Williams

Readings in Luke

Resting places and sacred spaces

1 The divine imperative to rest

Notes based on the *New Revised Standard Version* by
Members of the Bible Study group of South Street Baptist Church, Exeter, UK

Following discussion of the Bible readings for this week, these members of the group each wrote a day's notes: Norman Allnutt, former headmaster and lay pastor; Millie Hallet, retired nurse tutor in Australia and the UK; Sue Le Quesne, previously a missionary in Bangladesh; Verena White, a legal secretary; Ken and Marian Strachan, minister and wife.

Sunday 11 April: Preparing for the week

The scriptures contain many commands to rest, and the command applies not only to human beings, but also to animals and to the land itself. Jesus builds on the Jewish teaching of the sabbath in his own teaching about the need to abide or dwell in him.

Text for the week: *John 15:9*
'As the Father has loved me, so I have loved you; abide [stay, remain, rest] in my love.'

For group discussion and personal thought

- How do you rest? Do you make it possible for others around you to rest?
- Why do you think some people find it difficult to accept that there is strength in resting?
- Are there people in your church, or community, who have to work on Sundays but might like to worship, perhaps on another day (for example, hospital staff and carers, police or shop assistants)? How is your church looking after their need for worship and Christian fellowship?

Exodus 31:12-17

The sabbath rest

Most people enjoy holidays – to take a break from work, visit family and friends, or perhaps travel. Our God knows that we all need rest from daily work, for relaxation and refreshment. If we don't take time to renew our bodies, minds and spirits, we lose our enthusiasm, become tired and impatient with each other and become stale and unloving.

Christian people try to use Sunday, the first day of the week, which we call the Lord's Day, to celebrate Jesus' resurrection. We meet to relax and enjoy fellowship, to worship and to witness to God's love and presence in our lives and in our world. Our celebration of the Lord's Day owes much to the Jewish observance of the sabbath. On the seventh day of the week Jewish families, their slaves and even their animals were commanded to rest. The sabbath was to be a holy day, or a holiday: a time for refreshment.

Therefore the Israelites shall keep the sabbath . . . as a perpetual covenant. It is a sign for ever between me and the people of Israel that in six days the LORD made heaven and earth, and on the seventh day he rested, and was refreshed.

(part of verse 16, and verse 17)

In Old Testament times, the Jews were surrounded by, and constantly under threat from, neighbouring tribes. Sabbath rest and worship helped to mark them out as God's people. Sadly, God's gift of a day for rest became the target of very harsh Jewish laws and rules, which are reflected in this passage.

† Lord, as we worship on Sundays, help us to be mindful of and caring for those who want to worship but have to work.

South Street Baptist Church   Resting places and sacred spaces

Hebrews 4:4-11

The sabbath rest yet to come

When we are walking along a busy street, the best and safest thing to do is to keep looking forwards. If we try to look backwards, we might walk into a lamp post. If we look at our feet, we may easily bump into another person. In the letter to the Hebrews, we are reminded to keep looking forwards. We must never think that we have arrived at our final destination as Christians.

So then, a sabbath rest still remains for the people of God.

(verse 9)

What will take us to heaven, to share in God's rest? We may have been blessed and helped by God in the past, but that is the past. It isn't enough. God may have brought us to the place we are now, and to the service we are giving him. It isn't enough. We are always being challenged to keep moving forwards with God into the future. So the writer says,

Let us therefore make every effort to enter that rest.

(part of verse 11)

We must be like Christian in the book *The Pilgrim's Progress*. He was on a continuous journey, with ups and downs, successes and failures. But he kept striving forwards until he reached the celestial kingdom. He didn't stop halfway, or give up when difficulties arose. If we think we have arrived as Christians, then we need to be careful. The writer reminds us of the need to always be moving on – learning, exploring, expanding and growing.

† Dear Lord, help me to keep moving forwards with my eyes fixed on you, until I come to your eternal rest. Amen

Resting places and sacred spaces   South Street Baptist Church

Wednesday 14 April

Leviticus 25:1-7

The land's rest

The LORD spoke to Moses on Mount Sinai, saying: Speak to the people of Israel and say to them: When you enter the land that I am giving you . . . in the seventh year there shall be a sabbath of complete rest for the land, a sabbath for the LORD: you shall not sow your field or prune your vineyard.

(part of verse 2, and verse 4)

Experience has taught us that, just as people and animals need to rest, so does the land. The sabbath, intended by God as a time for refreshment and renewal, included a period of regeneration for the land. Cattle ranchers understand the importance of rotational grazing. Farmers know that periodically the land needs to lie fallow.

Sadly, there are many examples today, in different parts of the world, of misuse of the land. Overproduction takes so much goodness from the soil that it is often worked out and becomes barren. Dust bowls and desert areas may be the result of humanity's greed and insensitivity. They bear witness to the folly of failing to recognise the land's need for periods of rest. The land must have respite from constant use and fertilisers. Since the land is God's gift to us, he requires us to use it responsibly, so that it can be passed on from generation to generation in good condition. It is in our care, given to us in trust by God, to help feed our own and future generations.

† Lord, help us to use the land wisely and understand that it, like us, needs rest, respect and care.

South Street Baptist Church   Resting places and sacred spaces

Strength in resting

In returning and rest you shall be saved;
in quietness and in trust shall be your strength.

(part of verse 15)

April

In my Bible, the title of this chapter is 'A rebellious people'. I smiled as I read this because it reminded me of how stubborn and self-willed many of us can be at times. I know that I often make the mistake of wanting to rely too much on my own resources and abilities, forging ahead with ideas of my own, forgetting to seek God's counsel and to trust in him. Rest and quietness are not words we usually associate with strength and successful living. We want action, to move forwards, make plans.

The Israelites, in today's reading, thought that their fast horses and alliances with foreign powers would solve their problems and save them. But God warned that they were heading for disaster by trying to sort matters out by themselves, carrying out plans that were not his, refusing to seek his help. God speaks to each generation, and to each one of us, asking us to return to him, to trust, to receive his help, guidance and strength.

Therefore the LORD waits to be gracious to you;
Therefore he will rise up to show mercy to you.
For the LORD is a God of justice;
blessed are all those who wait for him.

(verse 18)

† Loving, gracious God, forgive us when we rely too much on ourselves and other people. Teach us to trust you, to rest with confidence in your promises, and in our weakness to know your strength.

Resting places and sacred spaces   South Street Baptist Church

Friday 16 April
Matthew 11:28-30

Jesus' promise of rest

'Come to me, all you that are weary and are carrying heavy burdens, and I will give you rest. Take my yoke upon you, and learn from me; for I am gentle and humble in heart, and you will find rest for your souls.'

(verses 28-29)

We have a lady in our church who is 80 years of age. After working for many years as a nurse tutor in England and Australia, she volunteered to work for a short time at a children's hostel in India. She now helps in a local hospice and serves as a deacon in our church. From many years' experience of living and serving her Lord, she writes: 'In our busy lives, with so many demands on our time and so many things to think about, it seems increasingly difficult to keep a space for quietness and relaxation, and for time to reflect and pray. It is so easy to forge ahead with plans we have made. But unless we ask for guidance from God, we may not achieve his purposes, and we may feel stressed from our efforts.'

Jesus advised his disciples to 'come apart and rest awhile' (Mark 6: 31). We all need to find a quiet place and a quiet time each day, to remind ourselves of God's promises and to rest confidently in him and his love for us.

† Lord, I want that rest you promise to all who come to you. Help me to seek and trust your guidance as I follow the path you open before me.

South Street Baptist Church   Resting places and sacred spaces

Abide in me

Aeroplanes cannot fly without aviation fuel. All motors need a reliable source of energy to function continuously and effectively, otherwise they splutter and come to a halt. If we drive a car, we are very aware of the need to supply fuel to keep it running.

The fuel for a Christian's life journey, and the energy needed for fruitful service, come not only from the food we eat, to meet our physical needs, but from resting, staying, remaining or abiding in Christ. Jesus used the example of the vine to teach this.

Abide in me as I abide in you. Just as the branch cannot bear fruit by itself unless it abides in the vine, neither can you unless you abide in me. I am the vine, you are the branches. Those who abide in me and I in them bear much fruit, because apart from me you can do nothing.

(verses 4-5)

When the branch is attached to the vine, it receives life and energy from the sap that flows through it. Jesus challenges us to be so joined with him that we will bear fruit, as his life and love flow through us to others.

† Living, loving Lord, we thank you that you have called us to be living branches by abiding in you, the vine. Help us each day to live fruitful lives so that you may be glorified.

Resting places and sacred spaces

2 Resting places in the Old Testament

Notes based on the *New Revised Standard Version* by
Marcel Valentin Măcelaru

Dr M V Măcelaru is a Romanian theologian living in Osijek, Croatia, where he teaches Old Testament at the Evangelical Theological Seminary. He is also a visiting lecturer at Elim Evangelical Theological Seminary in Timišoara, Romania.

Sunday 18 April : Preparing for the week

The biblical concept of 'rest' is not simply a call to leisure or inactivity, but is closely connected with the presence of God in the life of the community. 'Rest' is the time when God manifests himself, the place where he dwells. So, 'rest' is primarily a theological concept. It has a historical dimension, for history begins in the book of Genesis with God establishing a day of rest. It has a redemptive dimension, for divine acts of redemption restore creation to its initial state of rest. And it has an eternal dimension, for the goal awaiting faithful believers is God's eternal rest. 'Rest' represents God's plan for humanity, from the beginning to the end. 'Rest' in the Bible may be defined practically as an experience of order, wholeness, security, joy and peace – the place where life receives meaning through the assurance that God rules benevolently and powerfully over the entire creation.

Text for the week: *Psalm 131:3*
O Israel, hope in the Lord from this time on and for evermore.

For group discussion and personal thought

• Do you find time to rest and enjoy God's presence?

• Do you trust God to provide for your needs? Are you content with what you have?

• Is there any situation of chaos in your life? Can you rest assured that God will intervene?

Genesis 2:1-3

Finding meaning in life

So God blessed the seventh day and hallowed it, because on it God rested from all the work that he had done in creation.

(verse 3)

April

In the Bible, history begins with a series of marvellous acts of creation through which God brings into being a perfect, ordered universe. The culminating act inaugurates a state of being that describes God's intention for the creation: rest.

This is a peculiar vision for many of us. We live in a world where intense, constant activity is associated with quality, productivity and ultimately significance: the busier you become the higher your status in the society may be. Sometimes we call such people 'workaholics', a word meant to belittle those whose obsession with work has become an addiction, but in reality we all admire them, because we also define ourselves by what we do, by the array of duties and responsibilities we take upon ourselves.

However, I believe that meaning in life is not found in an endless pursuit of accomplishments. After creating the universe God rested. Similarly, sometimes we also must stop creating. Of course, God's rest is not a simple moment of inactivity. Rather, it is a time of joy and reflection, for God looks back at what he has accomplished, decides that it is all good and delights in his creation. In the same way, we are called to stop and reflect on what we do, on the quality of our work, and to enjoy the things we have accomplished. To find meaning in life, sometimes we simply have to rest.

† Lord God, you have ordained from the beginning a time for work and a time for rest. Help us to live accordingly. Make our work count but also give us true rest.

Resting places and sacred spaces   Marcel Valentin Măcelaru

Genesis 28:10-22

Surprised by God's presence

'Know that I am with you and will keep you wherever you go, and will bring you back to this land; for I will not leave you until I have done what I have promised you.'

(verse 15)

Today's reading shows Jacob on the run. This may come across as a paradox given the fact that our theme this week is 'rest'. However, Jacob's experience teaches us a great spiritual truth. That is, God manifests himself when one least expects him to do so.

The story behind today's reading shows Jacob as a scheming trickster who steals from his father the blessing rightfully belonging to his brother Esau. For all his efforts, however, Jacob ends up alone and without the blessing he so much sought. At that point God appears to him and promises him a blessing of his own. What I find interesting is where and how God does this. Weary of running, Jacob stops to rest for the first time since he ran away. Or maybe for the first time in his life, for here Jacob is finally unable to find a solution. Unexpectedly, this is the time and place that God chooses to appear to him.

I believe there is a lesson here for all of us. In order to experience the blessing of God in our lives we must learn to stop, we must learn to rest from any pursuit that keeps us too busy to notice that we are lonely and in need of God's presence.

---

† Heavenly Father, I am weary of running. Bless me with your presence. Open my eyes to see you.

Marcel Valentin Măcelaru   Resting places and sacred spaces

Wednesday 21 April

Exodus 15:27 – 16:26

Trust God and be content

[T]hose who gathered much had nothing over, and those who gathered little had no shortage; they gathered as much as each of them needed.

(part of verse 18)

Today's reading teaches us four principles of divine economy. First, it calls us to trust that God will provide for all our needs. As the Israelites learnt in the wilderness, when there seem to be no resources left, God is able to provide food for everyone. Second, it encourages us to be content with what we receive from God. God did not provide, either in variety or in quantity, more than the Israelites needed. Third, it tells us that there is a limit to how much one can and should accumulate. Whether gathering a lot, or gathering a little, all the Israelites had just as much manna as they needed. Fourth, it teaches us the importance of putting aside a time for rest, a time when all work must cease. At such times what remains is humble acknowledgement of God's provision, peaceful satisfaction with what is available and joyful use of what we have. From this perspective, the Sabbath rest described in today's reading is nothing less than a celebration of life lived in abundance under the care of God. People living according to these principles will never want (see Psalm 23:1)!

† Heavenly Father, thank you for your care and provision. Teach me to be content with what you have given me, and I shall never want.

Resting places and sacred spaces   Marcel Valentin Măcelaru

Finding rest amidst chaos

I went down to the land
whose bars closed upon me for ever;
yet you brought up my life from the Pit,
O LORD my God.
As my life was ebbing away,
I remembered the LORD;
and my prayer came to you,
into your holy temple.

(part of verse 6, and verse 7)

Every once in a while, regardless of how safe we think we are, our lives turn into chaos. For Jonah this was a life-threatening experience as he was sinking to the bottom of the sea. For some of us the chaos we experience may be caused by sickness, poverty, oppression, depression, or confusion. Nevertheless, no matter what is causing it and how it is manifested, today's reading teaches that even amidst the darkest, deepest chaos there exists the possibility of rest.

Of course, in order to experience such rest one needs to learn from Jonah to cry out to God for help, to rely on God's mercy and power to save. To someone who has not seen God at work this may seem an incredible idea, for how can a simple cry move God to act on our behalf? The Bible teaches, however, that asking God for help is an action that never fails to bring the desired deliverance (see, for instance, Psalm 107). So, dear believer, rest assured: there is hope even amidst the worst chaos!

† Help me, Lord Jesus! Bring order to the chaos in my life. My hope is in you, Lord.

Marcel Valentin Măcelaru   Resting places and sacred spaces

Resting in the presence of God

As an apple tree among the trees of the wood,
so is my beloved among young men.
With great delight I sat in his shadow,
and his fruit was sweet to my taste.

(verse 3)

What a wonderful image of loving reunion! At first glance today's reading depicts two lovers enjoying each other's presence. However, from ancient times Jewish rabbis commenting on this text rightfully understood that it talks about the spiritual dimension as well. They understood that the intimacy described in it is that of the believer who delights in the presence of God and that the sweet fruit referred to is the word of God encountered in the study of scripture.

Whether we accept the interpretation of the rabbis or not, two things are clear from the passage. First, the feelings the author wishes to convey are joy, trust, comfort and, most of all, love. Are not these the feelings we experience when in the presence of God? Second, the decision seems to be entirely in our hands. God has already opened his arms to receive us. His love towards us will never end. Shall we not run to sit at his shadow? Shall we not find rest in his embrace?

---

† Thank you, Lord, for your kind love. Here I am, sitting at your feet, resting in your arms. I desire your presence more than anything else. I love you, Lord.

Resting places and sacred spaces   Marcel Valentin Măcelaru

Saturday 24 April

Psalms 127:1-2; 131

The choice is yours!

*It is in vain that you rise up early
and go late to rest,
eating the bread of anxious toil;
for he gives sleep to his beloved.*

(Psalm 127, verse 2)

*I do not occupy myself with things
too great and too marvellous for me.*

(Psalm 131, part of verse 1)

The readings for today present us with two alternatives. The first is a life of worthless labour, full of fatigue and worry, too tiring to be enjoyable. Whether we recognise ourselves in this description or not, we are constantly in danger of living such a life. Of course, no one would deliberately choose this. What we need to realise, however, is that the choices we make each day may lead us there.

The readings also offer an alternative to such a life: 'rest'. In the context of Psalm 131 such 'rest' means knowing when to stop working and to start trusting in God that things will run well without any human assistance. It means not worrying about tomorrow. It means not undertaking to do more than is possible within normal work limits. It means not doing what is unsuitable, given your skills and abilities. Rest means knowing and respecting your limits. Which alternative will you pursue? The choice is all yours!

† Lord God, we live in a world where economic instability and low wages force us to seek more and more work. However, your word teaches us to know our limits, to know when to stop. We put our trust in you, Lord, to care for our needs.

Marcel Valentin Măcelaru   Resting places and sacred spaces

Resting places and sacred spaces

3 Resting places in the New Testament

Notes based on the *Contemporary English Version* by
Elizabeth Bruce Whitehorn

Elizabeth Bruce Whitehorn grew up in Edinburgh. After many years working as a teacher and adult educator, she was Senior Editor for NCEC and IBRA (now Christian Education) until 2005. She then 'retired' to Cambridge and has revived and developed a variety of interests, including exploring different approaches to Christian prayer and spirituality. She is a member of the United Reformed Church.

April

Sunday 25 April: Preparing for the week

This week, with the help of the Gospels of Mark and John, we consider the nature and importance of rest. What one person considers rest may be boredom for another and over-stimulation for someone else. Similarly, people have different ideas about sacred space: one may feel closest to God in his or her own home, another may find God in nature, and someone else may feel God's presence most easily in a church or at an ancient place of pilgrimage.

The notes this week are written as personal reflections to encourage you to examine your own faith and experience in the light of your relationship with God. Try to take time each day to focus on the Bible reading and the notes, and ask God to speak to you through them. You could begin your 'quiet time' by focusing on a flower or a lit candle, or listening to a calming piece of music or the natural sounds around you.

Text for the week: *Mark 6:31*

Jesus said, 'Let's go to a place where we can be alone and get some rest.'

For group discussion and personal thought

Each day's reflection contains several questions for personal thought. Take time to ponder them prayerfully.

• What action(s) do you need to take, individually and together?
• How can you help and encourage each other?

Monday 26 April

Mark 4:26-29

A regular resting place

The farmer sleeps at night . . . Yet the seeds keep sprouting and grow-ing and he doesn't understand how.

(part of verse 27)

Sleep seems so easy, a natural part of life's daily rhythm, yet it can be so elusive:
the harder I try to get to sleep, the more awake I become.
The more I worry about things, the 'seeds' I have planted or have yet to plant,
the less likely I am to reap the benefits of sleep and rest.
Do I worry about things over which I have no control?
What can I learn from this farmer who worked hard during the day and slept at night,
not worrying that he didn't understand everything?

Sleep is vital for my physical, mental and spiritual well-being:
what is the right amount of sleep for me?
If I lie awake worrying, what does that say about my attitude to God?
If I don't allow time for enough sleep, what does that say about my attitude
to myself, to those around me and to God?

† Teach me, O God, what is the right balance of rest and activity in my life. Help me to share my worries with you and leave them with you while I sleep, to do what I can and leave the results to you.

Elizabeth Bruce Whitehorn   Resting places and sacred spaces

Mark 1:9-13

A difficult resting place

Straight away God's Spirit made Jesus go into the desert. He stayed there for forty days while Satan tested him.

(verses 12 and 13)

How did Jesus feel about being 'made' to go into the desert?
After the 'high' of his baptism and God speaking from heaven,
he might have expected to start preaching and working straight away.
Instead he had to spend many days in the desert,
a place of loneliness, physical hardship and danger,
as well as being tested by Satan.

In the midst of a busy, pressurised life, filled with noise and distraction,
spending time alone in a deserted place can seem very attractive:
just me and God, enjoying quality time.
In reality it can be difficult to unwind, slow down,
depend on my own resourcefulness, enjoy my own company,
hear God speaking through the clamouring voices that have
come with me.
Far from being restful, it can be a time of wrestling with issues I have been
avoiding.

Do I find it easier to recognise God's presence in busyness or in quietness?
How important is it for me to find solitude and where do I find it?
How can I make better use of solitude?
Do I need to make more space and time for being with God?
Am I afraid of being alone, with myself and with God?

† Teach me, O God, what is the right balance of solitude and busyness in my life. Help me
   to face issues I would rather avoid, drawing strength and courage from you.

Resting places and sacred spaces   Elizabeth Bruce Whitehorn

Wednesday 28 April

Mark 4:35-41

A strange resting place

Jesus was in the back of the boat with his head on a pillow, and he was asleep.

(part of verse 38)

Oh to have such peace of mind that I could sleep in the midst of a storm at sea!
I love the sea, but if I had taken part in this story I would definitely have reacted as the disciples did.
It must have been bad to make experienced fishermen panic;
in spite of all their efforts the boat was about to sink.
How could a storm-tossed boat be a place of rest?
How could Jesus carry on sleeping?
Even if he didn't care about his own safety, surely he ought to be concerned about others?
Sometimes I panic over the smallest ripple that rocks the boat of my life, fearing the worst.
Sometimes I behave as if I think that my problems aren't serious enough to trouble Jesus about, but my actions end up making the situation worse.

Jesus asked, 'Why were you afraid? Don't you have any faith?'
How would I have answered that question the last time I was afraid or in a panic?
What does this say about my view of Jesus and my relationship with him?

---

† Teach me, O God, what is the right balance of faith and self-reliance in my life. Help me to focus on you more deliberately as I go about my daily life.

Elizabeth Bruce Whitehorn   Resting places and sacred spaces

No resting place

Jesus said, 'Let's go to a place where we can be alone and get some rest.' . . . People from every town ran on ahead and got there first.

(parts of verses 31 and 33)

The disciples must have been looking forward to some much-needed rest, but once again it had to be postponed.

No wonder they suggested sending the crowds away to find food for themselves at the end of the day.

Was there no end to the demands of living close to Jesus?

Were they expected to perform miracles too, in spite of being tired and having no resources?

Couldn't they have even a few minutes' rest away from the needy crowds?

Even if Jesus didn't need to rest, couldn't he see that they did?

Today's Western culture values 'me time':

time when I can focus on things I enjoy, things that refresh and restore me.

The Bible encourages me to love my neighbour as I love myself.

How do I balance my need for rest with my Christian responsibility?

---

† Teach me, O God, what is the right balance of self-protection and self-giving in my life. Help me to react to life's demands in Christ-like ways.

Resting places and sacred spaces — Elizabeth Bruce Whitehorn

Friday 30 April

John 14:1-6

A promised resting place

'There are many rooms in my Father's house . . . I am going there to prepare a place for each of you.'

(part of verse 2)

I love the picture described here:
Jesus himself will come and take me to a room which he has prepared for me in his Father's house,
and we will be together there.
How wonderful! How reassuring!

But wait: Jesus was speaking to his disciples here, all of them except Judas.
Jesus was talking to them equally and honestly while they were still in a place of rest,
preparing them for the difficult and bewildering hours ahead:
his arrest, trial, crucifixion, death.
What a way to end an evening of friendship and fellowship!

For me today as for the disciples then, Jesus' promise can be an anchor, keeping me connected with the source of true peace of mind whatever happens.
But am I assuming too much?
Am I taking too much for granted?
Do I need to examine my relationship with Jesus in the light of this promise?
While I can never deserve this promise, how can I try to ensure that it is for me?

---

† Teach me, O God, what is the right balance of effort and faith in my life. Help me to live now in ways that prepare me for the future and for eternity.

Elizabeth Bruce Whitehorn   Resting places and sacred spaces

Saturday 1 May

John 19:38-42

An unexpected resting place

The two men wrapped his body in a linen cloth, together with the spices, which was how the Jewish people buried their dead. The tomb was nearby . . . [they] put Jesus' body there.

(verse 40 and part of verse 42)

At last Jesus is at rest, but it is the rest of death.
Here is Jesus' final resting place, or so it seemed to the disciples:
fear in place of hope;
emptiness in place of purposeful activity;
the end of their dreams of a glorious future.
But God was working secretly in this seemingly empty place,
working to accomplish a far more wonderful purpose than they could ever have dreamt of.
Now this empty space has become a sacred place,
drawing crowds of pilgrims and tourists from all over the world.
Some find it easier to feel Jesus' risen presence in the simple rock tomb in a garden,
while others prefer to worship in an ornate building representing centuries of tradition.
I offer to God my hopes and dreams,
so that God may guide and inspire me through them.
I offer to God my emptiness,
so that God may have space to work secretly within me.

† Teach me, O God, what is the right balance of dreams and emptiness in my life. Help me to make space for you to work in and through me.

Resting places and sacred spaces   Elizabeth Bruce Whitehorn

The Jesus way

1 Seeing, touching and tasting

Notes based on the *New International Version* by
John Birch

John Birch is a Methodist Lay Preacher and worship leader based in
South Wales, who enjoys writing and music, and hosts a prayer resource
website www.faithandworship.com.

Sunday 2 May: Preparing for the week

It has been said that becoming a Christian is a journey, rather than a
destination. If we think we've already 'made it' then the chances are that
we've merely sat down somewhere along the way, and it's time to get up
and start walking again!

Travelling with Jesus and in the company of others, we learn a little more
each day not only about Jesus but also about ourselves. Not the 'meek and
mild' Jesus we learned about in Sunday school, but a Jesus who challenged
people, occasionally got angry and overturned tables. But also a Jesus
who enjoyed the companionship of his disciples, and showed a love and
compassion that we can only hope in faith to emulate.

Text for the week: *John 1:43*

*The next day Jesus decided to leave for Galilee. Finding Philip, he said to
him, 'Follow me.'*

For group discussion and personal thought

• Do you feel as if you are on a journey? What can you share with
  others about where you are now?
• What do you bring with you on this journey?

May

Come and see

As a child I loved reading about explorers discovering new lands or crossing uncharted waters, with the ultimate hope of fame and fortune at journey's end.

There are three basic types of explorer. There are those who enjoy walking in the countryside with a good map, following paths that others have trod before. There are those who prefer an accompanied walk, with an experienced guide. Lastly, there are those who boldly go where no one has gone before.

> *Philip found Nathanael and told him, 'We have found the one Moses wrote about in the Law, and about whom the prophets also wrote – Jesus of Nazareth, the son of Joseph.' 'Nazareth! Can anything good come from there?' Nathanael asked. 'Come and see,' said Philip.*

(verses 45-46)

As Christians on our journey of faith we experience, at one time or another, all three types of exploration. For many their journey of faith is accompanied by their study of the Bible, our map and compass for keeping us on the right path, written by those who have walked this way before. Many have become Christians because they have been guided towards Jesus by a friend, as was the reluctant Nathanael by Philip (would he have gone if a stranger had pestered him?). Lastly, some are called to step out boldly in faith, to become intrepid explorers – putting their whole trust in God rather than in their own abilities. It makes for an interesting journey!

† Be with me as I travel on my journey of faith, Lord.

The Jesus way

John Birch

May

John 20:19-31

Touch and see

The journey of faith is not always smooth, but that's no reason to stop or go back. Thomas was a natural pessimist; when Jesus proposed travelling to Judea after the news of Lazarus' illness reached them, his reaction was, 'Let us also go, that we may die with him' (John 11:16). Yet Thomas was also courageous and loved Jesus enough to journey with him into danger. After the crucifixion he couldn't even face being among the fellowship of believers, simply wanting to be alone with his grief.

Now Thomas (called Didymus), one of the Twelve, was not with the disciples when Jesus came. So the other disciples told him, 'We have seen the Lord!' But he said to them, 'Unless I see the nail marks in his hands and put my finger where the nails were, and put my hand into his side, I will not believe it.'

(verses 24-25)

So Thomas wasn't there when Jesus first appeared to his disciples. We can all be like that sometimes, in our darker moments unable to face even other Christians. In doing so we can miss out on so much that might help us back on the road again.

Fortunately Jesus doesn't give up on us that easily! A week later and Thomas was with the other disciples when Jesus appeared. This time there are no doubts – Thomas sees Jesus and believes. We don't know what happened to him afterwards, but one thing we can say is that a Thomas who could now declare the risen Jesus as 'My Lord and my God' without any trace of doubt was going to be a wonderful guide for anyone walking the journey of faith.

† Lord, in my darker moments be with me and let me touch you.

John Birch

The Jesus way

Wednesday 5 May

John 9:1-17

Seeing differently

When I was eleven I realised that I could no longer see the blackboard at school, and it's been downhill ever since! Without glasses everything is out of focus, and I am unable to do so much that I take for granted.

'How then were your eyes opened?' they demanded. He replied, 'The man they call Jesus made some mud and put it on my eyes. He told me to go to Siloam and wash. So I went and washed, and then I could see.'

(verses 10-11)

The glass that enables me to see clearly has connections to the mud that Jesus rubbed over the blind man's eyes – it's a natural substance, made from silica and other materials. Mixed together in their raw state with water they would probably resemble mud!

This story shows Jesus' compassion and his power to heal, but it's also a message about spiritual blindness. The Pharisees and Jewish leaders saw Jesus walking among them and yet were blind to who he was. They were spiritually short-sighted, unable to focus on anything but their own interpretation of scripture, unwilling to accept that they were wrong.

'While I am in the world, I am the light of the world.'

(verse 5)

The world I see now is not only clearer because of the glasses I wear. I now look at the world through the lens of Jesus, who is the light that makes all things clear. Seen through this lens, I can understand so much more about God and my place in his world, and on my journey of faith I can now recognise and overcome the obstacles that stand in my way.

† Lord, if I suffer from spiritual blindness then help me to see more clearly.

The Jesus way

John Birch

John 2:1-11

Wine overflowing

On the third day a wedding took place at Cana in Galilee. Jesus' mother was there, and Jesus and his disciples had also been invited to the wedding.

(verses 1-2)

There are some who think that the Christian journey is rather dull and wander off the road to find something 'a bit more interesting'. Yet here we have Jesus and his disciples enjoying a local wedding party, close to Nazareth. I'm guessing that this was not the only time Jesus enjoyed a party, but this story is here because of the miraculous changing of water into wine.

He thus revealed his glory, and his disciples put their faith in him.

(part of verse 11)

This story tells us something about the trust that Mary had in her son; it speaks of Jesus' authority and his power in changing water into wine; and the disciples' growing faith. But it does so much more than this, because the writer has woven his own spiritual lesson into the story. There were six stone water pots used for ritual washing, yet six is an imperfect number to the Jews. Jesus came to do away with the imperfections of the old life, and bring something new – washing water turned into something glorious. And no small wedding party was going to get through 180 gallons of finest wine!

What Jesus brings to the world is more than we can ever imagine, his grace is in abundance. One commentator says: 'Wherever Jesus went and whenever he came into lives it was like water turning into wine.'

† Lord, take my imperfections and transform them from water into wine!

John Birch   The Jesus way

John 2:13-22

Turning tables

So he made a whip out of cords, and drove all from the temple area, both sheep and cattle . . . Then the Jews demanded of him, 'What miraculous sign can you show us to prove your authority to do all this?'

(part of verse 15, and verse 18)

It's perfectly OK to feel angry now and then, as long as your anger is turned in the right direction. Jesus walked into the Temple at Passover and was met by the noise, smell and bustle of a market. Money changers were making vast profits; traders were selling sheep, oxen and doves at inflated prices. When Crassus captured Jerusalem and raided the temple in AD 54 he took around £2 million from its coffers. Jesus had good cause to feel angry!

We also have times on our journey with Jesus when we feel the need to stand up and shout out when we see injustice or evil around us; yet so often we sit down again and hope someone else will take the initiative. Oh for the courage that Jesus showed!

The Jews were horrified at what Jesus did, and demanded an explanation, even a miracle! Yet all they got was this mysterious response from Jesus: 'Destroy this temple, and I will raise it again in three days' (verse 19). Jesus didn't mean that he was going to physically destroy and then rebuild the Temple, but looked forward to a time when Temple worship would pass away, when animal sacrifices and ritual would be replaced with a spiritual worship, and when Christians could bow their heads and worship God wherever they were. The presence of the risen Christ is with us wherever we journey.

† Lord, enable me to worship in all circumstances and in all places.

The Jesus way

John Birch

John 6:1-15

Eating faithfully

Then Jesus went up on the hillside and sat down with his disciples.

(verse 3)

When we set out on a long walk we need to think ahead about where would be a good place to sit down and enjoy our packed lunch! Jesus was no different; he enjoyed sitting down with his friends, relaxing and sharing food. However, on this occasion there was a slight problem – an extra 5000 mouths to feed.

However we interpret this story, there are three characters that stand out. There's Philip who, when asked how they were going to feed the people, says, 'It's impossible!' How like so many Christians when faced by a daunting task, who fail to recognise in whose company they travel! Then there's Andrew who assesses the situation and says to Jesus, 'OK, I'll see what I can do, and then it's over to you!' Lastly there's the small boy with his cheap barley rolls and two pickled fish, who was brought to Jesus by Andrew and through whom the miracle was made possible.

'Here is a boy with five small barley loaves and two small fish, but how far will they go among so many?'

(verse 9)

Andrew didn't know the consequences of bringing that boy to Jesus, and the boy himself couldn't see what Jesus could do with the little he had to offer. But Jesus found in his offering the ingredients for a miracle! What can we offer on this journey? Who can we bring to Jesus?

† Lord God, take the little I have and use it to your glory!

John Birch

The Jesus way

The Jesus way

2 Showing, walking and praying

Notes based on the *New Revised Standard Version* by
Kavula John

Kavula John is a Methodist minister based in London. As well as having
pastoral charge of two churches, she is Chaplain to a Methodist Homes
residence. She was born and brought up in a village in Kenya.

Sunday 9 May: Preparing for the week

We may be able to quote biblical passages about the Christian life by heart
and give theological explanations of how to walk the Christian journey. But
really what matters is walking it, not just knowing about it. To drive a car in
London, you need an A to Z map, and know how to read it. But you never
really know what the journey from one place to another is like unless you
actually get into the car and do it. Otherwise it will stay head knowledge.

Walking with Jesus requires us to first to know him, and then to walk
his way. And the walk includes all aspects of the way Jesus walked and
talked about the kingdom of God. There will be times of great joy and
wonder, and other times of trial and even carrying the cross, falling down
and picking it up again. But we never walk alone: God has promised us his
presence always, and has given us sisters and brothers for fellowship on
the way.

Text for the week: *Mark 8:34*
*He called the crowd with his disciples, and said to them, 'If any want to
become my followers, let them deny themselves and take up their cross
and follow me.'*

For group discussion and personal thought
• Do you trust Jesus' call and promise, and are you willing to follow him
  all the days of your life? What might hinder you?

Matthew 23:1-12

Learning together

The religious world has always been divided between those who proclaim themselves as leaders and those who become their followers. Jesus was right to draw attention to the hypocrisy of many religious scribes and Pharisees of his time who overburdened their followers with rules and regulations, making a show of their own religiosity while failing to keep the standards set by their own teaching – all in pursuit of the kingdom of heaven.

But you are not to be called rabbi, for you have one teacher, and you are all students.

(verse 8)

By contrast to the Pharisees and the scribes of the day, Jesus offers his followers a very different model of discipleship, one that presents us even today with a serious challenge. According to the Jesus model, all disciples are learners together; there is no need of a dividing line between teachers and students because the goal to which we aspire, the kingdom of heaven, is so vast and all inclusive that it renders all of us lifelong students. To this end, the Jesus model or 'way' acknowledges only one 'Father' and only one 'Teacher' – the Messiah – and the key to being his disciples is neither religious display nor the exercise of institutional power, but an inner disposition of the heart that manifests itself in service and humility.

† Father God, make me aware of the dangers of drawing attention to myself. Fill me with the humility that seeks to serve you in all sincerity in my daily living and a learning spirit that seeks your wisdom and appreciates what others have to offer in your name. Amen

Kavula John

The Jesus way

Mark 1:1-8

Making way by walking the way

A true messenger not only knows the message and believes in it, but is also passionate about it. In Jesus' day, messengers on foot or on horseback were an essential part of the network of government and commerce. They were ambassadors for queens and kings. Messengers and ambassadors: that was the role of the Old Testament prophets and of John the Baptist in the New Testament. Forerunners go ahead of the person they represent, they travel the same route. How true this is of John and Jesus!

> [John] proclaimed, 'The one who is more powerful than I is coming after me; . . . I have baptised you with water, but he will baptise you with the Holy Spirit.'

(part of verse 7, and verse 8)

The messages of John and Jesus were essentially the same: 'Make straight the way of the Lord' – a metaphor for preparing the heart.

Unlike Jesus, however, John the forerunner led an ascetic existence in the desert. People were drawn to him from the towns and villages not because of his appearance, but because John, like the coming king Jesus, proclaimed a powerful message of repentance and forgiveness, as well as the coming of the 'one more powerful than I'. As the forerunner, every aspect of John's life was dedicated to preparing the way for Jesus who 'will baptise you with the Holy Spirit'. All God's messengers, ourselves included, must walk the way that they claim to prepare.

† Lord, make me a messenger of your peace. Teach me to live like Jesus, in humility, truth and love, as one who has been baptised with Holy Spirit, so that in all I do I may commend the way of the Lord. Amen

The Jesus way   Kavula John

Matthew 6:25-33

Consider the lilies

Walking the way of Jesus involves both courage and self-sacrifice: the courage to be different and the willingness to surrender 'self'. In this passage Jesus draws attention to the inner conflict between worry and trust. We may worry about, in the sense of striving after, basic necessities such as food, clothing and shelter, but Jesus clearly teaches that such worry achieves nothing positive; it serves only to blunt our trust in God. As followers of the way, if we say that we have faith in God, then we must trust him.

But if God so clothes the grass of the field, which is alive today and tomorrow is thrown into the oven, will he not much more clothe you – you of little faith?

(verse 30)

Our basic human requirements, like those of plants and animals, will be provided by God. Jesus' call to consider the lilies of the field and the birds of the air, which magnificently fulfil their purpose without worrying, has a twofold significance: it reminds us that God can be trusted as the one who sustains all creation, and it teaches us to reside in God's purpose rather than struggle to possess all we can. Worrying is a wholly negative exercise that does nothing but rob us of vital life force; the followers of the way should instead trust God and strive for 'the kingdom of God and his righteousness'. While the lilies of the field fulfil the purposes of God by their display of beauty, human beings can fulfil God's purpose only when they are clothed in righteousness.

† Lord, help me to rejoice in your provision and deliver me from unnecessary worry and complaining. May your righteousness cover me so that I display your beauty and become more and more the person you created me to be. Amen

Kavula John

The Jesus way

Praying the way

This intercessory prayer of Jesus overflows with spiritual intimacy, genuine concern and love for his disciples, and profound eschatological significance. They were his followers and would walk his way and therefore needed not only to be prayed for, but to learn that prayer was a key ingredient in walking faithfully.

Holy Father, protect them in your name that you have given me, so that they may be one, as we are one.

(part of verse 11)

May

This prayer is a very private conversation between Jesus and his Father, whose name he has fearlessly made known. The knowledge of God imparted by Jesus has been responsible for the faith of his disciples. That faith is the key to our Lord's intercession, as he prays for the safety of his disciples in the world and protection from the evil one. Faith has so transformed the disciples that Jesus can say 'they do not belong to the world just as I do not belong to the world' (verse 14). And so he continues to pray that the disciples will be 'sanctified' or made holy just as he has been made holy.

This is a prayer about living and transforming faith, and in so far as we share this faith, we can feel ourselves included in Jesus' prayer, as the following verses make clear. While Jesus is here 'praying the way', praying for his disciples' spiritual journey, he is also teaching us about the 'way of prayer'. If Jesus could pray for his disciples like this, so we must learn the importance of praying not only for ourselves but for all fellow travellers on the 'Way'.

† Dear God, there are times when I have overlooked prayer in my journey. Revive my prayer life; teach me how to pray not just for myself but also for others and their needs. Amen

The Jesus way   Kavula John

Friday 14 May

Mark 8:27-38

Who do you say?

Most of us have been in big gatherings where hardly anybody knows who we are. We try to make conversation and people ask polite questions: 'Where are you from? How long have you been in this country?', but no one knows who we really are. But then someone appears and says, 'I think I know who you are, we met a couple of years ago, do you remember?' Even in that large crowd someone has recognised us, someone knows who we are.

> On the way he asked his disciples, 'Who do people say that I am?' And they answered him, 'John the Baptist, and others, Elijah, and still others, one of the prophets.'

(part of verse 27, and verse 28)

Jesus and his disciples were on the way to Caesarea Philippi, evidently attracting attention. Their replies to his question indicate that the people were expecting great things from Jesus, longing to be liberated from their present Roman overlords. 'John the Baptist, Elijah or one of the prophets' would certainly have given the people renewed hope.

Peter's confession, 'You are the Christ (Messiah)', is even more significant because for the Jews that title brought not only hope, but assurance of God's ultimate victory. Messiah's kingdom would see the end of oppression and injustice.

As we follow the Jesus way, we shall hear that question over and over again, 'But who do you say I am?' If we can meet it with the assurance of faith, with heartfelt recognition – 'You are the Christ' or 'My Lord and My God' – then we shall no longer be alone in the crowd, for he is with us and will never leave us.

---

† Loving God, thank you that you know me by name and that through Jesus I am your child, loved and accepted. Help me to surrender my life to you, my Lord, my God. Amen

Kavula John

The Jesus way

John 15:9-17

Unexpected companions

Jesus followed the path of love, loving not only those close to him but everyone, everywhere he went. With Christ at the centre of a person's life, the Jesus way follows a path of obedient love.

If you keep my commandments, you will abide in my love, just as I have kept my Father's commandments and abide in his love.

(verse 10)

May

As Jesus obeyed the Father, so we must obey him. But this is not the kind of obedience that robs us of free will; rather, it is the obedience that assures us of spiritual blessing. Commitment to Christ is a commitment to love. By making this commitment we receive the spiritual benefit of remaining in God's divine love, and an assurance of true joy that flows from Christ. In the best human relationships there is a commitment that acts as an antidote to selfishness and self-seeking, reminding us that the other person is just as important and that we ought to speak and act for their benefit. True friendship is built upon this kind of equality and mutual understanding. Those who hear the call to walk the Jesus way will not walk alone. By obeying Jesus' command to love others we find ourselves in the company of those who love us, and so learn the meaning of true friendship.

† Dear Lord, I stand amazed at your love for me, even me. Help me to acknowledge sincerely those I meet on this journey of life. Give me grace, understanding and love for others. Fill me with joy and a longing to follow your commandments. Amen

The Jesus way   Kavula John

The Jesus way

3 Living and loving

Notes based on *Today's New International Version* and *The Message* (ed. Eugene Peterson, 2007) by
Chris Duffett

Chris Duffett is an evangelist who founded The Light Project, a charity that aims to demonstrate actively the Christian message and to train others in evangelism (www.lightproject.org.uk). He is also a Baptist minister and a sculptor and is married to Ruth. They have three children: Seth, Beatrice and Milly.

May

Sunday 16 May: Preparing for the week

This week's readings come with a caution: dynamite! They challenge how we live up to the teaching of our master. In order to bring change to a fallen world through the salvation of our family, friends and neighbours, God calls each one of us to partner with him, to show through our words and actions the wonder that a mighty God should become a man and restore to people a relationship that has been tainted. Whoever we are and in whatever way we have been gifted by God, he desires that we live out the good news in which we have believed. The gospel message is best preached through the everyday routine of our lives, so that people can encounter the living Christ through us.

Text for the week: *Matthew 5:1-3 (taken from The Message)*
When Jesus saw his ministry drawing huge crowds, he climbed a hillside. Those who were apprenticed to him, the committed, climbed with him. Arriving at a quiet place, he sat down and taught his climbing companions. This is what he said: 'You're blessed . . .'

For group discussion and personal thought
• 'God loves the world and chooses to show this love through my words and actions.' What does this mean for you?

Matthew 5:1-12

Show what you believe!

I have met some preachers who have spent a whole year preaching from the Beatitudes every week. These verses are packed full with the DNA of what it means to be a follower of Christ. Following this teaching of Jesus is much more than a theological nod and agreement to a statement of faith; rather, it serves as an 'action list' launching us out into a world that is needing, longing and 'waiting in eager expectation' (Romans 8:19) for redemption and will see such emancipation through our own lives flowing with blessing. One way in which we can show what we believe is through our attitude to others:

'Blessed are the pure in heart for they will see God.'

(verse 8)

How we look upon God and have a closer relationship with him depends on how we look upon others. Too often I find myself questioning people's motives and judging people through how they talk, what car they drive and how they look. Is this also true of you? Let us examine our hearts and be pure in how we see others, so that as we see God, others may see God in us.

May

† Father, you want me to show my faith to those around me. Help me to love others in my heart so that bad attitudes are kept at bay and I may see you more and more as my heart becomes increasingly pure. Amen

The Jesus way   Chris Duffett

Luke 14:25-33

The cost of discipleship

Too often, evangelists on TV shows and platforms present Jesus as the panacea for all things difficult in life, as if becoming a follower suddenly inoculates an individual from hard times. Truly following Christ is not trouble-free and to pretend that it is denies a central feature of being a disciple:

'And whoever does not carry their cross and follow me cannot be my disciple . . . those of you who do not give up everything you have cannot be my disciples.'

(verses 27 and 33)

A teenager called Jonny sat in my office. He wanted to follow Christ but wanted to keep it a secret from his friends and family. I read these verses from Luke with him and he decided that the cost was too much. For me to have 'sweetened' what it means to be a follower, without mentioning the cause and cost, would have misrepresented Christ. As people who have chosen to follow Christ we must show, rather than just explain, the cost of giving up everything. For example, this may mean moving into a smaller house as we set aside more time to serve and less time to make money. Or risking rejection by our family as we proclaim our new-found life.

† Jesus, your call to me to follow you is full of joy, yet also full of hard choices. You beckon me to leave all my comforts and to find my true home within you. You summon me to deny my life and to give it for this broken world in service of you. Jesus, help me to follow you. Amen

Chris Duffett   The Jesus way

Wednesday 19 May

Mark 9:38-50

Choices

I could be typing these notes with one hand, squinting out of one eye! All Christians sin, and today's reading shows how severe our reaction should be:

> *'And if your eye causes you to stumble, pluck it out. It is better for you to enter to the kingdom of God with one eye than to have two eyes and be thrown into hell.'*

(verse 47)

Plucking out our eyes or performing major surgery on our limbs may not be accepted practices for a follower of Christ, but there are other ways of ensuring that we remain pure and don't stumble. When my wife goes to visit her family and I can't join her, I ask her to take the remote control with her so that I am not tempted to flick aimlessly through the TV channels at night and watch things that would cause me to stumble. A 'safe search' facility for the internet will help you not to be tempted to look at pornography (as so many Christians are). If you do find yourself faltering over what you look at online, try:

• admitting your struggles and stumbling to a fellow Christian; if we confess our sins God will forgive us

• setting up a free accountability account through www.xxxchurch.com

• not going online if you are HALT: Hungry, Angry, Lonely or Tired.

Let us not live double lives – Christian in public but stumbling in private.

† Compassionate Father, I acknowledge before you what makes me stumble. Guide me by your Holy Spirit to be active in removing temptation and wise about what will cause me to stumble. Thank you for your forgiveness and the power at work in me that makes me more and more like Jesus. Amen

The Jesus way   Chris Duffett

May

Reaching out, moving on

Like Jesus, we need to allow others outside our usual social circles to experience the gospel through our lives. Today's reading describes a busy late night followed by an early morning, with an urgency reflected in the disciples' desperate search for Jesus:

> and when they found him, they exclaimed: 'Everyone is looking for you!' Jesus replied, 'Let us go somewhere else – to the nearby villages – so that I can preach there also. That is why I have come.'

(verses 37-38)

As followers of Christ we need to follow his example. The story of Jesus 'going somewhere else' also needs to be our experience. You cannot spell gospel without the 'GO'! Whether you offer practical help at a drop-in for homeless people or take part in a mission team as a once in a lifetime experience, each of us needs a story of how we went. Please offer to God your availability to reach out to those with whom you wouldn't usually spend time. Would you be willing to join a team to serve overseas short term, if the opportunity arose? At home or abroad, each of us has a role to play so that people are not excluded from the best news that the world has ever heard and seen.

† Lord Jesus, where your great commission has been my great omission, help me to remedy it and go to people who need help and have still to hear the wonderful story of the good news of Jesus. Amen

Chris Duffett   The Jesus way

John 3:4-21

Love for the whole of the world

One of the first Bible verses that many Christians learn is John 3:16; I learnt it through songs, games and stories when I was growing up! It is a key verse to being a follower of Christ:

This is how much God loved the world: He gave his Son, his one and only Son. And this is why: so that no one need be destroyed; by believing in him, anyone can have a whole and lasting life.

(verse 16, from *The Message*)

May

The giving of Jesus for the world continues today. Jesus spent three years ministering in one place the size of Wales. Yet he was given for the whole world. If every single person on earth is to understand this wonderful news, we have to continue the story. The world still has to learn that Jesus was given for it! According to the Joshua Project (www.joshuaproject.net) there are still 2.6 billion people in 6 859 people groups in the world who have not yet heard the name of Jesus. For example, in the UK population of 123 000 Kashmiri people, there is not a single Christian. Such statistics are not unique. In each of our countries there are tens of thousands of people who still do not know that 'God so loved the world' (verse 16, TNIV). Sent out by God, may you go to people and let them know that he loves them.

---

† The hand of God keeping me,
  The love of Christ in my veins,
  The strong Spirit bathing me,
  The Three shielding and aiding me,
  The Three shielding and aiding me;
  The hand of Spirit bathing me,
  The Three each step aiding me. Amen

(An old Celtic prayer taken from
www.mindburp.com/xian/celticprayer/celtic1.html)

The Jesus way   Chris Duffett

Ingredients for church growth

Luke reveals the secret of success for people who want to see their church swell with more and more people:

Every day they continued to meet together in the temple courts. They broke bread in their homes and ate together with glad and sincere hearts, praising God and enjoying the favour of all the people. And the Lord added to their number daily those who were being saved.

(verses 46-47)

The Greek word used for 'added' indicates that it is plural – more than one person was added daily. Even if it was only two people, that is still a staggering 700 people a year! As an evangelist who likes to be busy letting others know the good news, I get very frustrated when I read these verses. 'Where are the evangelistic projects?', I cry! It just doesn't seem to add up.

The early Christians simply met together, shared meals and praised God – and hundreds of people were added to the church. These verses challenge us to rethink our relationships with our brothers and sisters in Christ. The more we can vulnerably share our lives with others, including our meal times, the more the Lord will bring people to join us. I am humbled by this. Rather than 'evangelistic projects', church growth seems to need our missionary Father to bring his lost children to a safe and loving church family. Who will you invite to 'break bread' together in your home this week?

† Lord, bring to our church many more people who will experience the saving grace that you have poured out on me. Just as you have added me to the church, please add others, and show me with whom I may break bread together and celebrate your life. Amen

Chris Duffett   The Jesus way

Romans 1–8

1 Good news for sinners

Notes based on the *Good News Bible* by
Iain Roy

For Iain's biography see p. 52.

Sunday 23 May (Pentecost): Preparing for the week

The letter to the Romans has been a pivotal document
in the history of the Church ever since Paul wrote it as preparation for a
proposed visit to Rome. It became so again at the time of the Reformation
with Martin Luther's great commentary on it, and again, when Karl Barth
wrote his commentary on Romans against the backdrop of the questions
raised for the German church by the rise of Fascism.

Text for the week: *Romans 1:9-10*

*God is my witness that what I say is true – the God whom I serve with all
my heart by preaching the Good News about his Son. God knows that I
remember you every time I pray.*

For group discussion and personal thought

• What particular Christian beliefs do you find difficult to understand?
  Could your group look at one or two of them and get someone to lead a
  Bible study on them?

• In your Christian fellowship what are the things that you and others
  find you have most cause to give thanks for?

• The Acts of the Apostles and the letters of Paul reflect some deep
  divisions in the Early Church. It could be a profitable study in conflict
  management to look at one or two of these and see how Paul and others
  tackled them. Here are some passages that could be looked at: Acts 15;
  Acts 18:1-17; Galatians 2:1-14; and 1 Corinthians 3.

A tour de force

The opening verses of Paul's letter remind me of the opening notes of many great works of music. They focus the mind.

From Paul, a servant of Christ Jesus . . . The Good News was promised long ago . . . It is about his Son . . . This also includes you.

(part of verses 1, 2, 3 and 6)

With a great economy of words Paul states his sense of vocation, the long pedigree of his message, the great paradox of Jesus' humanity and divinity, and assures his readers that they have a place in God's love. It is a tour de force, especially to people he did not know. What it tells us about Paul is that he wanted to build the church on sure foundations. This was no evangelist looking for a glib response and commitment from those to whom he wrote. This was a man so enthralled by the gospel himself that he had to educate others to the same great truths he cherished, however difficult it might be for them to take them in.

---

† Lord, help us to build our own faith on sure foundations. Deepen our understanding that we may increase our love and trust of you.

Iain Roy

Romans 1–8

A word of encouragement

The church Paul wrote to in Rome is likely to have been small and struggling. But for Paul, a Roman citizen, it had great importance, situated as it was at the heart of the Roman Empire. His gratitude for the church's existing witness must have been very encouraging for its members.

First, I thank my God through Jesus Christ for all of you, because the whole world is hearing about your faith.

(verse 8)

May

Nothing strengthens any Christian fellowship more than encouragement, and nothing is more encouraging than gratitude for what has already been achieved. Paul's real desire to visit this church is also apparent. But it is his insight into the mutual benefits of such a visit that we should note. It would strengthen *his* faith as much as *theirs*. There is a certain humility here that we can sometimes be blind to in Paul. This ought to be the aim of every Christian fellowship, to strengthen each other's faith through sharing.

† Lord Jesus, encourage us in the faith that we may encourage others and be encouraged by them.

Romans 1–8   Iain Roy

Romans 1:18-27

Deep divisions

This passage clearly raises divisive issues for Christians today. The Anglican Communion, in particular, has become deeply divided over same-sex relationships and the ordination of homosexual bishops.

> *And so God has given those people over to do the filthy things their hearts desire, and they do shameless things with each other. They exchange the truth about God for a lie; they worship and serve what God has created instead of the Creator himself, who is to be praised for ever! Amen.*

(verses 24-25)

Placing this issue firmly in the historical context of Paul's day, however, what we see is an evangelist who believes that his Christian mission involves confrontation with others on a serious issue. It would be wishful thinking on our part to believe we can always avoid confrontation. Indeed, as Christians with deeply held views, conflict must be inevitable with those who differ from us and whose views are equally strongly held. What is important is how we handle our conflicts of opinion. We must always debate with humility, knowing none of us has a monopoly on truth, and we must always treat others with respect and love.

† Lord, heal our divisions and, when we remain divided, help us to respect each other and to continue being humble seekers after truth.

Iain Roy

Romans 1–8

Self-awareness and positive thinking

It may seem a strange way to win friends and influence people, to write as vigorously and polemically as Paul does here, especially to folk he does not know, and has not seen.

Because those people refuse to keep in mind the true knowledge about God, he has given them over to corrupted minds, so that they do the things they should not do.

(verse 28)

May

Yet there is an echo here of something that Paul wrote about himself: 'I do the evil that I do not want to do' (Romans 7:19). Paul has a great awareness of human nature, even his own, and the depths to which humanity can sink. He does not offer a psychological explanation of why we sometimes behave as we do. Rather, he offers a spiritual explanation: our refusal to have the attitude that Jesus had.

If Paul is polemical here, it is a good thing to remember that he could be pastoral, urging the Philippians, for instance, to fill their minds with those things that are good and deserve praise (Philippians 4:8). It is not a bad thing to note the consistency of Paul's thinking as he writes to these different churches in the early days of Christianity.

† Christ Jesus, let that mind be in us which was also in you, that our lives and purposes may be directed by your love and truth.

Romans 2:1-11

God's kindness

Paul states here something fundamental for our understanding of how God relates to us.

Do you think you will escape God's judgement? Or perhaps you despise his great kindness, tolerance, and patience. Surely you know that God is kind, because he is trying to lead you to repent.

(part of verse 3, and verse 4)

There is no question mark at the end of this sentence but perhaps there ought to be, because so often we forget the essential truth that 'God is love'(1 John 4:8).

The church in Rome had some excuse for not knowing that. This message must have been strange to the ears of people living in a society that could be cruel, vengeful and uncaring, particularly to its ordinary citizens and its slaves. One of the attractions of Christianity to those early Christians was the worth God's love placed upon each individual life. It must still be the basis on which we try to build society in our own countries.

† Lord God, so patient in your love for us and so forgiving, help us even now to repent of our sins, and to be as loving and forgiving of each other.

Iain Roy

Romans 1–8

A little knowledge

Paul knew that a little knowledge can be a dangerous thing.

The Gentiles do not have the Law of Moses; they sin and are lost apart from the Law. The Jews have the Law; they sin and are judged by the Law. For it is not by hearing the Law that people are put right with God, but by doing what the Law commands.

(verses 12-13)

One of the great dilemmas for Paul, as for every preacher and missionary, was how to deal with those who had no prior knowledge of God, his truth and his ways. The Jews he met had an advantage, one he shared, of having been taught God's Law. But here was the strange paradox that Paul found: in the practice of daily living, some gentiles seemed nearer to God's ways than Jews who knew the Law. It is a phenomenon that can still be as true today. Those who do not claim to be Christian can sometimes shame those of us who do by the way they live their lives. What matters most to God is not what we say we are, but what we show we are day by day.

† Let the words of our lips, the meditations of all our hearts, and the actions of our lives be acceptable in your sight, O Lord, our Strength and our Redeemer.

Romans 1–8   Iain Roy

Romans 1–8

2 All have sinned and are now justified

Notes based on the *New International Version* by
Yordan Kalev Zhekov

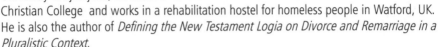

Yordan Kalev Zhekov is an Evangelical Christian born in Bulgaria. He holds a Doctor of Science degree in the field of theology, which he has completed with distinction in the Catholic Faculty of Theology of the University of Ljubljana, Slovenia. Dr Zhekov is a lecturer at South London Christian College and works in a rehabilitation hostel for homeless people in Watford, UK. He is also the author of *Defining the New Testament Logia on Divorce and Remarriage in a Pluralistic Context.*

Sunday 30 May: Preparing for the week

The problem of sin has been overlooked or denied by many and its impact on human life has been continually undermined. Human pride refuses to acknowledge one's sinful condition. Paul was tackling a similar situation with the Jews who had rejected the gospel, neglecting God's solution for the fulfilment of his promise. Paul's line of argument strikes deeply at Israel's national pride, exposing the Jews' misunderstanding of the Law, its purpose and its fulfilment, and redefining the real Jew and true circumcision. God's plan for all people, formulated in the gospel of Jesus Christ, is clearly presented and grounded on the Jewish scriptures.

Text for the week: *Romans 3:22*
This righteousness from God comes through faith in Jesus Christ to all who believe.

For group discussion and personal thought

• What is the future of Israel?
• How does Paul understand God's plan for the relationship between Israel and gentile Christians?

Romans 2:17-24

Human pride

The problem of self-righteousness and self-justification is universal, found in both non-religious and religious communities. As guilt appears to be unhealthy, sinlessness becomes something to brag about. The Jews who rejected the gospel appeared to believe that their special, divinely appointed status excluded them from the group of sinners. Paul confronts them on three grounds: the boastful claim, based on the Law, that they are a superior nation; individual failure to observe the moral demands of the Law; and the negative image of God this presents to the nations. The Jewish nation identified itself with the Law, which led to a distinctive perception of God's will and special favour. However, with rhetorical questions based on three of the Ten Commandments, Paul challenges individual Jewish failure to live up to this Law-defined status.

You who brag about the law, do you dishonour God by breaking the law?

(verse 23)

This conflict between their claim to a special position and their actual conduct brings God's image among the nations into disrepute and destroys the pedestal on which the Jews placed themselves. This problem of the duality of human life is faced by every individual, even the most devoted Christian. Hypocrisy is acknowledged as a vice but its power in an individual's life is difficult to overcome. The solution begins with recognition of the problem: sin. Recognising one's sinfulness should lead to repentance and a life empowered by Christ.

† Dear Lord, forgive my hypocritical dualism and help me live in sincerity through your righteousness.

Yordan Kalev Zhekov

Romans 2:25 – 3:8

The human heart

The tension between an outward religious appearance due to a particular rite and an inward, life-changing spiritual experience has always existed in Christian communities. It can be seen in the relationship between Jewish and gentile Christian communities, especially over the most significant Jewish rite of circumcision. Jews identified circumcision as the fulfilment of the Law, the mark of distinction that made them the favoured people of God.

Paul destroys this identification, arguing that the status given by circumcision depends on observance of the Law, not the opposite. He goes even further in redefining the covenant community, the mark of circumcision and the status of a Jew: those who experience the work of the Holy Spirit in their hearts are the real Jews, the true circumcised, and the covenant community of God.

a man is a Jew if he is one inwardly; and circumcision is circumcision of the heart, by the Spirit, not by the written code.

(part of verse 29)

This redefines the place of the Jews as the ones entrusted with God's word: it has been fulfilled in Christ, whom they rejected. God's faithfulness is seen in the light of Jewish unfaithfulness, which raises the issues of God's justice and its relation to human unrighteousness. According to Paul, God's faithfulness is independent of human unfaithfulness and God's justice and righteousness are fulfilled in the gospel of justification by faith. The dynamics of Christian faith become clear: it has its outward appearance, but is inseparable from the inner experience of the heart under the power of the Holy Spirit.

† Help us, Lord, to allow the Holy Spirit to impact upon our hearts.

Yordan Kalev Zhekov

Romans 1–8

Human plight

Many religious communities use their sacred texts to justify their actions. The Bible has been misused in the same way. Jews justified themselves through the written Law. Paul tackles the issue by defining their condition: both Jews and gentiles are identically sinful.

We have already made the charge that Jews and Gentiles alike are all under sin.

(part of verse 9)

The plight of sin defines both those who show explicit behaviour worthy of condemnation and those who through circumcision, covenant and Law attempt self-justification but fall under self-condemnation.

Against the defensive attitude of the Jews Paul offers a number of quotations from their scriptures to establish firmly his conclusion about the totality of the human plight. Most of these are taken from the psalms, used in the synagogues to promote Jewish righteousness over against gentile sinfulness. Paul's intention is to destroy the potential defence of the self-promoted religious Jew; he underlines that the very defence used by the Jews, the Law, condemns them for being under the Law. The actual role of the Law intended by God is to make those who follow it aware of their sinfulness – not, as the Jews misinterpreted it, to provide their self-righteous defence.

Are we using the biblical text for our justification or for our examination, repentance and life of faith?

† Please help us, Lord, to examine ourselves through your word.

God's solution

God's solution to the human plight was to re-establish the relationship with humanity that had been broken by humanity in the person of Adam and kept unresolved by the Jewish opposition based on misunderstanding of the Law. God has done this act of grace in spite of humanity's disobedience and faithlessness demonstrated by the covenant people. God's act of salvation impacts the present and has been fulfilled in the event of Christ, who reveals the righteousness of God apart from the self-righteous misinterpretation of the Law, and at the same time in continuation and fulfilment of the scriptures, namely, the Law and the prophets.

The proper response to God's act of salvation is faith in Jesus Christ.

This righteousness from God comes through faith in Jesus Christ to all who believe. There is no difference, for all have sinned and fall short of the glory of God.

(verses 22-23)

The believer's faith becomes the foundation and maintaining force of the relationship with God through Jesus Christ. Faith is the solution offered to all who in the person of Adam lost the intended eternal relationship with God. The results embrace present and future in the judge's pronouncement of humanity's acquittal from the bondage of sin through the price paid by Christ.

Christ's death was in continuity with the sacrificial system that dealt with the sins of Israel, exceeding and completing it by providing the solution for the sins of all humankind. The response of faith excludes any of the boastful reliance on the Law embraced by the Jews; it includes everyone who practises faith in Christ in actual continuity and completion of the Law and the scriptures. To accept God's solution for my problem is to believe in Christ.

† Thank you, God, for your profound solution.

Yordan Kalev Zhekov

Romans 1–8

June

God's righteousness

In our commercially defined culture it is almost impossible to think of getting anything without work. God offers us his righteousness only through faith. Paul demonstrates from scripture that the righteousness of God is based on faith, not on the works of the Law. His example is a key element in the story of Abraham, one of the most prominent characters in the Jewish scriptures, and father of the nation. Paul points out the absurdity of the Jewish understanding of Abraham's faithfulness as based on works of the Law; instead in Romans 4:3 he uses Genesis 15:6 to explain God's response to Abraham's faith.

Employing a commercial term that implies payment for work, Paul parallels and contrasts works of the Law, human merit, and the due reward for faith, which is God's unmerited grace and free gift. Paul also cites Psalm 32:2, which underlines that God's forgiveness is based on God's grace, not on counting the number of sins or works based on the Law. He argues that God's answer presented by David in the psalm was the same for Abraham before his circumcision, which represents the works of the Law. Therefore Abraham's fatherhood can be extended to include all gentiles who like Abraham obtain God's righteousness through faith and apart from circumcision.

> So then, he is the father of all who believe but have not been circumcised, in order that righteousness might be credited to them.

(part of verse 11)

† Thank you, God, for making your righteousness available to us simply through faith in Jesus.

God's promise

In our contemporary human relationships trust has suffered much damage because of our failure to keep our promises. Paul reveals a different approach in the example of Abraham's dealing with God's promise. God's promises, according to the Jewish understanding, were closely related to the Law and particularly linked to the distinctiveness of the Jewish covenant community as marked through circumcision. This, Paul argues, is a misinterpretation of the scriptures because Abraham and his offspring received God's promise through faith. The actual role of the Law is to expose sin, bring wrath and lead to faith for the fulfilment of God's righteousness. Hence God's promise does not require entry into a distinctively marked community; it embraces all Jews and gentiles who follow the example of Abraham.

Clarification comes by comparing God's acts of creation and salvation. The power of God as a creator, giving life and making the existing from non-existing, parallels his power as a saviour to grant righteousness on the basis of faith. God's promise was entirely based on his power, without any dependence on the abilities of Abraham, who acknowledged that he and Sarah could not themselves create life from their bodies. Abraham's faith was entirely based on his understanding of God's power and his trust in God's promise. He is a model for the Christian faith that trusts in God's power in raising Christ from the dead, faith that brings righteousness and justification based on the work of Christ without any human merit.

God will credit righteousness – for us who believe in him who raised Jesus our Lord from the dead.

(part of verse 24)

The Christian life is based on trust in God's power in spite of all the difficulties.

† Please help us, Lord, to exercise our faith in Jesus in our daily life.

Yordan Kalev Zhekov

Romans 1–8

Introduce a friend to

Light for our path 2010 or *Words* for today ■■■■2010

For this year's books, send us just £3.00 per book (including postage), together with your friend's name and address, and we will do the rest.

(This offer is only available in the UK, after 1 June 2010. Subject to availability.)

International Bible Reading Association

Order through your IBRA representative, or from the UK address below.

Do you know someone who has difficulty reading *Light for our Path*?

Light for our Path and *Words for Today* are both available to UK readers on cassette.

For the same price as the print edition, you can subscribe and receive the notes on cassette each month, through Galloways Trust for the Blind.

Please contact the IBRA office for more details:

International Bible Reading Association
1020 Bristol Road, Selly Oak, Birmingham B29 6LB

0121 472 4242

sales@christianeducation.org.uk

IBRA International Appeal

Imagine the only book you have to help you read the Bible is in French (or if you're a French speaker, try Tagalog!). Maybe you can understand bits of it, but imagine your joy when you discover someone has translated it into English for you!

Hundreds of thousands of people around the world experience similar joy when they discover the IBRA books and readings lists have been translated into their language. And this is all through the generosity of IBRA readers.

Each year, the IBRA International Fund provides funds for local groups to translate, print and distribute IBRA Bible notes and reading lists. Last year more than 68000 people in eleven different countries received copies of the IBRA books which had been translated, printed and distributed by IBRA partners. The reading list was also translated into French, Spanish, Telugu (India), Tokelau (Samaoa) and several Congolese languages, enabling 250000 people to receive them in a language useful to them.

The funds are given exclusively by IBRA readers like you, who give generously towards the fund, raising over £20000 each year. With your gift, more people will be able to experience the joy of reading the Bible using notes or a list of readings in a familiar language.

Please consider either giving for the first time, or increasing your donation this year. You can donate using the envelope which is part of the leaflet insert that came with this book, or add your donation to your order for next year's books.

Thank you!

International Bible Reading Association
1020 Bristol Road
Selly Oak
Birmingham
B29 6LB
Tel. 0121 472 4242

Romans 1–8

3 We have peace with God

Notes based on the *New Revised Standard Version* by
Alec Gilmore

Alec Gilmore is a Baptist minister, Senior Research Fellow at the International Baptist Theological Seminary in Prague, and author of *A Concise Dictionary of Bible Origins and Interpretation* (Continuum).

Sunday 6 June: Preparing for the week

'The peace of God' is an increasingly familiar eucharistic greeting. What are you offering? Or receiving? If asked, what would you say? Paul's reputation had gone before him. For a converted Jew on his way to a gentile church, Romans is his letter of introduction, setting out what he believes at a time when the emerging Christian community was split between those who saw Christianity as a sect within Judaism and others ready to accept gentiles becoming Christians and remaining gentiles.

Paul was 'piggy in the middle'. Jewish orthodoxy had taught him what to understand by peace (shalom), but experience, first on the Damascus road, then in close contact with gentile Christians, led into new territory. Rejected by his former associates for desertion and under suspicion by those to whom he turned because they were unsure of him, he struggles with what it means to have 'peace with God'. We benefit from his struggle as we travel with him.

Text for the week: *Romans 5:1.*

Therefore, since we are justified by faith, let us have peace with God through our Lord Jesus Christ.

For group discussion and personal thought

• Reflect on ways in which a sense of the peace of God has brought about a revolution in your thinking and attitudes to life, to people and to the world.

• What did you miss most once you ceased to be a slave to Adam, and what might make you want to return?

It starts with justification

Justification means acknowledging that we are sinners, but peace does not come through good resolutions, trying to make amends, pretending it doesn't matter or carrying a burden of guilt. Peace comes from learning to accept ourselves as we are, and where we are, and once we know that God accepts us like that then we have peace with him and can move on, responding to his love by walking in the steps of Jesus who has revealed this to us in all its fullness, and thereby growing in goodness and the likeness of God.

> *And not only that, but let us also boast in our sufferings, knowing that suffering produces endurance, and endurance produces character, and character produces hope, and hope does not disappoint us, because God's love has been poured into our hearts through the Holy Spirit that has been given to us.*

(verses 3-5)

Most of us know this at first hand. Maybe you fell out with a friend, confronted each other, sorted it out and found a new relationship. Perhaps a crisis of health led you to become a different person. Or you simply stuck at something against all the odds and then suddenly knew it was all worthwhile. Peace is the moment when the clouds roll away and the sun comes out, all bright and warm.

† Father, thank you for Paul who shows me the way and for Jesus (verse 11) who shows me how it works.

Alec Gilmore

Romans 1–8

Tuesday 8 June

Romans 5:12-23

The new and the old

Paul is trying to root the new faith in his old faith. His problem is that, if the new is right, how does it relate to what he had always been taught? His theological argument is somewhat tortuous, not easy to understand and difficult to express in practical terms.

Try thinking of Adam and Christ as symbols of two kinds of people or possibly two attitudes within yourself. Dictators, for example, can destroy a country or even a continent. One gunshot can transform the lives of a whole family or even a nation. Evil thoughts can spread like wildfire and do enormous damage. So much for Adam.

But then so it is with goodness. A smile, a bunch of flowers, a kind word (at one extreme) or an act of incomprehensible self-sacrifice (at the other).

Therefore just as one man's trespass led to condemnation for all, so one man's act of righteousness leads to justification and life for all. For just as by the one man's disobedience the many were made sinners, so by the one man's obedience the many will be made righteous.

(verses 18-19)

Find some examples in your own life or in the lives of your friends. Of course we are still sinners. We stray on both sides of the line rather than going down a one-way inescapable route, but thanks to Paul we have found a new peace.

† Father, thank you for a new awareness of the power of goodness and for an awareness that our greatest moments are when we contribute to it; let me never forget that the consequences are always far reaching and beyond my knowing or comprehension.

Romans 1–8   Alec Gilmore

Wednesday 9 June
Romans 6:1-14

Yes, but . . .

Like every good teacher, writer or preacher, Paul knows only too well what his readers are thinking. Is peace just a matter of being ourselves and doing what we like?

What then are we to say? Should we continue in sin in order that grace may abound? By no means! How can we who died to sin go on living in it? Do you not know that all of us who have been baptised into Christ Jesus were baptised into his death?

(verses 1-3)

Paul's answer seems to be that once you discover this peace you just cannot 'carry on as before' and live with yourself. Nobody who embraces the Christ-way can return to the Adam-way and there are no short cuts, half measures or easy answers.

Peace is not just doing what Jesus did, obeying what he said, as if it were a piece of ethical teaching or wise philosophy. It is a wholly different approach to life, as different as chalk from cheese, a veritable revolution in living, heart and soul, body and mind. It is learning to love with the power of love and the hope that springs from it, and a commitment to the positive rejection of everything that stands in the way.

Evil and sin are out. Goodness and love are in. We will not always make it, but this is where we are and where we know we are going. Embrace that and life just is different.

† Father, grant me this peace.

Alec Gilmore

Try again

Perhaps Paul feels the reader is not persuaded, because he returns to the point in a different way. Paul, always a hard-liner, sees things in black and white, so think of two ways of living and see them as mutually exclusive – living for self (Adam) and living for others (Jesus). The choice we have is which of the two we embrace, and it is fundamental. We have to be one or the other, at least in conviction and intention, and whichever we choose we will be slaves to that way of life.

Before coming to Christ we were slaves of Adam. That is how we are all made. Self-interest predominates in all of us, even if only at the level of survival, procreation and the protection of our own. That is the slavery we inherited. Embrace Christ in baptism (or confirmation), experience the peace of God, and you become a slave to him. From that moment there is no way we could revert to Adam, and why ever would we want to?

When you were slaves of sin, you were free in regard to righteousness. So what advantage did you then get from the things of which you now are ashamed? The end of those things is death. But now that you have been freed from sin and enslaved to God, the advantage you get is sanctification [peace?]. The end is eternal life.

(verses 20-22)

† Father, I want to believe that Paul is right, but please can you give me strength to believe it when the temptation to doubt is strongest.

Romans 1–8   Alec Gilmore

From death to life

For those still having difficulty with doctrine, Paul tries again, this time with imagery: marriage. Under Jewish law a married woman was bound to her husband. Once he died she was free. Death changes everything, says Paul, and once you embrace Christ the Law is dead. You are no longer tied to it. You are free to engage in a different way of living.

> While we were living in the flesh, our sinful passions, aroused by the law, were at work in our members to bear fruit for death. But now we are discharged from the law, dead to that which held us captive, so that we are slaves not under the old written code but in the new life of the Spirit.

(verses 5-6)

So what is this 'law' to which Christians are no longer answerable? Think of it as a summing up of all those things (old ideas, traditions, habits, superstitions and neuroses) that hold us in chains, prevent us from becoming the wholesome characters God intended us to be, and which in the end destroy us. To sharpen your understanding, spend some time trying to identify those former 'sinful passions'. For example, self-centredness (as individuals, families or nations), fear of others, anxieties about the future, or ways in which you are more aware of darkness, despair and gloom than of the light, hope and anticipation.

---

† Father, show me what I no longer need to worry about and grant me the joy of the light that comes with the new day.

Alec Gilmore   Romans 1–8

Saturday 12 June
Romans 7:13-20

Still confused?

If you are still confused, so was Paul. He may have died to the Law (the old) but he could not escape its influence. The past was past. The old was gone. He knew it. He had denounced it. But its impact and its influence were still strong and he knew there was no getting away from it.

I do not understand my own actions. For I do not do what I want, but I do the very thing I hate. Now if I do what I do not want, I agree that the law is good. But in fact it is no longer I that do it, but sin that dwells within me.

(verses 15-17)

So he takes refuge in dualism (or denial). 'I didn't do it – something inside that took control.' 'Eve tempted me . . .' The difference now is that Paul knows that whatever drove him to it is his enemy, not his friend.

He also knows that sometimes he cannot help himself, and that while that persists there is no peace – not inside, not with his friends, and certainly not with God. But how to get out of it? He no longer has to. Christ has set him free. God still loves him. No longer a slave to rules and regulations, traditions, rituals, tensions and anxieties eating away at him, he is free to grow in humanity, to be himself and not the person others want him to be and try to make him – he is on the road from death to life.

† Father, thank you for Paul and for the new ray of light he has brought into my life.

Romans 1–8   Alec Gilmore

Romans 1–8

4 Life in the Spirit

Notes based on the *New International Version* by
Meeli Tankler

For Meeli's biography, see p. 87.

For Meeli's biography, see p. 87.

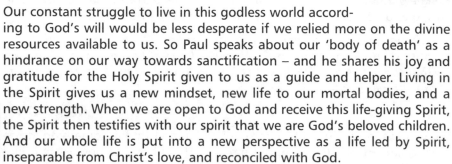

Sunday 13 June: Preparing for the week

Our constant struggle to live in this godless world according to God's will would be less desperate if we relied more on the divine resources available to us. So Paul speaks about our 'body of death' as a hindrance on our way towards sanctification – and he shares his joy and gratitude for the Holy Spirit given to us as a guide and helper. Living in the Spirit gives us a new mindset, new life to our mortal bodies, and a new strength. When we are open to God and receive this life-giving Spirit, the Spirit then testifies with our spirit that we are God's beloved children. And our whole life is put into a new perspective as a life led by Spirit, inseparable from Christ's love, and reconciled with God.

Text for the week: *Romans 8:1-2*

Therefore, there is now no condemnation for those who are in Christ Jesus, because through Christ Jesus the law of the Spirit of life set me free from the law of sin and death.

For group discussion and personal thought

• How would you understand Paul's words about the Spirit controlling one's mind? Is there anything in your mind that needs this kind of divine control?

• What does it mean for you to belong to God's family? What associations does the word 'family' create in you? Would you rather relate with God from a distance?

• How do you understand the thought that 'in all things God works for the good of those who love him' (verse 28)? Have you had moments when it was hard to believe that?

June

Rescue from the body of death

Paul complains:

When I want to do good, evil is right there with me.

(part of verse 21)

However good our intentions, as human beings we can never be certain that we are able to carry on with them in our own strength. In this godless world we are too often carried away from our good and noble goals, and we struggle constantly to stay on the right course. Paul is being very honest here – he calls himself 'a wretched man', and pleads for rescue 'from the body of death'.

This seems quite desperate. Since Adam's fall, there is this dreadful 'human factor' influencing everything we think or say or do. Even the best of us fail from time to time, and every failure reminds us about our imperfection again and again. We were created in God's own image but we have gone astray. And we struggle from day to day to keep our integrity intact as much as possible – but alas, our human strength and resources are so very limited!

And yet, there is the solution: God has reached out to save us. There is the good news: we do not have to remain prisoners of sin any more. We do not have to rely only on our own limited human resources. Through Jesus Christ our Lord, this battle is won already. Thanks be to God!

† Lord Jesus, thank you for this wonderful assurance that we do not have to be prisoners of sin any more. Help us to claim the rescue from the body of death, and accept your salvation. Amen

Tuesday 15 June
Romans 8:1-11

Receiving the life-giving Spirit

Paul continues to explain how the life-giving Spirit is working in us. First, the Spirit gives us an assurance that now it is possible to break free from the law of sin. For God himself has dealt with the problem of our sinfulness, and we can trust his solution as the best possible solution. He sent his own Son 'in the likeness of sinful man to be a sin offering' for us all (verse 3).

Therefore, there is now no more condemnation for those who are in Christ Jesus.

(verse 1)

There is a new era dawning, a new beginning made possible for us all through Christ Jesus, and his sacrifice. If only we open ourselves to God and his life-giving Spirit, something wonderful begins to happen inside us. It is a process of real renewal. Instead of struggling on our own, and failing, there is now divine help available for us.

Gaining freedom from sin opens a totally new way of life for us. God's Spirit provides us first of all with a new mindset characterised by 'life and peace' (verse 6). And instead of being in confrontation with God while living according to our sinful nature, from now on we shall be able to please him with our life, using his Spirit's help and guidance. And not only our spirit but also our mortal bodies become alive in this process.

† Our Father in heaven, thank you for solving the problem of our sinfulness for ever. Thank you for sending your son Jesus into this world as a sin offering for us. Thank you for giving your Spirit to make us alive. Amen

Meeli Tankler

Romans 1–8

Being led by the Spirit

There is a real life-and-death question here. Paul reminds us once more that living according to our sinful nature will ultimately lead us into death. But if we, by the Spirit, 'put to death the misdeeds of the body' (v.13), we shall certainly live. And there is no middle road available. Some people have understood all 'bodily deeds' to be unclean and sinful. However, if we read carefully, Paul is speaking about 'misdeeds' of the body here, contrasting the body with the spirit:

For if you live according to the sinful nature, you will die; but if by the Spirit you put to death the misdeeds of the body, you will live.

(verse 13)

June

Our body is 'a temple of God's Spirit', he reminds us elsewhere (1 Corinthians 6:18).

The main question is about right guidance. Are we led by our sinful nature, or do we open up to God, and invite the life-giving Spirit to be our ultimate guide? God's Spirit makes and keeps us alive, both our minds and bodies. And as soon as we accept the Spirit's guidance, we are welcomed into the family of God himself. Now we belong there as beloved children. We do not have to be afraid or hesitant – we can call God our father, and nothing separates us from his love. However, Paul reminds us that in the family, everything is common. There is not only God's glory for us to share – there are also Christ's sufferings to share.

† Thank you, Lord, for welcoming us into your family. Help us to be truly God's children in our daily life in a way that brings glory to God's name. Amen

Romans 1–8   Meeli Tankler

Waiting in the Spirit

Living as children in God's family, we still have to go through difficulties from time to time. Paul is again very straightforward here – he does not promise us only prosperity and mountain-top sensations. Even though we are led by the Spirit, and belong to God's family, Paul speaks in a matter-of-fact way about our present sufferings and frustration, our inward groaning as we wait for the freedom God has prepared for us.

But God's Spirit is able and willing to give us endurance and hope and patience to live under stress and frustration. This is good news. For it is easy to believe in God when everything goes well – when we experience great things, and blessings flow, and everybody is friendly and nice to us. But the truth is that we often realise the real blessing of God's presence in just those moments when we have to 'walk through the valley of the shadow of death' (Psalm 23:4). It is then we discover with great joy that we are not alone. Paul reminds us here that the richness of God's life-giving Spirit opens up new dimensions for us in difficult times. 'Hope that is seen is no hope at all' (verse 24). In a seemingly hopeless situation we need patient hope for the better days to come. And with the Spirit's help, we can hope and wait – patiently and eagerly at the same time. There is the future to be revealed in us:

the glorious freedom of the children of God.

(part of verse 21)

God will stand behind his promises.

---

† Lord Jesus, we pray for your children who are in difficult and hopeless situations. May your Spirit bring them hope, and may they experience your presence in a special way. Amen

Meeli Tankler

Called to glory

Our way towards God's glory begins from the realisation of how weak we actually are. We are weak and often confused – we do not even know what we ought to pray for! But the same Spirit who has brought us freedom from sin and hope for the future is now willing to help us pray in accordance with God's will. And it is interesting that Paul insists that God uses his great power not to change circumstances but to bring good out of all things – in all situations of life.

[W]e know that in all things God works for the good of those who love him.

(part of verse 28)

This puzzled me for a long time. I would have preferred God to intervene mightily, and turn bad things into good. But Paul gives us a picture of a far more powerful God – a God who does not have to change things in order to utilise them. In all things – good, bad or just insignificant – God is able to find the little something that will work for the good.

God has called you and me – and he has called us for his glory. With the help of God's Spirit we can respond to this call, and experience God's powerful hand in our life. And by admitting our own weakness, we can learn to trust God's mightiness. When there are no more thoughts or words left, the Spirit will come and intercede for us.

† Search me, O God, and know my heart; test me and know my anxious thoughts (Psalm 139:23). Come, Holy Spirit, and help me in my weakness to stay close to God. Amen

Romans 1–8   Meeli Tankler

Immersed in God's love

Today's passage begins as a battle-cry and ends as a love song. But it is first of all a love song: it tells us all about God's wondrous love. Nothing in this universe can separate us from God's love, Paul says. God did not spare even his own Son. His love is stronger than any hindrances we could imagine. God has deliberately opened his heart to us, and he never takes his offer back.

There is no change in God. When we look at God, the loving relationship is as strong as it can possibly be. If God is with us, who can be against us? We have entered into alliance with the greatest power in the whole universe. And at the same time, this is an alliance with the greatest love in the whole universe. But although there is every guarantee in place from God's side, we have to stick to this loving relationship from our side also – with all our hearts. Even though we may sometimes feel that we are 'more than conquerors', we always need to remember that we are strong only as long as we stay inside this loving relationship with God. Then indeed,

> neither death nor life . . . nor anything else in all creation, will be able to separate us from the love of God that is in Christ Jesus our Lord.

(part of verses 38-39)

Only if we stay close to God can the Spirit give us all we need for life and victory.

† Thank you, God, for loving us in Jesus Christ. Thank you for offering us this love that never changes or fades. Help us to love you with all our hearts and souls and minds. Amen

Meeli Tankler

Romans 1–8

Peter the Apostle

1 Peter and Jesus

Notes based on the *New Revised Standard Version* by
Robert Draycott

Robert Draycott is a Baptist minister who has had a varied ministry over thirty years, first as minister of a church in Northamptonshire, England, then as a lecturer in Theological Education in Brazil, before returning to Britain to be Chaplain of Eltham College in London.

Sunday 20 June: Preparing for the week

Peter is a legendary character in more ways than one. Recognised as the leader of the disciples, renamed as 'the rock', revered as the first Bishop of Rome, reputedly crucified upside down in that city, a role model in many ways, both positive and negative.

Reflecting on Peter and Jesus inspires us, warns us, and encourages us in equal measure. This is because Peter had his ups and downs, and comes across as one whom Christians today can relate to because his faults and failings did not disqualify him. If someone like Peter could be called, chosen and commissioned, then there is hope for us all.

Text for the week: *Matthew 16:15-17*

'Who do you say that I am?' Simon Peter answered, 'You are the Messiah, the Son of the living God.' And Jesus answered him, 'Blessed are you, Simon son of Jonah!'

For group discussion and personal thought

• 'Reflecting on Peter and Jesus inspires us, warns us, and encourages us.' What inspiration, warning and encouragement have you found in this week's readings?

Someone who needs no introduction

The surprising thing here is that Luke feels that Simon Peter needs no introduction. He simply states that Jesus entered Simon's house and cured his mother-in-law. Then almost incidentally we learn that Simon has a boat. Simon begins well: he allows Jesus to teach from his boat, then he obeys Jesus when he is told to put out into deep water. Simon's first words are memorable: 'Master, we have worked all night long but have caught nothing. Yet if you say so, I will let down the nets' (verse 5). Such unquestioning obedience leads to a catch so great that both boats begin to sink under the weight of the fish.

When Simon Peter saw it, he fell down at Jesus' knees, saying, 'Go away from me, Lord, for I am a sinful man!' For he and all who were with him were amazed at the catch of fish that they had taken . . . Then Jesus said to Simon, 'Do not be afraid: from now on you will be catching people.'

(verses 8-9 and 11)

Luke's account introduces the essential character of someone who was well known in the Early Church: obedient, yet aware of his own weakness. Like a cartoonist, in one picture Luke captures both the essence of Simon's character and how Jesus relates to him. 'Do not be afraid.'

Fear, not doubt, is the enemy of faith. Jesus did not go away from Simon. That can encourage us today, but it also challenges us because we find it easier to see other people as sinners. If, like Peter, we understand that *we* are sinners, we might be of more use as Christians.

† Lord, give us eyes that see the best in others, and beyond our own sins to our potential.

Robert Draycott

Peter the Apostle

Matthew 14:22-33

In stormy times

On holiday in Scotland, we went on a boat trip to the Isle of Staffa to visit Fingal's Cave. The outward journey was quite rough; the return journey was worse. Some passengers were seasick, others were frightened. Two things helped me: looking back at the fixed landmark of Staffa, and trusting the skill of the boatman.

Today's reading is Matthew's second account of a similar storm on Lake Galilee. The key difference here is that Jesus does not immediately calm the storm; instead he is in it with the disciples.

> Jesus spoke to them and said, 'Take heart, it is I; do not be afraid' . . . Peter . . . started walking . . . towards Jesus. But when he noticed the strong wind, he became frightened, and beginning to sink, he cried out, 'Lord, save me!'

(verse 27, part of verse 29, and verse 30)

For Peter, Jesus was both the fixed landmark and the one in whom to trust. As long as he kept his eyes on Jesus he was all right. When he lost that focus he began to sink. For Christians the message is clear: the secret of weathering the storms of life is to know that Jesus is there with us; and when we launch out in faith great things can be done, as long as we keep trusting in him. This story appears to revolve around Peter, but in reality it points away from him to the one who is Lord and Saviour:

> Jesus immediately reached out his hand and caught him

(verse 31)

† Father, we give you thanks for bringing us safely through the storms of life. We pray for those encountering times of trouble – may they know your presence and peace.

Peter the Apostle

Robert Draycott

Blessed and rebuked

Here Matthew uses the name Simon again in order to emphasise the significance of the name Peter. Jesus asks his disciples a key question: 'Who do you say that I am?' Simon's answer, 'You are the Messiah, the Son of the living God' (verses 15-16), is blessed by Jesus, who goes on to say:

> I tell you, you are Peter, and on this rock I will build my church and the gates of Hades will not prevail against it. I will give you the keys of the kingdom of heaven.'

(part of verses 18-19)

Peter's name is emphasised, as a rock on which Jesus will build his Church.

So far so good, and yet the next few verses describe a stinging rebuke when Peter refuses to accept the idea that his Master must suffer. The rock has become Satan (verse 23). It is not clear how we should interpret this puzzling reversal. Perhaps it reminds us that the Church is both human and divine, it is not perfect, and sometimes 'gets it wrong'. Often the Church can appear to be seduced by power, keener to use the keys to lock doors on those deemed unworthy than to use them to unlock the gates barring those considered 'the wrong sort of people' and give them opportunities to grow and flourish within the Church. Perhaps the key phrase is 'my church'. It belongs to Jesus; he is the one who builds it.

† Lord, forgive us when we forget whose church we belong to. May we be people who offer welcome and acceptance to all.

Robert Draycott

Peter the Apostle

Thursday 24 June

Mark 9:2-10

Not now, Peter

This passage, which occurs roughly at the central point in Mark's Gospel, is also central in that it reveals who Jesus is for the second time.

And he was transfigured before them, and his clothes became dazzling white . . . And there appeared to them Elijah with Moses, who were talking with Jesus. Then Peter said to Jesus 'Rabbi, it is good for us to be here; let us make three dwellings . . . He did not know what to say, for they were terrified.

(part of verses 2-5)

Jesus is centre stage, revealed in his true glory as God's son.

What are we to make of Peter's suggestion about making three dwellings? One suggestion is that Peter's timing is wrong, the time for building will come later. Not 'booths on the mountain' to which people have to travel, but the kingdom of God, where people are. A second suggestion is that Peter's real mistake is to think of the three figures as equal; the overshadowing cloud, symbolising the presence of God, makes clear the authority of Jesus as the unique son of God.

This passage reminds us that a healthy pattern of discipleship consists of glimpses of the glory of Jesus, listening to him, and 'doing in his name'. In other words, being inspired, instructed and enabled to live as Christians. How? Through worship, prayer, Bible reading as individuals, and through service and practical action as members of the Christian community, otherwise known as the 'body of Christ'.

† Father, we give you thanks for glimpses of your glory; may they inspire our worship and discipleship.

Peter the Apostle

Robert Draycott

Peter's denial

This is perhaps the best-known story about Peter. It is the night when Jesus was arrested and interrogated before the high priest. Before being arrested Jesus tells his disciples that they will all desert him.

Peter said to him 'Even though all become deserters, I will not.'

(verse 29)

Peter could not imagine denying his Lord and, unlike the other disciples, had the courage to follow Jesus 'right into the courtyard of the high priest' (verse 54). So far, so good.

But then came Peter's failure, which escalated from claiming not to understand, through a straightforward denial, to the traumatic emphasis of the third denial.

Then after a little while the bystanders again said to Peter, 'Certainly you are one of them; for you are a Galilean.' But he began to curse, and he swore an oath, 'I do not know this man you are talking about.' At that moment the cock crowed for the second time . . . And he broke down and wept.

(part of verse 70, verse 71, and part of verse 72)

Throughout the centuries Christians have been greatly moved by this episode. We have been able to see ourselves in Peter, with our petty evasions and unwillingness to speak up. Yet failure and denial were not the end of the road for Peter's discipleship. Nor should it be for us when we deny our Lord.

† Lord, forgive our failure to represent you as we should, and our silent denials when we fail to speak up as Christians.

Robert Draycott

Peter the Apostle

John 20:1-10

Peter at the tomb

Today's reading comes from John's Gospel and leaves us slightly puzzled about Peter's role. It is clear that a woman, Mary Magdalene, is the first witness to the resurrection. She ran back with the news:

> *'They have taken the Lord out of the tomb, and we do not know where they have laid him.' Then Peter and the other disciple set out and went towards the tomb . . . the other disciple outran Peter and reached the tomb first . . . but he did not go in. Then Simon Peter came, following him . . . and went into the tomb. He saw the linen wrappings lying there . . . Then the other disciple, who reached the tomb first, also went in, and he saw and believed.*

(part of verses 3-8)

No one really knows the identity of this other disciple. But John is saying something important about faith. Simon Peter went into the tomb and examined the evidence, but we are not told that he believed. The other disciple 'saw and believed'.

Christians cannot go back in time and see the evidence for themselves, but these verses make clear that this is not just impossible – it is unnecessary. The 'other disciple' serves as a model for all Christians who walk by 'faith' and not by sight. This points us forward to Jesus' declaration, 'Blessed are those who have not seen and yet have come to believe' (John 20:29).

† Lord, we give thanks for the example of Peter, for the encouragement we receive from his story. May his example draw us closer to our Master, the risen Lord Jesus.

Peter the Apostle   Robert Draycott

Peter the Apostle

2 Peter, a leader

Notes based on the *New Revised Standard Version* by
Philip G O'B Robinson

Philip Robinson is a former President of the Jamaica District of The
Methodist Church in the Caribbean and the Americas (MCCA) and of The
Jamaica Council of Churches. He is a Director of the National Religious
Media Commission. He is Methodist Chaplain to the University of the
West Indies (Mona Campus) and to the Excelsior Education Centre, the largest educational
institution of the MCCA. He is also teaches at Excelsior.

Sunday 27 June: Preparing for the week

Simon, whom Jesus surnamed Peter – the 'Rock', was the spokesman of
Jesus' disciples. Impetuous, bold, passionate, loyal and very human, that
was Peter. Jesus must have seen in this plain fisherman a potential gem of
a leader to have placed such confidence in him and to have made Peter's
function and leadership a pillar on which he would build his Church. Peter's
story is the story of one of the greatest leaders of the Church.

Text for the week: *John 21:17*

*[Jesus] said to him the third time, 'Simon, son of John, do you love me?' .
. . And he said to him, 'Lord, you know everything; you know that I love
you.' Jesus said to him, 'Feed my sheep.'*

For group discussion and personal thought

• Outline the qualities of a Christian leader anyone can trust.

• What can leaders in your congregation learn from the life of Peter, the
leader?

• How should the Church today fulfil Jesus' command to Peter to 'Feed
my sheep'?

June

Monday 28 June

John 21:1-17

Leader in the making

He said to him the third time, 'Simon, son of John, do you love me?' . . . and he said to him, 'Lord, you know everything; you know that I love you.' Jesus said to him, 'Feed my sheep.'

(part of verse 17)

When Jesus first met him (John 1:41-42) he knew what Peter was destined to become. Jesus gave him the name Cephas (the Aramaic translation of the Greek name, Peter) which means 'rock'. At Philippi Jesus affirmed Peter's designation and declared, 'You are Peter, and on this rock I will build my church' (Matthew 16:18). Jesus entrusted him with a mission and gave him authority.

Peter was not always a rock by nature; there were periods of weakness. Three times he denied that he was a disciple of Jesus (John 18:15-17, 25-27). Yet Jesus still had faith in this man. Three times he required Peter to declare his love – not casual love, but love that exceeded the love of his colleagues (verse 15). Peter declared his love and received his mandate; Jesus entrusted him with the task of taking care of his flock.

Love for Christ is vital to effective service and leadership in the Church. It is the motivating factor that urges us on, furnishing us with courage and determination. That is why St Paul declared with such boldness: 'the love of Christ controls us' (2 Corinthians 5:14). Nurturing God's people by the word of God, and pastoral care of the young in age and the young in the faith, are two awesome responsibilities given to leaders engaged in building up the kingdom of God. Such was the mandate given to the man Jesus called Peter.

† Lord, take what I am and make me into what you want me to be.

Peter the Apostle   Philip G O'B Robinson

Tuesday 29 June

Acts 2:14, 22-39

Peter's credible authority

But Peter, standing with the eleven, raised his voice and addressed them, 'Men of Judea and all who live in Jerusalem, let this be known to you, and listen to what I say.'

(verse 14)

On the Day of Pentecost, a bold Peter, as leader of the apostles, addressed the massive cosmopolitan crowd in Jerusalem. It was not the impulsive utterances of a zealous disciple; it was the authoritative pronouncements of an apostle that they had heard and to which they eventually responded.

At the end of Jesus' Sermon on the Mount (Matthew 5 – 7) 'the crowds were astounded at his teaching, for he taught them as one having authority, and not as their scribes' (Matthew 7:28-29). The scribes depended on other authorities (writings and traditions) in order to authenticate their teachings; Jesus spoke as one who had authority – real authority. It was his prerogative to confer such authority and power on Peter (see Matthew 16:18, 19).

In the Church, where Christ alone is the head, a leader exercises authority delegated by Christ. Peter 'raised his voice' not just for people in the crowd to hear him; it was a sign of how confident he was about the gospel of Christ – being neither afraid nor ashamed to embrace it for himself and to proclaim it to others. Effective leaders must be credible, and to be credible they must themselves believe what they have to offer to others, then they must lead and speak with authority.

† Sovereign Lord, we have no glory, power or authority of our own; they belong supremely to you. Give to all leaders in your church the grace to exercise authority with care and conviction so that your kingdom and its glory might be manifested in their service.

Philip G O'B Robinson

Peter the Apostle

Acts 3:1-16

To the greater glory of God

'You Israelites, why do you wonder at this, or why do you stare at us, as though by our own power or piety we had made him walk? The God of Abraham, the God of Isaac, and the God of Jacob, the God of our ancestors has glorified his servant Jesus.'

(part of verses 12-13)

Peter could have basked in the limelight. As he turned to address the crowd, with the healed man clinging to him and John, he could have played Jesus or savoured his influence over the curious and admiring crowd. Sometimes leaders develop an inordinate sense of personal power, which sometimes leads to their downfall. Peter's response made it clear that he had no such aspiration or intention. He pointed the people to God and to Jesus, the Christ, as the source of the power through which the man was healed. Peter saw himself and John as mere instruments of divine power and gave the glory to the Lord. Consequently, he was able to remain focused and true to the commission he had received from Jesus.

Paul advised that leadership in the Church should not be conferred on those who are young in the faith, one reason being the potentially damaging effects of unhealthy pride (1 Timothy 3:6). Leaders should beware the attractiveness of being popular. A leader driven by popularity is likely to sacrifice virtues such as truth and justice in order to maintain popularity. A Christ-inspired leader, such as Peter, lives and serves 'to the greater glory of God'.

† O God, we acknowledge the privilege that is ours to be instruments and channels of your gracious and powerful acts. May we always give you the glory and thank you for the blessings.

Peter the Apostle   Philip G O'B Robinson

Acts 11:1-18

A bold leader who thinks 'out of the box'

*'If then God gave them the same gift that he gave us when we be-
lieved in the Lord Jesus Christ, who was I that I could hinder God?'*

(verse 17)

Confronted by the apostles and other believers in Judea because he had taken the gospel to the gentiles, Peter explained his actions. He related his vision and the experience of Cornelius, a Roman army officer, to whom an angel had spoken and who was instructed to send for 'Simon, who is called Peter'. He also told them how the Holy Spirit had fallen on the gentiles gathered at Cornelius' house, just as he had on the apostles on the Day of Pentecost. Peter interpreted the vision to mean that God was showing him that no one should be considered profane or unclean (Acts 10:28).

Peter would have had in mind the Lord's purpose for him (Matthew 16:18, 19) as well as the Great Commission to 'make disciples of all nations . . . baptising them . . . and teaching them' (Matthew 28:19, 20), so he proceeded to analyse the current situation, in spite of common practice and existing regulations – he was a leader who was prepared to think 'out of the box' as long as the divine purpose was not compromised. He was not going to argue the will of God. This is the kind of leader that was required to move the Early Church beyond the narrow thinking of Judaism and prepare her to reach the whole world with the gospel of Christ; this the boldness we need today.

† O Holy Spirit, may we be endued with power from on high and be bold in witness and in the work to which God has called us.

Philip G O'B Robinson

Peter the Apostle

Galatians 2:6-14

I stand corrected

But when Cephas came to Antioch, I opposed him to his face . . . for until certain people came from James, he used to eat with the Gentiles. But after they came, he drew back and kept himself separate for fear of the circumcision faction.

(part of verse 11, and verse 12)

Peter made a bad decision to withdraw from the gentile Christians when Jewish Christians arrived from Jerusalem teaching that 'unless you are circumcised according to the custom of Moses, you cannot be saved' (Acts 15:1). He was afraid of what they would say about his association with the gentiles. Paul rebuked him for this apparent double standard.

This incident did not devalue Peter's leadership in the least. On the contrary, it showed the mettle of the man. The Bible does not tell us that Peter reacted negatively to Paul's rebuke, nor does it tell of any later disagreement between the two. It is reasonable, therefore, to assume that Peter, to his great credit, graciously accepted the correction. He did not make excuses or become defensive as many leaders would. This is supported by Peter's later reference to his 'beloved brother Paul' (2 Peter 3:15). It takes a humble and mature leader to accept correction gracefully – Peter was all of that. This is a leader who is worthy of respect and admiration. Peter the leader understood well the spirit and wisdom of Proverbs 15:31-32, which says: 'If you listen to constructive criticism, you will be at home among the wise. If you reject criticism, you only harm yourself, but if you listen to correction, you grow in understanding' (*New Living Translation*).

† Lord, we acknowledge our imperfections; grant us the grace and humility to accept correction, so that we may grow in wisdom and understanding.

Peter the Apostle   Philip G O'B Robinson

2 Peter 1:16-18

The eyewitness

For we did not follow cleverly devised myths . . . we had been eyewitnesses of his majesty.

(part of verse 16)

Peter's leadership role in the Early Church was based on his experience as an eyewitness, as well as his appointment by Jesus. He had been with Jesus for three years, he had seen him teaching and healing and listened to his words. However, the one event that seems to have really impressed itself on his memory was the more private occasion when Jesus took his closest disciples, Peter, James and John, with him when he climbed the mountain and was transfigured (Mark 9:2-8). There, Peter was given a glimpse of the real Jesus, the man who was also the glorious Son of God, the Father's beloved Son; and the evidence of the Acts of the Apostles is that the experience turned Peter into a passionate witness to Jesus.

All Christians are called by God to be witnesses. We cannot, like Peter, be eyewitnesses to the actual physical presence of Jesus and his earthly ministry; but we have all experienced God, and the Spirit at work in our lives. That is our witness, the good news we have to share with others.

† Lord, Peter was with you during your earthly ministry and witnessed your transfiguration. We have never seen your human form, but we too have plenty of experience of you to share with others. Help us, like Peter, to witness boldly for you, that others may be drawn to know and love you.

Philip G O'B Robinson

Peter the Apostle

Moods and emotions

1 From sorrow to joy

Notes based on the *New Jerusalem Bible* by
Sister Christopher Godden OSB

Having decided not to become a teacher, Sr Christopher worked for 13 years in the supply industry. It was the advent of computers. In 1982 she sold her house, bicycle, canoe and cat and entered the Benedictine Monastery at Talacre in North Wales. Shortly after her Final Profession she moved with the Community to Chester, where she does her best to live according to the Rule of St Benedict and to become a Christian.

Sunday 4 July: Preparing for the week

Darkness gives birth to light, and night to day (Genesis 1:1-5), a pattern that continues throughout life. Bad days, good days, ups and downs: life is no straight path but a creative balance of opposites in harmony. This appears repeatedly throughout scripture. The ancient yin/yang symbol illustrates it beautifully. The division between the two sides is shown as a curved line, each of the two sides containing a small 'seed' of its opposite. In life, periods of darkness hold a seed of light and at times of joy a grain of sorrow or darkness may be found. Even when all seems lost there is always hope.

Text for the week: *Psalm 30:5*
His anger lasts but a moment, his favour through life;
in the evening come tears, but with dawn cries of joy.

For group discussion and personal thought
• What is the difference between happiness and joy?
• You come across a would-be suicide, what do you do?
• Can war ever be justified?

Monday 5 July

Psalm 10:12-18

A real God

Rise, Yahweh! God, raise your hand,
do not forget the afflicted!

(verse 12)

The psalmist does not doubt God's existence – but where is he? Instead of life being a smooth path with no problems, it seems the wicked flourish and get away with it. So, where is God? Asleep? Forgotten about his people (verse 10)? Gone away? Hiding? Perhaps an appeal to his pride will work (verse 13)? The faith of the psalmist and his conception of God are very matter of fact and precise. He speaks openly of God's (seeming) absence in an unjust world – trusting that he will be heard and vindicated.

When life does not always turn out as expected or hoped for, many people find themselves puzzled and wonder if they have annoyed God and now he is 'punishing them'. But God does not work like that. His gift to us of free will means that he watches and cares but will not interfere unless asked.

It is the hard lessons in life that tend to help us mature and grow in faith. Outside my window as I write, rain pours down and wind tugs tree branches hither and thither; it's the sort of weather that encourages a tree to put down deep and firm roots to hold it steady. In times of darkness our job is to face the blackness with a candle of faith lighting the way until the end of the tunnel.

† Lord, there are those today who will feel that you are far away or have even deserted them; help them not to leave go of their faith but to trust in hope.

Sr Christopher Godden

Moods and emotions

Tuesday 6 July

1 Samuel 2:1-10

Gift of God

[F]or Yahweh is a wise God,
his to weigh up deeds.

(part of verse 3)

An unexpected windfall or something suddenly 'coming right' and we see the world with 'new eyes'. What previously was negative and seemingly impossible changes to become positive, bright and full of possibility. No longer the butt of Penninah's taunts and scorn, Hannah has returned to the temple, her prayer answered (1 Samuel 1:11). She returns to keep the promise she made to Yahweh should he see fit to give her the son she asked for. In her joy Hannah's vision expands to embrace the entire world. Her world turned upside-down, Hannah glimpses what will later be called 'the kingdom of heaven', where the attitudes and values of the present day are stood on their head(s) and injustice and unfairness redressed.

Not a mother myself, and never likely to be one, I don't know the joy of parenthood; however, I do know of the excitement and gratitude of those who, after many years, do find that at last they are to bear a child. In her darkness and anguish Hannah believed, trusted and acted (1 Samuel 1:9). At times that seems to be all one can do. But at the same time we have to keep our minds and hearts open because the answer we expect, and want, may not always come in the way expected or hoped for at the time, and only later on will we realise that God really does know what is best.

† Father, we pray for all parents who long for a family, and for the many children waiting for adoption and parents of their own.

Moods and emotions

Sr Christopher Godden

Start all over again

When Yahweh brought back Zion's captives
we lived in a dream.

(verse 1)

Freed from their captivity in Babylon and on their way home, the exiles dream of their triumphant arrival in Jerusalem. The reality is very different (Nehemiah 1:3). Desolation and despondency greet them. The dream must change from what was and now is to a vision of what can be. And that vision must lead to results. Anxious to show they have learned their lessons well in captivity, the returnees begin work on the restoration of the Temple, the resumption of the liturgy and the rededication of the people. Conscious of how far they have fallen from being God's chosen and special people, if they begin their task of rebuilding their lives and restoring national pride with a heartfelt return to God, then surely he will bless them in their task!

When things do not turn out as planned, dreams and hopes are shattered and life seems to fall apart at the seams, it may be that God is trying to get us to change direction or focus and try something new and unexpected. He is asking us to walk in faith and trust – even though it may feel like treading on water. New beginnings can be very hard, but we have to start sometime and somewhere and, with God alongside, it is amazing what can be done . . .

† Lord, we pray for all who have been forced to leave home for any reason but are now returning to build new lives and homes.

Sr Christopher Godden

Moods and emotions

A meal to remember

On this mountain, for all peoples,
Yahweh Sabaoth is preparing
a banquet.

(verse 6)

Today's reading comes from a short section of Isaiah headed 'Apocalypse'. This type of writing developed at times of great calamity and persecution, when the religious community was experiencing suffering or was victimised by some extreme form of deprivation. Apocalyptic writing diverted attention from the present distressful conditions to the (believed in) end of the present world, which would be a time of judgement of the wicked and vindication of the righteous, and would usher in a new era of prosperity and peace. The writing was not a flight from reality, more a way of coping with it and planning for the future. Because it was written in a time of danger and persecution, the message was often conveyed in symbolic form and not always explained or interpreted. In today's passage, verses 6-9 show the captives in Babylon the vision of a great mountain-top feast, when the entire world will finally turn towards Yahweh in faith and praise.

Food plays an integral part in Jewish culture and religion: holy days at synagogue are also honoured by special and symbolic food at home. So what better way to celebrate the inauguration of the longed-for Messianic age than a banquet?

I am also reminded of two other mountains: the one where Jesus fed the multitude; and the small hill outside Jerusalem where, after the meal now known as the Last Supper, through agony and death the seeds were sown for the fulfilment of Isaiah's words.

† We pray for those who will not get enough to eat today. May ways soon be found to share the plenty of some with the nothing of others.

Moods and emotions   Sr Christopher Godden

Exile to Exodus

Yahweh invites the world to witness the return of the exiles to the Promised Land. Their fortunes reversed, at last the captives were free to come home after 70 years of banishment in Babylon. Strangely – or maybe not so strangely – not all chose to go home. And, of those who did, great faith and hard work would be demanded when they saw the ruinous state of their once prosperous country.

But their time away has been, in part, preparation for this moment. The captives had to learn to see Yahweh in new ways – not only as the creator of the world who was so holy that his name could never be spoken, but also as Yahweh who had gone into captivity with them and remained with them to teach, encourage and be alongside them. Yahweh was not just someone 'up there' to be propitiated and satisfied with sacrifices offered through a temple hierarchy. He would 'shepherd' them home (verse 10), have gifts ready for them on their return (verse 12), comfort them and give them joy after their troubles (verse 14). When they are reunited with their own land and with those not taken into captivity, God will:

change their mourning into gladness,
comfort them, give them joy after their troubles.

(verse 13)

Even the land will celebrate (verse 12) as the people party. What a homecoming!

---

† We pray for all who have been forced to leave homes, families, jobs and friends and to seek somehow to pick up the pieces of shattered lives in strange and foreign places.

Sr Christopher Godden

Moods and emotions

July

Honest to God

I would hate to think that some of the mistakes I have made in life were still being read, written and talked about 3000 or so years after my death! Yet that is still happening with the errors of King David, author of today's psalm. But that, of course, is not the entire picture. Deeply religious and aware of Yahweh, David is also able to admit his faults and wrongdoing and seek forgiveness even though that may well involve punishment. When in trouble, be it from an enemy without or a sickness within, he turns to Yahweh in openness, trust and faith. Conversely, when all goes well David also turns to Yahweh but now in order to thank him for the blessings he has sent.

The story of David illustrates beautifully the living relationship between 'him who must not be named' and a mortal human being. So close does Yahweh feel to David, that when he seems absent David admits

you turned away your face and I was terrified.

(part of verse 7)

Is our notion of God merely 'top brain' – just a notion, an idea without any feeling or relationship? Or is it deep, at times bewildering, frightening but also very real? Yahweh was real for David. He longs to be real for us too. Good days and bad days. We need both. Thank God.

† Father, we pray for all who will not acknowledge you or are afraid of you. Help them to overcome whatever is stopping them from recognising you and your love in daily life.

Moods and emotions

2   From despondency to hope

Notes based on the *New International Version* by
Jember Teferra

Jember Teferra is an Ethiopian who has worked for 28 years in the poorest slums in Addis Ababa, promoting the philosophy of the Integrated Holistic Approach, which endeavours to address the root causes of poverty both through practical programmes and through advocacy on issues related to poverty.

Sunday 11 July: Preparing for the week

The major lesson we learn from this week's readings is that if we follow the Lord we must not assume everything in life will go happily ever after. That is the expectation of those who believe in the 'prosperity gospel' (a guarantee of being wealthy). God's uniqueness lies in knowing each one of his followers, allowing what grief, suffering and troubles they can bear, and carrying them through them, as the popular text 'Footprints' concludes: 'During your times of trial and suffering, when you see only one set of footprints, it was then that I carried you.'

Text for the week: *Habakkuk 3:17-18*

Though the fig tree does not bud, and there are no grapes on the vines . . . and the field produce no food, though there are . . . no cattle in the stalls, yet I will rejoice in the LORD, I will be joyful in God my saviour.

For group discussion and personal thought

• How would you behave, as a Christian, if you were in Job's place?

• As leaders, which is easier: to be a top-down planner and operate quickly and efficiently, or to listen to the 'still small voice', however long we have to pray and wait?

A cry of affliction

You have taken my companions and loved ones from me,
the darkness is my closest friend.

(verse 18)

C S Lewis's book, *A Grief Observed*, written under the pseudonym of Mr Clerk, attempted 'to argue out a grief'; Lewis, a man of spiritual depth hit by his wife's death, expressed the feelings of most Christians who have experienced bereavement. I can identify with Psalm 88's cry of affliction because I lost two loved ones – my husband and my son – on the same day from different causes in different geographical locations. What a great loss!

During his bereavement C S Lewis asked, 'Meanwhile where is God?' – identifying perhaps with Jesus, who had asked his Father 'Why have you forsaken me?' David the psalmist seems to be in the same position when he concludes Psalm 88 by saying 'the darkness is my closest friend' – the loneliness, fear and depression of darkness. But, thank God, the good Lord understands the downheartedness and total depression of the bereaved, and gives us comfort and victory over grief. The poet John Donne (1573–1631) affirms this victory in his poem 'Death':

one short sleep past, we wake eternally,
and death shall be no more: Death, thou shalt die!

† Our loving and caring heavenly father, thank you for being sympathetic and understanding with us when we grieve, as you also, yourself, experienced death and grief. Thank you for all the comforting words of scripture that assure us that the light overcomes darkness and death itself will be conquered.

Moods and emotions   Jember Teferra

Job 3:11-26

Death seen as the deliverer

Yesterday we saw death in its negative aspect. Today we see Job praying for death to deliver him from profound grief, physical agony and intolerable pain. St Francis of Assisi referred to death as 'most kind' and 'gentle', though his reasons were different: Job saw death as an escape from multiple sufferings, whereas Francis was longing to see God. But Job cries out:

'Why is light given to those in misery,
and life to the bitter of soul,
to those who long for death that does not come,
who search for it more than for hidden treasure.'

(verses 20-21)

How many of us are judgemental of Job? Or, like him, have prayed for the anaesthetic of death when life becomes too difficult to face? I did, following my double bereavement. I had four different illnesses, though when I recovered I soon remembered my three other children who would at one stroke be left without parents and a brother if I also died. I felt very guilty and asked God for forgiveness.

Most psychologists advise that quality of life is more important than being alive in Job's condition. However, as Christians we have seen Joni Erikson, totally paralysed and moving about in a wheelchair, witnessing for the Lord in a most unbelievably dignified way. So he uses us even in our most vulnerable state. God has a purpose for allowing suffering, as we see in Job's story. His quality of life changed and more blessings were bestowed on him; that was why God restored his life!

---

† O God, when you allow suffering in different forms – including death – help us
   to understand and trust that you have a purpose. Please also give us the ability to tolerate
   suffering until it is over.

Jember Teferra   Moods and emotions

Wednesday 14 July

1 Kings 19:1-8

Travelling with God

'Get up and eat, for the journey is too much for you.'

(part of verse 7)

Since childhood, when I began my journey with the Lord, this verse has been special to me. To each of us the 'get up and eat' means different things: we may need prayers for guidance, we may need to be open to listen and be instructed, we may be running out of energy and need more faith, strength and obedience.

When I began my present ministry, I clearly recall three simultaneous obstacles that I faced – a situation that could have stopped me starting at all. I felt much like Elijah – I just wanted to run away and leave it all. One day, at 4 o'clock in the morning, I sat up more or less having a long discussion with the Lord – almost like negotiating. When I finished my morning prayer I thought of a favourite poem by Kristone, called 'Don't quit', which speaks of how things at their worst can be about to change for the better. So we must stick to the fight. God will travel with us if we listen for wisdom and instructions and don't quit when things are hard; we must re-charge – 'get up and eat' – and press on for the unknown journey. God knows best.

† Thank you, Lord, for all we learn from those who travel with you through thick and thin. May we be open to respond to your Spirit and your angels as they constantly pass on your messages and instructions.

Moods and emotions

Jember Teferra

1 Kings 19:9-18

The still small voice

Then a voice said to him, 'What are you doing here, Elijah?' . . .
'Go back the way you came and go to the Desert of Damascus.'

(part of verses 13 and 15)

Elijah was in a state of confusion and depression after a series of horrific events. He sheltered from wind, earthquake and fire until the 'still small voice' gave him a plan of action. For those of us who are privileged to follow the Lord and are leaders or part of a team, when we try to make a wise plan of action we have to listen to the 'still small voice' of the Lord. One of my favourite verses was used by King George VI in his broadcast on Christmas Day 1939 ('The Gate of the Year' by Minnie Louise Haskins): it speaks of asking 'the man who stood at the gate of the year' for a light into the unknown future; he was told that the way forward was to put his hand into the hand of God, who would lead him towards the dawn. So we should be open to listening to the 'still small voice' for instructions and directions. He will give us holistic wisdom.

† Our Father, whatever strategies you plan, amid confusion and lack of clarity, for now and for the future, help us to be open to hear your 'still small voice', for your wisdom and direction will guide us through thick and thin.

July

Jember Teferra

Moods and emotions

Habakkuk 3:17-19

Choose to hope in the Lord

Though the fig tree does not bud
and there are no grapes on the vines,
though the olive crop fails
and the fields produce no food,
though there are no sheep in the pen
and no cattle in the stalls,
yet I will rejoice in the LORD,
I will be joyful in God my Saviour.

(verses 17-18)

What a faith! What an assured calmness! We can confidently say that personal faith is the best practical answer to trials, tribulations and unhappiness in life.

We also see the real meaning of love – come what may, we will love, trust and continue to follow the Lord. Unconditional love is what the Lord himself always gives us, and Habakkuk is a real role model. He has always been my challenge during suffering and leadership difficulties, showing us how one-sided loving and trusting would be if we dared to question God's enabling power to do the impossible. God does not let us suffer just for the sake of seeing us suffer – he has a reason. Habakkuk ends his writing by declaring: 'The sovereign LORD is my strength . . . he enables me to go on the heights'; when our recovery comes, we may even fly.

† 'O Jesus, thou hast promised to all who follow thee, that where thou art in glory, there shall thy servant be; and, Jesus, I have promised to serve thee to the end. O give me grace to follow, my Master and my friend.' (John Bode)

Moods and emotions

Jember Teferra

Lamentations 3:19-23

Trouble into blessings

I remember my affliction and my wandering . . .
Yet this I call to mind
and therefore I have hope . . .
his compassions never fail.
They are new every morning;
great is your faithfulness.

(part of verses 19 and 21-22, and verse 23)

I have been privileged to know and follow the good Lord from childhood to adulthood, but there is one negative factor that all human beings have in common: not just being sinful, but also forgetting, when we suffer, the many blessings God has given us. Jeremiah in his lamentations portrays God as a huntsman shooting arrows at his prey; like David in his grieving and depressed state, Job even questioned why was he born; and I can identify with those who ask God 'Why me?' or 'How can you do that to your followers?' Whenever suffering hits us, if we only remembered that yesterday we received so much blessing, we should be ashamed that, when we suffer, all that God did yesterday is totally forgotten. We all forget God's blessings, forgiveness and compassions at a time of sufferings and trials. Fortunately he knows, he cares, and he loves unconditionally. His compassion never fails.

† Our loving, caring and compassionate Father, forgive us when we suffer from short memories of your blessings; and equip us with adequate faith to see and fight trials and tribulations, knowing that you do not allow them without a purpose.

Jember Teferra

Moods and emotions

July

Moods and emotions

3 From anger to creative action

Notes based on the *New Revised Standard Version* by
David Huggett

For David's biography see p. 80.

Sunday 18 July: Preparing for the week

The theologians of the Middle Ages did us no favours when
they classified anger as one of the seven deadly sins. Like joy and sorrow,
anger is a normal human emotion. It is our reaction to what someone
says to us or about us, or to threatening circumstances or behaviour, or
perhaps when we fear the loss of our security. Words like wrath, fury and
rage indicate a range of levels at which anger can be experienced, just
as different people will experience it in a variety of ways and intensities
according to their personality. But the real question is how we handle it.
Do we control it or does it control us? Do we use it as a weapon to injure
someone or get our own back, or can it be used in a positive way to help
others?

Text for the week: *Romans 12:17*

*Do not repay anyone evil for evil, but take thought for what is noble in
the sight of all.*

For group discussion and personal thought

• What advice would you give to someone who said to you, 'I can't
control my temper'?

• Beverley Harrison said that anger is 'a vivid form of caring'. What do
you think she meant?

July

When I am the victim

I imagine myself playing a game of football. I accidentally trip up one of the opponents. He has every right to be angry but I apologise, admitting that I was in the wrong. However, his anger is still boiling and he won't leave it there. He goes on to accuse me of a deliberate foul and then turns to the referee demanding that I should be sent off. That is the kind of over-reaction the psalmist is suffering from. It can take many forms: we may unintentionally offend a neighbour, or make a foolish mistake at work. In doing so we possibly incur an angry response that is deserved. But provided we seek to put things right, that is where it should end.

It doesn't always. Anger is harboured. Forgiveness is denied. Relationships are soured. Whatever it was that led to the psalmist's prayer to God for vindication (verse 1), in verses 2-5 he turns to address those who have insulted him, told lies about him, and called his integrity into question. So in verse 4 he warns them that they should beware of letting their anger get out of hand. To do so is likely to lead to the sin of revenge. But, like Job, the psalmist knows that in the end his integrity will remain intact because his trust is in the God of integrity.

I will both lie down and sleep in peace;
for you alone, O LORD, make me lie down in safety.

(verse 8)

† Lord, when I am unfairly treated or criticised, when someone tells lies about me or insults me, help me to remember that you are the 'God of my right' so that I may experience your gift of peace.

David Huggett   Moods and emotions

When anger takes control

If you have difficulty understanding what Paul means by the word 'flesh' in verse 16 you are not alone. Modern translators are not at all certain, and Paul himself uses the word in different ways in his letters. What he seems to refer to here is that inner part of our human nature that is attracted to the kinds of thing listed in verses 19-21. Since we have already noted that human anger is a natural emotion, we may be surprised to find it in this list, but Paul is clearly thinking of anger that has got out of control. He uses a specific Greek word better translated as 'rage', and since he uses it in the plural he is doubtless thinking of repeated fits of rage.

Some of us have a real problem: anger keeps rearing its ugly head and we find it difficult to control. What particularly concerns Paul is that some of the Galatian Christians are claiming that because Jesus Christ offers us freedom we can do just what we like – including losing our temper. Paul rejects such self-indulgence (verse 13) because it is likely to lead to problems like those he lists in verses 19-21. Psychologists offer useful advice on the strategies we can adopt in what they describe as 'anger management', but Paul adds a strategy that is key for Christians:

Live by the Spirit.

(verse 16)

When the Spirit of Christ controls us, our natural emotions can develop in such a way that our lives and the lives of those around us, are enriched.

† Lord, I have often allowed one thing to lead on to another. I have lost my temper, and found myself going on to do and say things that later make me deeply ashamed. Forgive me and grant me grace that increasingly I may bear the 'fruit of the Spirit'.

Moods and emotions   David Huggett

James 1:12-21

How should I respond?

Watch a surgeon at work – the careful study of the X-rays, the calm cut of the scalpel, the step-by-step movement through each stage of the operation. Imagine the disaster if he or she grabbed the nearest knife and started hacking and slashing without that careful preparation and steady progress. We do best in dealing with our anger if we follow that sort of example. Often our problem is not so much the depth of our feelings of outrage as the haste with which we express our feelings in words we later regret. James gives us wise advice:

let everyone be quick to listen, slow to speak, slow to anger.

(part of verse 19)

Start by developing the gift of simply listening, not only to what the other person is saying, but also to what his or her body language and actions are telling us. And listen to what the circumstances or events that tend to make us angry are saying to us, for by so doing we may actually hear God saying something important. The simple act of listening can often defuse a tense situation. It also gives time for our anger to drain away, and enables us to listen to our own anger and so discover what that says to and about us. Such careful listening reaps rich rewards, but takes time and effort to cultivate.

† God of grace, in this hectic world that demands quick results, grant that I may develop a slow walk that keeps pace with you.

David Huggett

Moods and emotions

What should I avoid?

Without realising it, we may become addicted to anger because we find it pleasurable. Anger affects us physically. The greater our anger the redder our face becomes. The body releases adrenalin, which creates a surge of energy. As well as raising our blood pressure this can lead to a sense of power and control, and can also dissipate any feelings of frustration. It is wise, therefore, says Proverbs, to avoid developing a deep relationship with someone who is addicted to anger in this way ('given to anger', verse 24). The reason is simple:

you may learn their ways
and entangle yourself in a snare.

(verse 25)

Other people's emotions inevitably have an impact on us. We are much more likely to show warm affection to someone who is warm towards us; and the person who is cheerful often lifts our own spirits. So the danger is that we react to the angry outburst by irritation and anger ourselves. We cannot cut ourselves off from people, but we can avoid forming serious relationships with those who are in the habit of indulging their anger. Friendship demands mutual respect and commitment, both of which are difficult to maintain with someone addicted to anger.

† Lord, you have called us your friends, for which I thank you. Give me the wisdom to make good friends, and the grace to be a good and faithful friend to others. Help those who are addicted to anger, that they may find their deliverance through you.

Moods and emotions   David Huggett

Ephesians 4:25-32

The positive picture

In the days before digital cameras the photographer produced a black and white or colour negative. From this a positive image was produced. Looking at the negative in which the dark and light areas were reversed, it was usually quite difficult to make out any detail, and sometimes even to decide what had been photographed. Sadly Christians have sometimes presented a negative image to the world based on what we should not do rather than what we should be. From that negative too it can be quite hard to know what a Christian is really like.

Although in this chapter Paul does warn us against spiritual and moral things that will harm ourselves and others, his emphasis is on the positives. For example, he reminds us that our speech is to be truthful (verse 25) and helpful (verse 29), and that our work is to be honest and generous (verse 28). This is much more useful than merely being told that we must avoid falsehood, gossip or stealing – which we probably knew anyway.

The same principle is true in our dealings with anger. It is no accident that we often talk about 'losing' our temper. It is when our anger gets out of control – when we lose it – that it becomes sinful. We know that. What we also need to know is how to control it. Paul gives two positive suggestions. In verse 26 he accepts that we may have been angry but advises making up any differences that have arisen before the day is out. Most importantly he suggests that the best way of control lies in replacing anger with positive things:

> be kind to one another, tender-hearted, forgiving one another, as God in Christ has forgiven you.

(verse 32)

---

† May my life be increasingly filled with the qualities that I see displayed in Jesus Christ, so that anyone who looks at me may see a clear and positive picture of him.

David Huggett

Moods and emotions

Following the best example

Jesus was human too, so we need not be surprised that he got angry. The clearest example of this was his reaction to the money changers who had grossly abused their privileged position in the Temple courts (John 2:12-17). He was angry because they were taking advantage of the worshippers.

There were other occasions when he showed anger: he rebuked the wind and waves because they threatened his friends' safety (Matthew 8:26); when disease was the threat he rebuked that (Luke 4:39, 41); and when faced with a man disfigured and ostracised by leprosy, the word used to describe his compassion is so strong that almost certainly it would have included the anguish of rage. When confronted by evil and its effects on vulnerable people the adrenalin began to flood Jesus' veins, providing that surge of energy that helped drive him to action.

The most dramatic example, of course, is the cross. There God's anger against all that spoils his creation, all that is evil, morally, spiritually, and physically, is dealt with in the ultimate example of the words:

Do not be overcome by evil, but overcome evil with good.

(verse 21)

Rather than trying to overcome or quench our anger, perhaps we need to redirect it. Turning the other cheek is not a question of weak capitulation, but rather, like Jesus, overcoming violence and injustice with love.

† Lord, make me angry with those things that make you angry. Move me deeply when I am faced with all that oppresses the human spirit, and may I find ways in which to turn my anger into action on behalf of vulnerable and needy people.

Moods and emotions   David Huggett

Moods and emotions

4 From jealousy to contentment

Notes based on the *New King James Version* by
Deborah Dunn

Deborah Dunn is a licensed marital and family therapist in private practice in the USA. She has written several books for women about wise life choices, published by Simon and Schuster of New York/Howard Books under her trademark Smart About Life! You can learn more about her at www.deborahdunn.com.

Sunday 25 July: Preparing for the week

Our emotions can be a curse or a blessing. We can be inspired to do great things for God because we feel compassion, sorrow, and a passion for good works. On the other hand, as creatures of the flesh born into sin, we can also allow evil thoughts to dominate our thinking and drive us to evil actions. If we are damaged by traumatic life experiences, struggling with mental or physical illness, or grief-stricken, our resulting emotions can be intense, and this encourages fear, hatred, jealousy and anger. We can become a slave to our emotions, in bondage to our pain. Whatever the cause of our emotional problems, we can trust that Jesus Christ bore the stripes on his back for the healing of our minds as well as our bodies. It may take time, but the God of the universe can tame our moods and heal our minds, just as he tamed the tossing seas of Galilee for his disciples.

Text for the week: *Philippians 4:19*

My God shall supply all your needs according to His riches in glory by Christ Jesus.

For group discussion and personal thought

- If you have ever been so hurt or angry that you wanted to hurt someone, how did God deliver you from that rage?
- Are you are a person who is 'content' with your circumstances in life? What difference does contentment make?

July

Numbers 11:23-30

Jealous of spiritual power

'Oh, that all the LORD's people were prophets and that the LORD would put His Spirit upon them!'

(part of verse 29)

At this juncture in the Exodus, Moses was exhausted by his role of leader to the captives he had led out of Israel. He was angry, and desperate for relief from having to be the sole arbiter of justice and leadership. In response to his plea, God gave him seventy elders to help him and equipped them with a provisional anointing of the Holy Spirit. The Spirit fell on them, and they began prophesying in the tabernacle, something that only Moses had done until then. Unfortunately, this also stirred up the jealousy and outrage of some men in the camp who had not been so blessed.

The odd thing is that apparently this anointing of the elders only occurred once, and they never prophesied ever again. That raises some questions. Perhaps 'the anointing' was more than the elders could handle. Perhaps they realised what continuing in it would require, and were not willing to pay that price. If you crave spiritual power, God will give it to you, but you must be prepared to pay a terrible price. It is not for the fainthearted. But you can trust that God will be right there with you, just as he always was with Moses.

July

† Father, as the old hymn says, there is 'wonder-working power in the blood of the Lamb'. Forgive us if we have ever envied others that power, misused it when we had it, or failed to appreciate all its fullness and glory. Give us our portion, Father, and give us the strength to bear it when you do. Amen

Moods and emotions   Deborah Dunn

1 Samuel 18:5-16

Driven to murderous rage

[W]hen David was returning from the slaughter of the Philistine . . .
the women sang as they danced, and said:
'Saul has slain his thousands,
and David his ten thousands.'
Then Saul was very angry, and the saying displeased him.

(part of verses 6-8)

As a therapist, I'm convinced that Saul was not only tormented by jealousy and a 'distressing spirit from God' (verse 10) but was also a paranoid schizophrenic. The nature of the illness is extreme fear and irrational suspicion, especially fear that someone is plotting evil against you. One small thought or incident can convince schizophrenics that someone, even a close loved one or trusted friend, is out to get them, and no amount of reassurance will help. A whispered word, a seed of suspicion planted, a raised eyebrow – it doesn't take much to convince us that someone is talking about us behind our back or doing something to undermine us, especially if we are already plagued by self-doubt, lack of faith, or jealousy.

But the Lord can use these 'distressing spirits' to agitate us to the point where we change. Instead of changing for the better, however, Saul chose to give in to his murderous rage, and that choice led to his eventual suicide. In the face of jealousy or spiritual agitation we can choose love, forgiveness, faith and renewal, or we can spiral downwards into paranoia and fear. The choice is always ours, no matter what our mental state.

---

† Father God, help us always to choose to cast away fear, fight our tendency towards self-doubt, and embrace a goal to love others always, even those of whom we are envious.

Deborah Dunn

Moods and emotions

Repaying evil with good

Saul said, 'Is this your voice, my son David?' And Saul lifted up his voice and wept. Then he said to David: 'You are more righteous than I; for you have rewarded me with good, whereas I have rewarded you with evil.'

(part of verse 16, and verse 17)

All mature Christians will find themselves in situations where it would be so much easier – and satisfying – to 'even the score'.

About ten years ago I was hired as director of a women's shelter in the small town where we lived. The programme became very successful, but unfortunately, like David, I learned that success can be dangerous. When I least expected it, I was presented with all sorts of false accusations and fired without any warning – apparently through extreme jealousy. Of course, I was crushed and thought my career was over. I considered a lawsuit, but chose instead the much more difficult path of acceptance and forgiveness.

However, during that dark time without a job the seeds of my writing career were planted. Out of my pain the Lord has brought a splendid career. If David had killed Saul when he had the chance, I do not think the Lord would have blessed his eventual rule as King of Israel, just as he will never bless us if we take matters in our own hands. Let God deal with your enemies, and in the long run he will bring good out of evil.

† Father of the universe, help us to put our trust in the knowledge that in time you will bring about justice in an unjust world, if not in this life, then in the next, and lead us to repay evil with good, no matter how tempting it would be to retaliate.

Moods and emotions   Deborah Dunn

Philippians 4:2-9

Rejoicing brings peace

Be anxious for nothing, but in everything by prayer and supplication, with thanksgiving, let your requests be made known to God; and the peace of God, which surpasses all understanding, will guard your hearts and minds through Christ Jesus.

(verses 6-7)

Anxiety is one of the greatest curses of humanity, and probably one of the chief reasons people seek out my services as a therapist. Most of the time, anxiety is the result of sin. Someone did something to someone else that they shouldn't have. Often talking about it, repenting, and seeking to forgive or be forgiven goes a long way to remedy the situation, and to stop fear from breeding. Other more difficult cases benefit greatly from medication. But I've never found a better remedy yet than gratitude, thankfulness and prayer.

But read today's text closely. Not only does God promise peace; he promises, through Jesus Christ, that he will guard your hearts and minds. The Lord knows that an anxious spirit is the work of the enemy, and that he must guard us from that attack. Praise, prayer and peaceful thoughts are not only medications, they are weapons!

You can slay the enemy and his vexing anxious spirits. Let your tongue become a sword of peace. Give the enemy no room. Become a suppliant in the Spirit, letting nothing but praise, thanksgiving and gratitude flow from your lips. You will be surprised at how the imps of anxiousness will scatter in their wake.

† Father God, help us to remember what power we have to banish anxiety with our gentleness, kindness, gratitude and prayers of thanksgiving. We will become suppliants sitting at your feet, praising your holy name!

Deborah Dunn

Moods and emotions

The secret of contentment

And my God shall supply all your need according to His riches in glory by Christ Jesus.

(verse 19)

In times past, when I have become anxious about not having a job, or about a bill I needed to pay, I have realised two things: I was not trusting in divine provision; and I had probably got into trouble because I had indulged my wants instead of meeting my needs. I only had to look to myself to find the reason for my difficult circumstances. Even so, in spite of my lack of discipline or wisdom, God has been faithful to supply all my needs – not always in ways that I found pleasant or easy, but the provision was there, none the less. I believe that this is because for most of my life I have tried to serve God.

But how can we reconcile God's promise of divine provision with, for example, the existence of so many starving children in the world? Do these children not deserve to be cared for as well? We cannot allow ourselves to lose faith in God's provision because of the suffering we see around us. Instead, we must allow him to use us to provide for the necessities of others, and remember that we may be the instrument he is using to care for those less fortunate.

July

† Father in heaven, it is difficult to reconcile your words of divine provision when there are so many starving, sick children in the world. Yet we can testify that, as we meet their needs, ours are met as well. Let us give away what we have with wild joy and trust that you will meet our need as long as we always strive to reach out and meet the needs of others.

Moods and emotions

Deborah Dunn

1 Timothy 6:1-12

A radical way of life

For the love of money is a root of all kinds of evil, for which some have strayed from the faith in their greediness, and pierced themselves through with many sorrows. But you, O man of God, flee these things and pursue righteousness, godliness, faith, love, patience, gentleness.

(verses 10-11)

Much of the work I do involves responding to corporate crises. The saddest thing I've had to do was respond to a company whose founder committed suicide in his office one morning. The company was going under and he found no comfort except to end his life. How I wish he could have heard what his employees and family members said to me in our counselling sessions afterwards. In that moment, none of them cared anything about their jobs, or the money that was being lost. All they wanted was to have their beloved friend, father and co-worker returned to them. Their love for him far exceeded the wage that the company provided for them.

Sometimes the snares can be our wounded pride and the shame we feel because we do not have enough money. But if we succumb to shame and despair over money, then we are truly poor – not only in money, but in spirit as well. Riches come and go, but the love of God is constant. Our riches are in our relationships, not our bank accounts.

† Father, I pray for those who have allowed their financial losses to make them bitter and angry. Restore them to you, Father, and let them experience deep within the comfort that comes from storing up riches in heaven, instead of wealth on earth.

Deborah Dunn

Moods and emotions

Readings in Luke (4)

6 Forerunners and followers

Notes based on the *Jerusalem Bible* by
Anthea Dove

For Anthea's biography see p.38.

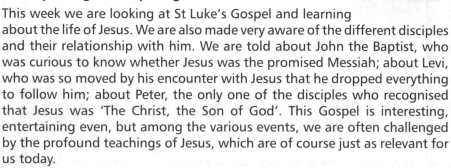

Sunday 1 August: Preparing for the week

This week we are looking at St Luke's Gospel and learning
about the life of Jesus. We are also made very aware of the different disciples
and their relationship with him. We are told about John the Baptist, who
was curious to know whether Jesus was the promised Messiah; about Levi,
who was so moved by his encounter with Jesus that he dropped everything
to follow him; about Peter, the only one of the disciples who recognised
that Jesus was 'The Christ, the Son of God'. This Gospel is interesting,
entertaining even, but among the various events, we are often challenged
by the profound teachings of Jesus, which are of course just as relevant for
us today.

Text for the week: *Luke 5:31-32*

*Jesus said to them . . . 'It is not those who are well who need the doctor,
but the sick. I have come not to call the virtuous, but sinners to repentance.'*

For group discussion and personal thought

• What have you learnt about the disciples of Jesus?
• Which of the teachings of Jesus has meant most to you in this week's
  passages from Luke's Gospel?

Monday 2 August

Luke 5:27-39

The virtuous and the sinners

The call of Levi (also known as Matthew) is particularly moving because the tax collector doesn't hesitate for a second. He drops everything, abandons his rich and successful career and without a backward glance accepts Jesus' invitation to follow him. This is surprising, especially as at that time tax collectors were notoriously grasping and greedy and wedded to their trade. It makes us wonder how we would have reacted if we had suddenly come face to face with Jesus.

But Levi continues to surprise us. He is so delighted to become a friend of Jesus that he immediately throws a party to which all and sundry, including the sort of people the 'virtuous' despise, are invited. When the Pharisees realise what is happening, they seize the opportunity to mock Jesus for the company he keeps. But he has a quick answer for them:

'I have come not to call the virtuous, but sinners to repentance.'

(verse 32)

It is easy for us who are Christians to forget this saying, especially if we spend our lives striving to be virtuous, to obey every rule so as to win a place for ourselves in heaven. We can become so intent on this that we fail to be aware of the needs of others and fail to realise that we are sinners too.

August

† Dear Lord, never let me fall into the trap of imagining myself to be virtuous.

Tuesday 3 August
Luke 6:12-26

Poverty

Some of the teachings of Jesus must have astonished his hearers. How did the poor, for example, feel when they heard him say this?

'How happy are you who are poor: yours is the kingdom of God.'

(part of verse 20)

How did the rich feel when they heard him say it? And we may well ask: How can the poor be happy? If we have seen the very poor existing in the slums of big cities like Mumbai or Nairobi, where they are forced to live in degrading conditions, we are likely to feel guilt, anger, even despair.

Yet we may have had the experience of meeting the very poor in African or South American countries where, although they have almost nothing, they are ready to give away the little they have in a spirit of generosity and hospitality. They are ready to celebrate and sing when someone has a birthday or comes home after a long absence.

Monks and nuns, and some lay people, choose a life of poverty so that without distractions they can give their lives more completely to God. More and more we are encouraged to take on a simple lifestyle and, as the slogan has it, 'Live simply so that others may simply live.'

† Dear Lord, keep us aware of the poor, in our parishes and communities, our towns and cities and in countries far away. Help us to translate our concern into action.

Anthea Dove

Readings in Luke

Wednesday 4 August

Luke 7:18 35

Channels of grace

When the disciples relayed John the Baptist's question to Jesus, asking whether he was truly the Messiah, Jesus did not answer with pride, saying 'Yes, I am the Messiah' or 'Truly, I am the Son of God.' Instead, he simply told them to give the following description to John:

'the blind see again, the lame walk, lepers are cleansed, and the deaf hear, the dead are raised to life, the Good News is proclaimed to the poor and happy is the man who does not lose faith in me.'

(verse 22)

We can learn from this. Jesus never boasted of his own powers. He knew that God was working in him. But we, in our weakness and vanity, sometimes forget this and enjoy basking in the praise of others. When we achieve success, when we are able to befriend or support or inspire others, it is as well to remember that it is only through the power of God's Holy Spirit that such friendship and support and healing and inspiration take place. We are simply instruments that God uses, channels of his love and grace.

† Dear God, help us to see clearly. Help us to realise that all our achievements and successes come from you, and that on our own we can do nothing. Make us receptive to all you wish for us, so that your message of love may reach others through us.

August

Readings in Luke

Anthea Dove

Thursday 5 August

Luke 8:22-25; 9:1-11

The calming of the storm

Today we are considering two episodes in the life of Jesus: the calming of the storm; and the mission of the twelve disciples to whom Jesus gave the power to heal and proclaim the kingdom of God to the people. They are linked by the theme of authority: the authority of Jesus, and the authority he gives to the disciples to share his ministry.

When he gave them this authority, the disciples were still getting to know Jesus. They called him Master, and they expected him to rescue them from drowning, but when they heard him scolding the winds and the stormy seas,

> *they were awestruck and astonished and said to one another, 'Who can this be, that gives orders even to the winds and waves and they obey him?'*

(part of verse 25)

We are told how the disciples reacted, but we may wonder how Jesus himself felt on this occasion. We know that, although without sin, he had all the attributes of a human being; naturally, after all the intense and draining work he did among the people, he must often have felt exhausted. So he fell asleep on the boat, and surely he must have been exasperated when he was wakened. When we reflect on this passage we become aware of the paradoxical nature of Jesus: he was a man like us, capable of feeling tired and cross, yet he also possessed a great and wonderful power.

† Dear Lord, increase in us our love for you and for Jesus. Keep us ever mindful of his humanity and vulnerability.

Anthea Dove

Readings in Luke

Friday 6 August

Luke 9:18-36

The Transfiguration

From today's readings we can learn a lot about Jesus, but the climax of the passage is the strange and wonderful event we call the Transfiguration. Today, 6 August, the Church celebrates this great feast; in an intertwining of glory and suffering, it is also Hiroshima Day.

On the mountain top, in the presence of Peter, James and John, Jesus was praying.

> *As he prayed, the aspect of his face was changed and his clothing became brilliant as lightning. Suddenly there were two men there talking with him; they were Moses and Elijah, appearing in glory.*

> (verses 29- 30, and part of verse 31)

Peter, always the impulsive disciple, wanted to do something. But they were all afraid when a cloud covered them and they heard the voice of God. Then the awestruck disciples were silent. All through this Gospel, the disciples are gradually realising who Jesus is, and for these three this tremendous experience must have been confirmation that he was in truth the Son of God.

It is an inspiring happening, but it leaves us with many questions. Why did Jesus take only three disciples with him? Why did he choose those particular three? How was it that even after this experience Peter let him down? We cannot know the answers to such questions. Perhaps it is wisest just to accept this wonderful story with thankfulness.

August

† Dear Lord, as we celebrate this great feast, keep us mindful also of the victims at Hiroshima who died on this day.

Readings in Luke

Anthea Dove

Saturday 7 August
Luke 10:1-20

The labourers and the harvest

Jesus realised that he could not accomplish his mission alone. So he chose a band of 72 (we cannot be certain they were all men) to go forth in pairs carrying the good news and preaching and healing. He said,

'The harvest is rich but the labourers are few.'

(part of verse 2)

Still in our time, two thousand years later, it is true that the labourers are few. This text is often taken to refer to the shortage of ministers and priests, especially in Western countries. But in truth, we are all called to be labourers, that is, people who work to draw others to the kingdom of God. We may be able to do this by preaching or healing, but for most of us the task is at once simpler and more difficult. If we truly love and care about our neighbours and if we ourselves are seen to live lives of compassion and generosity, then we may be able to draw people near to God's kingdom more readily than if we had gifts of eloquence and healing, or were recognised officially as ministers or priests. Very often it is the humblest people of integrity who most touch our hearts and inspire us to seek our God, and so come to love and worship him.

† Dear Lord, give us the courage and perseverance to do your will and to work for the coming of your kingdom.

Anthea Dove

Readings in Luke

Readings in Luke

7 Making people whole

Notes based on the *New International Version* and *Good News Bible* by

Aileen Khoo

Now retired, Aileen Khoo worked in the Methodist Church in Malaysia for over 30 years, and was Director of Christian Education at Trinity Methodist Church, Petaling Jaya. She particularly enjoys leading Bible studies, especially experimenting with participatory Bible study methods.

Saturday 8 August: Preparing for the week

Luke almost always shows contrasting personalities in his storytelling: the Roman centurion, and the widow of Nain; the Pharisee who invited Jesus, and the sinful woman; the demon-possessed man, and the villagers; Jairus, the ruler of the synagogue, and the woman with menstrual problems; the father of the sick boy, and the disciples of Jesus; the Samaritan leper, and the other lepers. Whoever you are, whatever your status, Luke is saying, God desires to make you whole! That is Luke's good news: God has acted mightily in Jesus so that everyone can be brought into a saved and saving community that both experiences God's joyous reign and awaits its complete fruition. God desires to make us whole financially, spiritually, psychologically, socially, physically and politically.

Text for the week: *Luke 9:42-43*
Jesus rebuked the evil spirit, healed the boy and gave him back to his father. And they were all amazed at the greatness of God.

August

For group discussion and personal thought

• Have you ever felt that you were in bondage and that God rescued you into a new freedom? How did he do this?

• Have you ever felt cut off, 'unclean' or outcast? What helped you to overcome this feeling?

Monday 9 August

Luke 7:1-17

God frees us from financial bondage and makes us whole

They were all filled with awe and praised God. 'A great prophet has appeared among us,' they said. 'God has come to help his people.'

(verse 16)

The centurion was a powerful man, with a hundred soldiers under his command. He must have been a man of courage and integrity to be a centurion. He was admired by the Jews even though he was a gentile. The woman, though, was a widow in a society where women counted for nothing apart from the wealth of the husband. As a widow, and now without a son, the woman would be all alone and would face much hardship. The centurion was a worthy man: 'he loves our people' and 'built our synagogue for us', said the Jewish elders; the widow could not afford to give two mites. The centurion had a home in Capernaum, a Jewish town on the Sea of Galilee; the widow lived in an obscure village in Galilee called Nain. The centurion had many servants; the widow an only son. God cares for the rich and powerful as well as the poor and defenceless, the economically deprived people. Jesus went beyond all social norms to express compassion, to make people whole.

Often we think we are all alone and no one understands our pains and struggles. Along comes Jesus, who reaches out to us without our asking, to touch our lives and make us whole as he did the widow.

† You, LORD, are all I have,
and you give me all I need;
my future is in your hands.
How wonderful are your gifts to me;
how good they are!
(Psalm 16:5-6, GNB)

Aileen Khoo

Readings in Luke

August

224

Luke 7:36-50

God frees us from spiritual bondage and makes us whole

Then Jesus said to her, 'Your sins are forgiven.' The other guests began to say among themselves, 'Who is this who even forgives sins?' Jesus said to the woman, 'Your faith has saved you; go in peace.'

(verses 48-50)

Here are a Pharisee and a woman. One is religious and morally upright but judgemental, rich enough to hold a dinner party but failing to extend hospitality. The other is a woman of ill repute and poor, but she gives all she has in extending hospitality to Jesus. Both needed forgiveness and to be made whole.

Simon the Pharisee missed the opportunity because he did not recognise this need. Jesus used words usually reserved for the conclusion of miracles or healing: 'Your faith has saved you.' He sent the woman away in peace and with the recognition that she had been made whole spiritually and socially.

† Hear my cry, O LORD;
   listen to my call for help!
   If you kept a record of our sins,
   who could escape being condemned?
   But you forgive us,
   so that we should stand in awe of you
                    (Psalm 130:2-4, GNB)

Readings in Luke   Aileen Khoo

August

God frees us from psychological bondage and makes us whole

When they came to Jesus, they found the man from whom the demons had gone out, sitting at Jesus' feet, dressed and in his right mind; and they were afraid.

(part of verse 35)

Gerasene was predominantly gentile. 'Son of the Most High God' (verse 28) was a term used by gentiles when addressing Jesus. The man was mentally ill, able at times to rip off the chains used to restrain him. When Jesus found him, he was naked, frightened, living in a cemetery. 'What is your name?' Jesus asked. 'My name is Legion.' Six thousand soldiers made up a Roman legion. The man's personality was so fractured, he did not know who he really was.

After he was made whole, he put on clothing and sat at Jesus' feet 'in his right mind'. The villagers found the presence of Jesus uncomfortable. Instead of welcoming Jesus for delivering one of their people from demons and restoring him into their community, they rejected him and sent him away. Sometimes our fragmented personalities drive us away from communities and into the wilderness of torment and self-destruction. But Jesus takes us from estrangement to reconciliation, from alienation and meaninglessness to wholeness.

† I will praise you, LORD, with all my heart;
  I will tell of all the wonderful things you have done.
                    (Psalm 9:1, GNB)

Aileen Khoo

Readings in Luke

Luke 8:40-56

God frees us from social bondage and makes us whole

Jesus said to Jairus, 'Don't be afraid; just believe, and she will be healed.'

(part of verse 50)

Things go well for a time and the future seems bright. Then comes a crisis when life seems hopeless. Everything we have dreamed of, worked for, even prayed for, falls apart. How are we to keep going?

Two healings are interwoven. The 12-year-old daughter of Jairus, a leader of the synagogue, and an unknown woman who had suffered haemorrhages and been a social outcast for 12 years. She had been sick as long as the young girl had been alive. She had spent all she had seeking a cure. Her discharge of blood would have made her 'unclean' and anybody she touched would have become 'unclean' as well. She would not be permitted to take part in Temple worship or offer sacrifices for purification. She was forbidden to mingle with people in case she defiled them by accidentally touching even their clothes. Thus, in touching Jesus, she was defiling him.

Jairus, 'ruler' of the synagogue, was responsible for the arrangements at the synagogue service. He was thus an important person in the community. Both his daughter and the woman were made whole the same day.

August

† You have changed my sadness into a joyful dance;
you have taken away my sorrow
and surrounded me with joy.
So I will not be silent;
I will sing praise to you.
LORD, you are my God;
I will give you thanks for ever
                    (Psalm 30:11-12, GNB)

Readings in Luke   Aileen Khoo

God frees us from physical bondage and makes us whole

Jesus rebuked the evil spirit, healed the boy and gave him back to his father. And they were all amazed at the greatness of God.

(part of verse 42, and verse 43)

The disciples, who were given power and authority over all demons, were incapable of casting this one out – only Jesus could do it.

The clouds blot out the sun. Is there any hope? Can anyone push back the greyness so we can smile and sing again? Can you see times and places where God carried you through a tough experience? Any security we have rests in God, the author of life, and not in the work of our hands. Can you see examples around you of the pride that says, 'I can take care of myself; I don't need God'? Look at your own life to see if you detect a pride that treats God as a back-up: 'I'll manage my own life; when I need help, God, I'll let you know.' Who comes to help us? Those who have not suffered but have ideological ideas about how they can change the world cannot help us. It is God who comes to save us because God knows suffering. Ever nursed a sick child? Can you be happy when your child is sick? God wants us to be happy. When we are sad, God is sad. Hand our hurts over to God and let God deal with them.

† Hear my prayer, O God;
   don't turn away from my plea!
   Listen to me and answer me;
   I am worn out by my worries.
            (Psalm 55:1-2, GNB)

Aileen Khoo

Readings in Luke

Luke 17:11-19

God frees us from political bondage and makes us whole

When [Jesus] saw them, he said, 'Go, show yourselves to the priests.'
And as they went, they were cleansed.

(verse 14)

This incident took place at the border between Samaria and Galilee. Samaritans and Jews would have nothing to do with each other. It takes a crisis for us to put our differences aside and work towards a common good. When the ten men were lepers, they lived together. They did not ask specifically for healing, but simply for mercy, for Jesus to take pity on them. When Jesus saw them, he responded by telling them to go and show themselves to the priests who would act as health inspectors to certify that the cure had taken place. On their way they were made clean.

A Samaritan came back to thank God. Jesus asked where the other nine men, presumably Jews, were and why they were not grateful enough to return to give thanks to God. Even when they did not thank him, God made them whole anyway. Jesus made insiders and outsiders whole. God intends political bonding, not bondage.

† You are my God, and I give you thanks;
   I will proclaim your greatness.
                    (Psalm 118:28, GNB)

Silence

1 Old Testament silences

Notes based on the *New Jerusalem Bible* and *Grail Psalter* by

Paula Fairlie OSB

Paula is a Benedictine nun and lives in Chester, England.

Sunday 15 August: Preparing for the week

Silence is defined as 'abstinence from sound and speech'. To abstain from speech can be very difficult indeed. We have to learn to be silent and listen to either interior promptings or verbal communication. Most biblical silence is imposed by God himself, and is not the sort of warm, reflective and consoling silence we expect! It is a discipline. The Psalms give very clear examples of our clamour: 'Lord, hear my prayer!' or 'Lord, listen to me!' He rarely gets a word in edgeways without some prior cataclysmic intervention, as the readings for the week will show.

A writer in the journal *Cistercian Studies* (22) said: 'Each word we speak is born in silence and returns to silence. And without the frame of silence there can be no human communication. Because silence is so tragically lacking in our times, the rhythm of human communication has become frenetic and disjointed. Our own noise and extraneous noises drive us to distraction.' Within this flurry of distraction, amid tumult, God tries to reach us and teach us trust.

Text for the week: *Psalm 46:11 (Grail 45)*
'Be still and know that I am God,
supreme among the nations, supreme on the earth!'

For group discussion and personal thought
• There are several sorts of silence: identify some of them.
• What sort of silence to you desire?
• Why does God impose silence upon us?
• Consider silence and darkness as creative gifts.

All passion spent

'Go out and stand on the mountain before Yahweh.'

(part of verse 11)

Elijah was suffering from exhaustion and depression. He fled into the desert wanting to die. The religious war raging between the prophets of Yahweh and the worshippers of Baal had not resulted in a decisive victory for Yahweh. Elijah, a hunted fugitive, was once again totally dependent upon God. Two parts of the religious battle had been won through drought and fire, and the spilling of blood What more could Elijah do? He had forty days in the desert to think about this. He could not depend upon his own judgement. Now that the internal clamour had died down, Elijah relinquished his own will and his confrontational righteous anger. He waited all night in a cave for Yahweh to reveal himself.

At dawn God did not come in hurricane, earthquake or lightning, the mantle of the storm-god. Instead Elijah heard 'a light murmuring sound' followed by words of instruction. Elijah was quietly told to anoint the rivals of the local kings, and a successor for himself, who would act on Yahweh's behalf. Silence was imposed upon him: he, too, was to whisper. He was committed to intrigue. After the clamour and inner turmoil, he could finally hear the quiet voice of inspiration but he could not see: his face was veiled.

The storm, earthquake and lightning were the heralds of Yahweh. 'The whispering murmur signifies that he converses intimately with his prophets; it does not mean that God's dealings are gentle – this common interpretation is refuted by the terrible commission of verses 15-17' (*JB* notes).

August

† Lord, help us to listen to you. Still the turmoil of our hearts and minds.

Silence

Paula Fairlie

2 Kings 2:1-11

He lost sight of him

'Yes, I know . . . be quiet.'

(part of verse 5)

In many ways the life and mission of Elijah were a foreshadowing of the life of Christ. Elijah had spiritually reached rock-bottom when he spent the night in a cave on Mount Horeb. In the symbolic womb/tomb he was prepared for revelation. He emerged from this darkness with eyes veiled to listen to Yahweh. He had renounced his own insights and died to himself. The time would come when he would make his ascension to heaven, watched by his most faithful follower.

Why did he not want Elisha to follow him? Was it because Elisha had ulterior motives, wanting to be recognised as Elijah's principal spiritual heir? (The eldest son always inherited two portions of the property when the father died: the others received one portion.) Was the mother of James and John similarly ambitious for her sons when she made a similar (and impossible) request of Jesus?

Elijah himself could not grant this: it was in the hands of God. Why did Elisha silence the other brotherhoods of prophets in Bethel and Jericho? Was it because he needed to concentrate on where Elijah was going and did not want to be distracted, or did he not want any rivals? Elijah, like Joshua, crossed the Jordan dry-shod but in the opposite direction. The desert was the place for theophanies, revelations of God, and Elijah was taken by a chariot of fire with horses of fire, going up to heaven in a whirlwind. Surely this passage merits more than the comment that there is a time to keep silent?

† Dear Lord, we do not know how to be silent before you. Help us to listen to you.

Paula Fairlie

Silence

True compassion

They sat there on the ground beside him for seven days and seven nights. To Job they spoke never a word, for they saw how much he was suffering.

(verse 13)

Our compassion is often accompanied by embarrassment: we simply do not know how to comfort a person in dire distress. So we begin with many words, all to no avail. Job's nagging wife asked him: 'Why persist in this integrity of yours? Curse God and die.' In this instant Job was indeed patient, but scathing, to his wife: 'That is how a fool of a woman talks. If we take happiness from God's hands must we not take sorrow too?'

Then the friends arrived, weeping aloud, tearing their robes and throwing dust over their heads in mourning. Having exhausted themselves, and presumably Job, they sat beside him. True compassion is often silent, manifesting wisdom. They saw how much he was suffering and kept silent, but inside their heads they were busily justifying God and mentally accusing Job of concealing some grievous wrongdoing. It all spilled out later: 'God is never unjust! You must have done something really grievous to merit such punishment. Admit it, and make amends!' But Job couldn't think of anything he had done wrong and refused to accept the argument. Would God have spoken if Job hadn't challenged him?

So many innocent people suffer, and many want to know why. But there is no earthly answer. Even Christ died quoting Psalm 21: 'My God, my God, why have you forsaken me? You are far from my plea and the cry of my distress.' Yet the last verse of this psalm admits of hope. Is the hope for this life or the next?

---

† Dear Lord, grant that we may not obscure your purpose with our empty-headed words.

Silence   Paula Fairlie

Thursday 19 August

Psalm 46:1-11 (Grail 45)

Pause for thought

'Be still and know that I am God,
supreme among the nations, supreme on the earth!'

(verse 10, Grail)

The psalmist, a man of faith, considers God's dealing with cataclysms on earth, his place in the holy city of Jerusalem, and his silencing and disarmament of hostile nations. All three remain a concern throughout the world today. But 'God is for us a refuge and strength, a helper close at hand, in time of distress' (verse 2). The psalmist is not considering suffering as such: he is looking at an overall pattern in which the people as a whole matter more than the individual. Modern people, especially in the West, find this difficult to understand because our society tends to value the individual more – although not always.

The psalmist simply says 'We shall not fear . . . the Lord of Hosts is with us' (verse 11). Basically he is saying: Be still, stop panicking, let the worst happen! We shall be cared for (as a nation). God's holy city has its own river (water supply), God resides there, so what does it matter if the surrounding kingdoms are menacing it? All the Most High has to do is to lift up his voice and 'the earth shrinks away' (verse 6). What does that mean? God has imposed order and silence, as though calming the sea. He can end wars, destroy all weapons – he is 'supreme on the earth'! But is this sort of belief really compatible with what we see around us?

† Dear Lord, please help us to really trust in you, despite the sorrow and anguish that rends the world with inexplicable tragedy. Help us to be still and not fear, truly believing that you are with us.

Paula Fairlie

Silence

Friday 20 August

Psalm 50:16-23 (Grail 49)

Should I keep silence?

'Do you think I am like you?'

(part of verse 21)

There are many forms of silence. In this psalm the Lord finally addresses the people who have made a covenant with him – which includes all the baptised – and tells them that he does not want formal worship. He wants loving service from the heart, expressed in obedience to his commandments and love of neighbour.

It seems that God keeps a more or less patient silence when we fail to understand his law and our place in the covenant. But the time comes when he 'keeps silence no longer' (verse 3); he sits in judgement, convicting us of wrongdoing: 'God says to the wicked. . .' (verse 16). There is always the hope that we shall 'come to our senses' in time and make amends but, when that fails, we need to be challenged, reprimanded and corrected. It is often our interior chatter that blocks out God and busily justifies our evil activities. 'Everyone does it! Office stationery is there to take home, another's wife/husband needs some variety in relationships. So and so is a prig and needs taking down a peg or two, even if he is my brother!' This inner corruption is like an apple that looks fine from the outside and yet is decayed inside. Sometimes a part can be saved but often the whole is thrown into the compost heap.

† Dear Lord, when you accuse us of evil doing, may we have the grace to be silent and amend.

Silence

Paula Fairlie

August

Saturday 21 August

Habakkuk 2:18-20

Lifeless gods

'Disaster to anyone who says to the log, 'Wake up!'
to the dumb stone, 'On your feet!'

(part of verse 19)

From childhood onwards we actually like to speak to inanimate objects, even if they have no specific anthropomorphic form. We like to communicate with our own imaginary creation, and actually come to believe that it is more real than the external world of duties and demands. We are 'god' in our own world. This can lead to superstitious fear, although the fear is real enough in a culture of witchcraft. The only convincing defeat of idolatry and evil practices comes from invoking a more powerful 'god'. The prophets had to ridicule the belief in dumb idols that gave people a false security, and to introduce them to the true God. Habakkuk asks the perennial question: 'Why do people trust in dumb idols when there is Yahweh in his Temple?' 'Let the whole earth be silent before him' (verse 20).

God's temple is not only the Temple in Jerusalem, which few people have actually seen, but the heavenly palace from which he will reveal himself to the whole world. 'You uttered your sentence from the heavens; the earth in terror was still' (Psalm 76:9, Grail 75). Theophanies are terrifying events and induce awe. Who can see God and live?

† Dear Lord, teach me the silence that is pleasing to you.

Paula Fairlie

Silence

Silence

2 New Testament silences

Notes based on the *New Revised Standard Version* by
Kate Hughes

Kate worked for the church in Southern Africa for 14 years. Returning to England in 1990, she is now a freelance book editor, and is also active in her local church and community. She is currently editor of *Light for our Path.*

Sunday 22 August: Preparing for the week

The American monk Thomas Merton wrote that 'It is not speaking that breaks our silence, but the anxiety to be heard.' All too often the words we speak are not meant to help the other person but to make our presence felt, to boost our self-image or our self-esteem. There is 'a time to keep silence, and a time to speak' (Ecclesiastes 3:7), and we need to learn when to do both – especially in our conversations with God. This week's readings give us a variety of examples from the New Testament.

Text for the week: *Revelation 8:1*

When the Lamb opened the seventh seal, there was silence in heaven for about half an hour.

For group discussion and personal thought

• How much of your personal prayer time is spent simply being silent with God?

• How much silence is there in your church worship? Would it be good to have more?

• What experiences in life reduce you to the silence of adoration?

The silence of defeat

When I was a child, my mother always refused to argue. If I had a tantrum, she simply walked out of the room (sometimes having boxed my ears before she left!). I found this very frustrating – you can't have a good fight with someone who isn't there. But refusing to be drawn into an argument is often the best way of silencing your opponents. They come spoiling for a fight, armed with arguments to humiliate and discredit you – and the object of their attack simply isn't there.

This was the tactic that Jesus employed when the scribes tried to trap him into a discussion of Jewish politics. They were clever: whichever way Jesus answered their question, it would get him into trouble. If he said it was right to pay taxes to the hated Romans, he would alienate his followers. If he said that it was wrong to pay taxes, he would be arrested for treason. So Jesus threw their question back at them. There are secular authorities and there is the authority of God. Both can demand their dues, but it is your responsibility to decide what is due to which of them. Jesus' opponents were defeated; he had seen through their question to the malice that motivated it and had simply refused to play their game.

[B]eing amazed by his answer, they became silent.

(part of verse 26)

There was nothing left for them to say.

---

† Thank you, Lord, for this reminder that we do not always need to out-argue those who oppose us, or defeat them with clever words; often we simply need to refuse to be drawn into arguing, so that our opponents can find nothing more to say.

Kate Hughes

Silence

Luke 22:54-62

Silence convicts

The LORD turned and looked at Peter . . .
And he went out and wept bitterly.

(part of verse 61, and verse 62)

I live in Coventry and, in our cathedral, covering the whole of the east wall, is Graham Sutherland's vast tapestry of Christ enthroned in glory. Not everyone likes it: some feel that Christ's white robes dominate too much; others don't like the modern figures of the four evangelists that form part of the design. But I love the face of Christ. It is a serious face, which gazes straight down the long nave of the cathedral, but it looks directly at me, and at everyone who sits in front of it. The eyes look straight through you, seeing everything that is in you, knowing all about you – the good and the bad. But they do not condemn; they are eyes filled with love and compassion and understanding. And you gaze back at them, holding a silent conversation with Christ, content just to sit with him. These are the eyes that looked at Peter when, out of fear, he had denied that he even knew the man he had followed for three years. There were no words; there was no need for words. Jesus simply looked at him with love and compassion and understanding, and with infinite sadness for the weakness of humankind. No wonder Peter went out and wept.

August

† Lord, the world is full of speech and talk. But you can say so much more through your silence, your quiet presence with us. Help us not to be so busy talking to you that we cannot share your silence.

Silence

Kate Hughes

Wednesday 25 August

Luke 23:6-12

Truth in silence

[Herod] questioned him at some length, but Jesus gave him no answer.

(verse 9)

When one of my nephews was young, I used to babysit him quite often. Sometimes he would ask me a serious question, and I would take time to answer him carefully, in words suited to his limited understanding. If I went on too long, he would look at me and say 'Auntie Kate, why are you talking?' All he wanted was a short, straight answer to his question – not my detailed explanation. There was a mismatch between our expectations.

Herod had the same problem with Jesus. He wanted an answer – but not the answer that Jesus was prepared to give him. He did not want to hear the truth, he did not want a message from God, he would not hear what Jesus said to him; he had his own agenda. He was looking for excitement, for signs and wonders, for instant answers – perhaps even for an interesting theological discussion. By his refusal to answer, by his silence, Jesus showed Herod his own shallowness and evasion of truth. His silence judged Herod. And rather than hear the truth about himself contained in the silence of Jesus, Herod reacted with contempt and cruelty.

† Lord, so often in our prayer we demand that you speak to us, we ask you for this and that, we require an instant response. Is it surprising that your response is so often silence? Why should you speak when we are so unprepared to listen? Your very silence is a truth about ourselves, and about you, that we need to hear. Thank you.

Kate Hughes

Silence

The silent suffering of Jesus

Jesus valued silence. He would get up early in the morning to go out into the dawn silence to pray. He is shown walking by himself on the road, while his disciples chatted and squabbled behind him. When talking was pointless, or a trap, he stayed quiet. Above all, he endured his pain and suffering in silence. And it was this refusal to rant and rave, or scream and shout, during his trial and death that seems to have impressed others, as it impressed the Ethiopian eunuch in today's reading:

Like a lamb silent before its shearer,
so he does not open his mouth.

(part of verse 32)

Jesus moves through the Gospels, through his busy, noisy, hectic three years of ministry, with an inner calm, an inner silence that perhaps grew out of his focus on his Father. Only by clinging to his conviction that what was happening to him was the Father's will, by holding grimly on to his Father's hand, could he endure betrayal, desertion, arrest, accusations, mockery, suffering, momentary separation from the Father, and death. He could not waste his energy on noisy protest, only hoard it in silence and get through the day. Perhaps it was this silent concentration that impressed the centurion (Matthew 27:54), as it impressed the Ethiopian. This man was no ordinary criminal.

August

† Lord, when times of suffering come, help us to cling to you and focus on you, not in the silence of the 'stiff upper lip' but in the silence of faith and trust.

Silence

Kate Hughes

A model for prayer

*Since he would not be persuaded, we remained silent except to say,
'The LORD's will be done.'*

(verse 14)

When my mother was diagnosed with terminal lung cancer, naturally I prayed for her. But I found that, much as I wanted to, I simply could not pray for her recovery. It somehow seemed much more important to hold her silently up to God so that he could work in her life during her few remaining months in this world. And he made such a good job of it! Apart from a brief visit home shortly after the diagnosis, I was in South Africa and she was in England, yet in God's silence I was so aware of her, aware of lifelong barriers against him coming down, of God gently leading her and loving her into the next world. Our instinct in a crisis is to bombard God with words: Do this, do that, give us this or that, save us, please, please, please. Yet so often we have no idea of what God is intending to do, indeed what he is capable of doing. To fall silent and simply hand the crisis over to him is often all that we can realistically do. It is a prayer that requires much faith and trust – and readiness to be used when God speaks. There comes a point in our relationships with other human beings, also, when, like Paul's friends, we have to hand them silently over to God and trust him to look after them.

† Father, I hand over to you all those I love, all who are in need, trusting them to the silence of your love, believing that you can do what is best for them in ways beyond our understanding.

Kate Hughes

Silence

August

Silence as reverence

When the Lamb opened the seventh seal, there was silence in heaven for about half an hour.

(verse 1)

Revelation must be one of the busiest and noisiest books in the Bible. But at its centre is silence – only half an hour, but it comes as the climax of the sealing of the faithful and the glorious worship of the 'great multitude that no one could count' (verse 9), the angels, the elders, and the four living creatures. Sometimes, in a church or a concert hall, a piece of music rises to a glorious climax, ending on a note of triumph. No one claps; there is a total, focused silence as the audience's hearts and minds expand and lift, reaching out without words or noise to embrace the beauty, the force, the harmony, God – whatever they believe is behind the glory of the music. A door opens on to eternity, leaving us speechless. Then slowly we come back down to earth, and a ripple of clapping begins and grows.

In silence, we can draw closer to God than we can with words. The rush of love, satisfaction, expansion, joy that we feel when we watch our children, see a beautiful flower or a lovely landscape, hear tremendous music, read a well-written, wise book, look at something good that we have created – hundreds of different experiences that connect us momentarily with God – leaves us without words. The only possible response is the silence of adoration and gratitude.

August

† Amen! Blessing and glory and wisdom and thanksgiving and honour and power and might be to our God for ever and ever! Amen

Silence

Kate Hughes

Rivers of the Bible

Notes based on the *New Revised Standard Version* by
Gloria Barrett-Sobers

Gloria Barrett-Sobers lives in Kingston, Jamaica, with her husband, Peter. A former Registrar of the University of the West Indies, she is now retired and a full-time housewife and guardian to her two grandchildren, Ashlee and Jerome. A church leader and chorister at Providence Methodist Church in Kingston, she also serves on the boards of the United Theological College of the West Indies and Excelsior Community College.

Sunday 29 August: Preparing for the week

The Bible begins and ends with rivers. In Genesis 2 the river flowing through the Garden of Eden splits into four to go to the four corners of the earth – water is essential for life to exist on earth. Equally the river of the water of life is essential for the life of heaven (Revelation 22). In between, certain rivers play a key part – either actually or symbolically – in what the Bible tells of the truth about God. The rivers we encounter in this week's readings are instrumental in helping us understand more about God's sovereignty, providence, faithfulness and constancy. We also learn lessons of obedience and humility, of hope and the blessings of a Spirit-filled life.

Text for the week: *John 7:38*

'And let the one who believes in me drink. As the scripture has said, "Out of the believer's heart shall flow rivers of living water."'

For group discussion and personal thought
• What does 'a Spirit-filled life' mean, and how apt is the analogy of 'rivers of living water' flowing out of the believer's heart, to such a life?

The river Nile

A few years ago, while attending a conference in the beautiful Rockies resort of Banff, I became seriously ill and was admitted to a hospital in Calgary, Canada. After doing all they could for me, the hospital dismissed me, forbidding me to travel until I had completed the prescribed outpatient treatment. Here I was in a strange city, getting ready to move from the hospital to a hotel to await clearance to travel back to Jamaica, when someone came asking for me. It was an old university acquaintance whom I had not seen for decades. He had heard of my predicament from one of our mutual friends from our student days, and had come to invite me to stay with his family until I was well enough to travel. Divine providence at work, indeed!

Today's reading recounts the story of the baby Moses, born soon after Pharaoh's decree that all Hebrew baby boys should be killed. His mother, distressed at the possible demise of her lovely son, deliberately works out a scheme for his reprieve from this murderous decree. Placing her son in a basket on the river and awaiting God's providence reflect this mother's great hope that the Egyptians will not prevail against him.

Then God intervenes and how providentially he works! To some it may seem ironic that it is Pharaoh's own daughter who comes to bathe in the river and saves young Moses.

> She named him Moses, 'Because', she said, 'I drew him out of the water.'

> (part of verse 10)

His mother, like so many others of faith, knows, however, that it is God who uses the river for his own purpose, as he will use it later (Exodus 7:14-24) to thwart Pharaoh's stubborn intent by making the waters of the Nile undrinkable when they are turned into blood.

August

† Lord, thank you for the reassurance of your providence, however hopeless our situation may seem.

Rivers of the Bible

Gloria Barrett-Sobers

The river Jordan

The river Jordan is highly symbolic for the people of Israel: it represents the boundary between their landlessness and wanderings and their becoming a settled people in the Promised Land. Crossing the Jordan and conquering the land east of the river was the finale to their 40 years of wanderings since the miraculous parting of the Red Sea allowed them to escape slavery in Egypt. It signalled God's fulfilment of his promise to give the land to Abraham's descendants.

The crossing of Jordan as described in today's reading is one of the most stirring and dramatic accounts of the Lord's dealings with his people. The river is in spate because it is the time of harvest. The ark of the Lord, representing his presence among his people, was to go ahead of them and as the feet of the Levites bearing the ark touched the water it would recede and 'stand in a single heap' (verse 13), supernaturally dammed up, allowing the people to cross. Beyond the action-packed historical facts, there is much to learn of the conditions under which God's greatest spiritual blessings are gained. The people were told to purify themselves for the divine presence:

> 'Sanctify yourselves, for tomorrow the LORD will do wonders among you.'

(part of verse 5)

They were to follow the ark at a given distance. Joshua was given clear instructions to lead and direct the people, but also the promise that God would exalt him in the sight of the people. Purity and obedience are reasonable and required responses to God's faithfulness and providence.

---

† Sanctify us and help us to be obedient as we seek your continued presence and guidance in our lives, Lord, God of our salvation.

Gloria Barrett-Sobers

Rivers of the Bible

The rivers of Syria

Naaman was clearly a very important person in Syria: supreme commander of Aram's army; a 'great man', implying high social standing; highly regarded by his master, the king; a successful military man and a courageous warrior (verses 1-2). Plagued by leprosy, he is prepared to try the suggestion of the little Israeli slave girl and seek help from Elisha, the prophet in Israel. In grand style and with much fanfare and many gifts he goes directly to the king of Israel – no second-level official for him! When Elisha offers to deal with the matter for the king and sends a message to Naaman to dip seven times in Israel's muddy Jordan river, Naaman feels insulted.

'I thought that for me he would surely come out and stand and call on the name of the LORD his God and would wave his hand over the spot and cure the leprosy.'

(part of verse 11)

He has not been dealt with according to his station in life, and imagine bypassing the great rivers of Syria, Abana and Pharpar, to bathe in muddy Jordan! Thankfully, his caring servants persuaded him to obey the prophet's simple instructions. What a difference it made to his life! In obedience he is miraculously healed and the once proud and self-important Naaman is transformed: 'Now I know that there is no God in all the earth except in Israel' (verse 15).

† Before your great might and power we bow in humble adoration and offer ourselves in service. May we be obedient and faithful to your precepts and directions for our lives.

●

Rivers of the Bible   Gloria Barrett-Sobers

The rivers of Babylon

Bob Marley, Jamaica's best-known music icon, immortalised in haunting melody the sadness and despair of Psalm 137, sung by the Hebrews exiled in Babylon. The psalm expresses the hopelessness and frustration of a people far from home and from the culture, comfort and care that home represents. Students studying abroad, émigrés and refugees will no doubt identify with the sentiments and mood of the writer.

How could we sing the LORD's song in a foreign land?

(Psalm, verse 4)

Once again the river plays its role, for as the people sit by the rivers of Babylon, they are reminded bitterly of their homeland and of their status as slaves in a foreign land. Thankfully, however, today's readings do not end on this note of despair because, seated by the Chebar, one of Babylon's rivers, Ezekiel is reminded that God is the God of all the world and is with his people, wherever they find themselves, even by the rivers of Babylon.

The word of the LORD came to the priest Ezekiel, son of Buzi, in the land of the Chaldeans by the river Chebar; and the hand of the LORD was on him there.

(Ezekiel, verse 3)

We do not have to be in a foreign country to feel despondent and distant from God. So when frustration and despair threaten to overtake us, let us be reminded that God is with us wherever we are.

† Come, speak to us, Lord, and place your hand of comfort upon us, so that we may know that whatever the circumstance, however far we have wandered, you are still close to us and will hear us when we turn to you.

Gloria Barrett-Sobers

Rivers of the Bible

The river Jordan

The rivers of the Bible have often been the setting for important events, discussions and reflections. The Jordan, perhaps more than any other river, has great significance for the Hebrews. As we read earlier this week, it marked the final leg of their odyssey from Egypt to the Promised Land and the boundary between their being a nomadic tribe and becoming a settled people.

Today's reading brings us once again to the river Jordan, now the setting for people to respond to John the Baptist's plea to repent, turn again to God and be baptised. People began to ask whether John might be the long-awaited Messiah, or the promised return of Elijah, but John quickly declared that he was but the messenger preparing the way for the one who would bring the message of hope. On several occasions when John had the opportunity to focus on himself, he shifts the focus on to the Messiah, declaring that he is simply 'the voice of one crying out in the wilderness, "Make straight the way of the Lord"' (verse 23). On another occasion,

John answered them, 'I baptize with water. Among you stands one whom you do not know, the one who is coming after me; I am not worthy to untie the thong of his sandal.'

(verses 26-27)

John's humility as he testifies to the Christ and insists on giving him the pre-eminence is something that all of us would do well to emulate, whether we are preachers, evangelists, church leaders or simply homemakers who love and serve the Lord.

September

† Dear Lord, help us, like John, to point others to you and in humility to give you the pre-eminence, seeking no glory for ourselves.

Rivers of the Bible

Gloria Barrett-Sobers

John 7:37-39

Rivers of living water

Water is essential for life on earth. After Hurricane Gilbert devastated Jamaica in 1988, it took days for water to be restored to my home. I remember the desperation with which I used to drive around town seeking out friends who had water to spare. Jesus, knowing the indispensability of water, issues a generous invitation:

> 'Let anyone who is thirsty come to me, and let the one who believes in me drink. As the scripture has said, "Out of the believer's heart shall flow rivers of living water."'

(part of verse 37, and verse 38)

Jesus is addressing the crowds during the week-long celebration of the Festival of Booths (verse 2), during which the Jews commemorated their wanderings in the wilderness after fleeing Egypt. Rites involving fetching water were a key part of these celebrations, recalling the water coming from the rock in the desert. In the midst of this comes the message that Jesus is the true water, embodying the power to which the festival actually points.

As believers, we can become the channels of life to others, through Jesus' Spirit, according to his promise. Note, however, that it is only as we accept Jesus' invitation to come to him, believe in him and drink of him, that his Spirit will flow from us to bring life to others.

† Lord, we come to you thirsty and believing that only you can quench our thirst. Fill us as you have promised, and make us channels of your love and Holy Spirit. Let rivers of living water flow from us to others, so that your name may be glorified.

●

Gloria Barrett-Sobers

Rivers of the Bible

Writing

1 Stones, letters and graffiti

Notes based on the *New Revised Standard Version* by
Julie M Hulme

Julie M Hulme is a Methodist minister, following a call to live a life of prayer through writing and art. She says, 'Prayer is not something I do, but rather a way of paying attention to God in everything I do. That's the theory, anyway. There are moments of inspiration, but it can also be hard work.' She lives close to Birmingham, England, with her husband, David, also a Methodist minister. They have two adult daughters.

Sunday 5 September: Preparing for the week

Today, the ability to read and write is so widespread that in many contexts it is taken for granted and people who lack this ability suffer many disadvantages. However, in the ancient world the written word was relatively rare and surrounded with awe and wonder. Reading and writing allowed the truth of God to reach people in new ways, stretching the mind, nourishing the spirit and challenging them to hear and obey.

Text for the week: *Deuteronomy 31:12*

Assemble the people – men, women, and children, as well as the aliens residing in your towns – so that they may hear and learn to fear the LORD your God and to observe diligently all the words of this law.

For group discussion and personal thought
• What are the 'words of grace' that have comforted or inspired you most? Is there a promise that you could pass on to encourage a friend?

September

Read – and remember – the word of God

Then Moses wrote down this law, and gave it to the priests, the sons of Levi, who carried the ark of the covenant of the LORD, and to all the elders of Israel. Moses commanded them: 'Every seventh year, in the scheduled year of remission, during the festival of booths, when all Israel comes to appear before the LORD your God at the place that he will choose, you shall read this law before all Israel in their hearing.'

(Deuteronomy verses 9-11)

Writing enables words to outlast the one who writes them. Moses puts the law into writing so that the message he has received from God can survive for future generations. However, at first there is only one copy, and few people can read. So every seven years the law is read in public, during a festival, so that all can hear – and remember – what the Lord commands.

Writing also tells us something about the author. Moses and Joshua want people to remember the character of God who gives the law. God has liberated the people so that they can enjoy abundant life in the Promised Land. Every seven years, debts are remitted as a way of celebrating this vision and making it real. At such a time, when the people gather together to worship God, the law is read to remind them how God has saved them, and to show them how they should respond.

† Liberating God, through saving acts you set us free. Through words of grace, you show us how to use our freedom.

Julie Hulme

Writing

September

Finding the word of grace

Because it was written down, the law survived even when the people neglected it and eventually abandoned it. A copy of the law lay, forgotten, in the Temple treasury. Then, during an audit initiated by King Josiah, the book was found.

When the king heard the words of the book of the law, he tore his clothes. Then the king commanded the priest Hilkiah . . . saying, 'Go, inquire of the LORD for me, for the people, and for all Judah, concerning the words of this book that has been found; for great is the wrath of the LORD that is kindled against us, because our ancestors did not obey the words of this book, to do according to all that is written concerning us.'

(verse 11, part of verse 12, and verse 13)

Josiah fears what the wrath of God will bring upon them all.

We too can find the word of God demanding, daunting, even terrifying. Fear can alert us to what is wrong, but to act in faith, we need words that will build us up, not beat us down. Like Josiah, we need those who can apply its truth to our situation in a way that will help us do the right thing. We must look beyond the words of judgement to the mercy in God's promises. The grace of God meets us here and now to encourage us. God is generous so that we can be generous to ourselves – and to others. By remembering the love and mercy of God, we deepen our humility and renew our obedience.

September

† O God of mercy, show me your word of grace for me today. May I take it to heart, and grow in grace to bear the fruit of love.

Writing

Julie Hulme

Words from the highest authority

Belshazzar, king of Babylon, wants to impress his supporters, so he decrees that they shall drink wine out of the treasure that his father, Nebuchadnezzar, had taken from the Temple in Jerusalem.

> *Immediately the fingers of a human hand appeared and began writing on the plaster of the wall of the royal palace, next to the lamp stand. The king was watching the hand as it wrote. Then the king's face turned pale, and his thoughts terrified him. The king cried aloud to bring in the enchanters, the Chaldeans, and the diviners; and the king said to the wise men of Babylon, 'Whoever can read this writing and tell me its interpretation shall be clothed in purple, have a chain of gold around his neck, and rank third in the kingdom.'*

(verses 5-7)

Words written in stone – on walls, pillars or cliffs – were signs of royal authority. The words that appear on a wall in the heart of the palace, while Belshazzar himself is watching, show that the power of God is far greater than that of the king. Moreover, the king's advisers cannot interpret them. Only Daniel, a Jew, understands that they proclaim God's judgement on Belshazzar and his rule. And that God who wrote the words has the power to implement them.

† O God, our Saviour King, glorify your name in all the earth.

Julie Hulme

Writing

September

Take the word to the people

[T]his word came to Jeremiah from the LORD: Take a scroll and write on it all the words that I have spoken to you . . . Baruch wrote on a scroll at Jeremiah's dictation all the words of the LORD . . . And Jeremiah ordered Baruch, saying, 'I am prevented from entering the house of the LORD; so you go yourself, and on a fast day in the hearing of the people in the LORD's house you shall read the words of the LORD from the scroll . . . It may be that their plea will come before the LORD, and that all of them will turn from their evil ways, for great is the anger and wrath that the LORD has pronounced against this people.'

(part of verses 1-2 and 4, verse 5, part of verse 6, and verse 7)

Jeremiah is forbidden to preach in the Temple. However, because he causes the words of God to be written down, the message can go where the prophet cannot go. It is a fast day. The crowd in the Temple is larger than normal, and in a thoughtful mood. When Baruch reads the scroll, the word of God is proclaimed as if Jeremiah is there, speaking to them. This is an awesome act in solemn surroundings. Through this prophetic message, God is urging the people to change their ways. But how will they respond?

† O God of truth, speak to us. Let your people hear your voice. And help us to respond with reverence, love and praise.

September

Writing   Julie Hulme

Hear the word with humility

News of Jeremiah's scroll reaches officials of Jehoiakim, king of Judah, and, eventually, the king himself, who sends for the scroll and has it read to him. There was a convenient fire in the king's winter apartment:

As Jehudi read three or four columns, the king would cut them off with a penknife and throw them into the fire in the brazier, until the entire scroll was consumed in the fire that was in the brazier. Yet neither the king, nor any of his servants who heard all these words, was alarmed, nor did they tear their garments . . . And the king commanded Jerahmeel the king's son . . . to arrest the secretary Baruch and the prophet Jeremiah. But the LORD hid them.

(verses 23-24, and part of verse 26)

When we hear the word of God, we have to choose how to respond. How do we react when it tells us what we do not want to hear? Sometimes it takes courage to hear the word with humility. Sometimes it is hard to receive and respect God's instruction. There are so many reasons why we might fail to take it seriously. We might be afraid of what we think it is demanding of us. We might prefer to dismiss it, disregard it, even destroy it. It can be painful to accept the challenge, to live with unanswered questions and remain open to fresh insights.

September

† O God of life, may we receive your truth with reverence, and obey your word with courage.

Julie Hulme

Writing

We are in conversation with God

King Jehoiakim believes that by burning the scroll he has destroyed, not just the words themselves, but also the power they contain to influence events. However, he is mistaken.

> The word of the LORD came to Jeremiah, 'Take another scroll and write on it all the former words that were in the first scroll, which King Jehoiakim of Judah has burned. And concerning King Jehoiakim of Judah you shall say: Thus says the LORD, You have dared to burn this scroll, saying, Why have you written in it that the King of Babylon will certainly come and destroy this land, and will cut off from it human beings and animals?

(part of verse 27, and verses 28-29)

No one, not even a king, has the power to destroy the word of God. God's word lives on, because God is eternally alive. When God commands Jeremiah to fill another scroll, the message includes God's judgement of Jehoiakim's action: what was threatened in the first scroll will come to pass.

God's word is alive, responding to events as they unfold. We are in conversation with God. As we respond to God's word, so God responds to us. God lives with us and within us, longing to be heard. God asks us to listen with humility, honesty, attention and trust. So that mercy and grace might be ours.

† Living God, help us to hear you. Loving God, help us to love you. Gracious God, help us to live in your strength for ever.

September

Writing

Julie Hulme

Writing

2 Keeping what is important

Notes based on the *New International Version* by
Selina Samuel

Selina is from New Delhi, India. She is a housewife and a
freelance editor.

Saturday 12 September: Preparing for the week

Think of times when you have read a thank you note, a letter, a card, and
been refreshed; or a book that has made an impact on your life. Think of
times when you have refreshed the heart of a family member or friend by
your written word. There is power in the written word that gives it a sense
of permanent importance. Nations, communities and organisations are
bound by the agreements they sign on paper. History has been kept alive
for us by the written word.

This week's reflections are on the importance of the Bible, the written word
of God. If the words of mere human beings can refresh, imagine what the
word of God can do for us in our lives if we take God at his word. The Bible
is an amazing source of life, hope, encouragement, strength and guidance
for our daily living.

Text for the week: *John 20:31*
*But these are written that you may believe that Jesus is the Christ, the
Son of God, and that by believing you may have life in his name.*

For group discussion and personal thought

- What does it mean to have the written word of God as 'a lamp to my
  feet and a light for my path' (Psalm119:105)?

- How can we use scripture better in our teaching, rebuking, correcting
  and training in righteousness (2 Timothy 3:16)?

An encouraging word

This is the text of the letter that the prophet Jeremiah sent from Jerusalem to the surviving elders among the exiles and to the priests, the prophets and all the other people Nebuchadnezzar had carried into exile from Jerusalem to Babylon.

(verse 1)

Jeremiah's prophecy came true regarding the Exile as a punishment from God. He now has a word from God again. This time the word of God is a word of hope and encouragement. God wants them to live normal lives even though in exile.

There were many false prophets but Jeremiah knew his message was from God and, though it was in complete contrast to the other messages, he wrote down what God told him to and sent it across. To know that the 'Lord almighty' was still interested in them was a message of hope. God expected them to live the present in peace and patient waiting with meaningful involvement, and not in fruitless complaints. This word was from God who wanted them to live in spite of the circumstances.

The word creates hope, giving us strength, courage and guidance for the present. Whatever your circumstances, be encouraged to continue to trust in God. Read the written word of God and apply it to your hearts. 'Your word is a lamp to my feet and a light for my path' (Psalm 119:105).

† Father, we want to thank you for giving us your word, written down and kept for our life and encouragement. Help me to take you at your word and experience abundant life. Amen

September

Writing

Selina Samuel

Proverbs 22:17-21

The practical word

Have I not written thirty sayings for you,
sayings of counsel and knowledge,
teaching you true and reliable words?

(verse 20 and part of verse 21)

The book of Proverbs challenges us to a better way of thinking and living – not as the foolish do, but recognising wisdom and becoming wise. This book helps us to think on a variety of issues, including wealth, speech, justice and character. This word of knowledge and counsel gives us the understanding we need to live lives that are transformed and pleasing to God.

But is it enough to read the written word? Does information transform lives? The author tells us of a few steps needed for this transformation. We need to listen, pay attention, apply the word to our heart, preserve it in our hearts. This is pleasing to God and helps us to put our trust in the Lord and be able to give sound answers. It equips us to be always ready to share and talk about the reality of the goodness of God. 'I have hidden your word in my heart that I might not sin against you' (Psalm 119:11). The privilege of having the word of God with us is not just to pull out a verse or two in times of crisis; verses like these from Proverbs are counsel and wisdom that totally influence our everyday lives.

† Father God, help me to search the scriptures so that my life may be shaped by your wisdom and counsel, and make a difference to the lives of everyone with whom I share this. Amen

September

Selina Samuel

Writing

The truthful word

Therefore since I myself have carefully investigated everything from the beginning, it seemed good also to me to write an orderly account for you.

(part of verse 3)

Luke was a physician and had a friend or friends in mind who needed to hear the reality of Jesus. He wanted to persuade and convince them of this truth. So he was not in a hurry to present a half-done project; he did all he could to get the details correct – an accurate account is what he calls it. Care was taken in the way information was collected. The word of God is not just thoughts and incidents put together. It is about God acting in history.

The character of God is truth. The three lessons one can learn from this are: first, this is God's word, take it seriously. Second, take pains to be accurate and truthful in your words, both spoken and written; this is a reflection of God's character. Let your 'yes' be 'yes' and your 'no' be 'no' (James 5:12). Third, write or speak to persuade people. It is important to share, to talk to people about the truth of Jesus Christ. The Holy Spirit will do the convincing or convicting but let our efforts be complete and accurate. Study the word so as to be able to give correct and complete answers to anyone who may have questions about our faith.

† Father, help me to be absolutely truthful in my spoken and written words. Help me to understand the importance of words and use them wisely. Amen

September

Writing

Selina Samuel

Thursday 16 September

John 20:30-31; 21:20-25

The life-giving word

But these are written that you may believe that Jesus is the Christ, the Son of God, and that by believing you may have life in his name.

(verse 31)

John the disciple was with Jesus through all the years of his ministry. He was a witness to the miracles, and listened to the teaching of Jesus. He must have seen and heard a lot and yet when he writes his Gospel narrative for us he is very selective: it is purposeful and just enough. His concern and desire were for all to believe that Jesus is the Christ, the son of God, and to have life in his name.

John's life had changed drastically when he encountered Jesus. From a man who wanted to call for fire from heaven he became a man who constantly said, 'Dear children, love one another' (1 John). John the disciple is very forthright and has written to give us information for life and not to tickle our brains with meaningless discussions. He wants to persuade the unbeliever to see the miracles and believe, and the believer to be assured of life abundant and eternal. John 6:68-69 says, 'Simon Peter answered him, "Lord, to whom shall we go? You have the words of eternal life. We believe and know that you are the Holy One of God".' Read through the Gospels again and have a fresh encounter with the Jesus who changes and transforms lives.

September

† Father God, help me to believe in you and live a meaningful and abundant life. Amen

Selina Samuel

Writing

The exciting word

Blessed is the one who reads the words of this prophecy, and blessed are those who hear it and take to heart what is written in it, because the time is near.

(verse 3)

The author of this book is the disciple John, who is now writing from the island of Patmos. He was there because of the terrible persecution that the Christians were facing under the Roman Empire. He is writing about his vision of the Lord Jesus, the Lamb of God. It is a series of images: war in heaven between God and Satan, worship, the prayers of the saints being given as incense, the angels bowing down and crying 'Holy, holy, holy', the saints worshipping him, monsters ravaging the earth. It is an amazing book. It is a prophetic or futuristic book and the emphasis is on worship, obedience, and the ultimate victory of the Lamb upon the throne. It speaks of the completion of God's redemptive plan, his expectations of us as his children, his plans for the future, and the concerns of his heart.

John's writing is faithful to the vision and has captured for us its excitement. This word inspires hope and blesses those who read and listen to it. Read it, talk about it, take it to heart and be encouraged and excited by this written word.

† Father God, help me to live a life that waits excitedly for your plan of redemption to be completed.

September

Writing

Selina Samuel

The word of God

For everything that was written in the past was written to teach us, so that through endurance and the encouragement of the Scriptures we might have hope.

(verse 4)

'All Scripture is God-breathed and is useful for teaching, rebuking, correcting and training in righteousness, so that the man of God may be thoroughly equipped for every good work' (2 Timothy 3:16-17). In the midst of a world that looks grim with wars, hate, crime, racism, ethnic cleansing, poverty, oppression, corruption, and the like, we have the Bible, the written word of God that gives us instructions for living a life that is different and godly. This written word of God opens our eyes to learn about God, his character, to know how we ought to live, to be encouraged and to continue in hope.

'For the word of God is living and active. Sharper than any double-edged sword, it penetrates even to dividing soul and spirit, joints and marrow; it judges the thoughts and attitudes of the heart. Nothing in all creation is hidden from God's sight'

(Hebrews 4:12-13)

† Dear God, thank you for your word. Thank you that you love us so much. Help us, God, to read, follow and apply your word to our lives so that we can truly be your children, transformed and living lives that are meaningfully involved and portray your character to the world. Amen

Selina Samuel

Writing

Old age

1 Reflections on old age – God is there

Notes based on the *New Revised Standard Version* by
Kate Hughes

For Kate's biography see p. 237.

Sunday 19 September: Preparing for the week

One of the things I have enjoyed most about growing old is that many of the preoccupations, hassles and upsets of my younger self have simply dropped away. And I think I know myself better, and can admit more easily to my faults and weaknesses – I no longer have any need to impress people. I have a sense of being stripped for action, for the important activity of the last stage of my human growth and the gradual slowdown towards death.

Young people often view old age as a boring period of inactivity, but old people are on a journey in the company of God, or in the final year of school with the best of all teachers.

Text for the week: *Psalm 71:17*

O God, from my youth you have taught me, and I still proclaim your wondrous deeds.

For group discussion and personal thought

- If you are an older person, what have been the pluses and minuses of growing old?
- What difference has it made to your relationship with God?
- If you are a younger person, what are your feelings about growing old?

September

The faithfulness of God

I spent almost all my school days at the same Church of England school in London, from the age of 6 to 18. Our school motto came from the last verse of this psalm: 'Prosper for us the work of our hands' (verse 17). Although I am not quite 70, so not yet really old, I still find it amazing to look back at the years I have lived: at my childhood, my schooldays, going to university, starting work, living in Africa, coming back to England. Like everyone else, I have had my share of problems and difficulties, but the thread that runs through all my life has been, and still is, God.

The writer of this psalm knew that God was there all the time, even when life was at its most difficult, and that he would continue to be there as life moved to a more peaceful end. In the same way, in spite of my failures, God has always been there, guiding, correcting, telling me what he thinks of me when I am at my worst, providing the right people to help me on my way, using the dark times to help me grow, and also giving me plenty of light and joy to encourage me. It is only when I look back that I can see this pattern, and know that God will be with me in the same way as I get older.

Let your work be manifest in your servants.

(part of verse 16)

---

† Lord, the person I am now is the product of your loving care and guidance over the years. Continue to be with me as I get older and face new difficulties and challenges, and new opportunities to witness to your love.

Kate Hughes

Old age

Learning from experience

I cringe at the sort of old people who do nothing but grumble and never have a good word to say about anyone. Joking, I say to my friends that, if I ever get like that, will they please knock me over the head with a (full) bottle! The writer of this psalm has the right attitude: he or she looks back over their life and is filled with gratitude:

My mouth will tell of your righteous acts,
of your deeds of salvation all day long,
though their number is past my knowledge.

(verse 15)

God has been there right from the beginning: 'it was you who took me from my mother's womb' (verse 6). He has been someone to lean on, to rely on for guidance and protection.

But now the psalmist wavers: will God still be there in old age, when strength is spent and there is even more need of his protection? The evidence comes from the past: God has always been faithful, why should he change now? It is our past experience of God that enables us to go hopefully into an unknown future – with him.

† You, O Lord, are my hope, my trust, O Lord, from my youth; thank you that you will not forsake me in old age, but we will continue to journey together.

September

Old age   Kate Hughes

Ecclesiastes 12:1-7

Remote preparation

Old age isn't always much fun. Your body starts wearing out; you go to a lot of funerals; you can be short of money; you can be sidelined by the people around you; your ability to get out can be limited. Sometimes it seems as if we lose something or someone from our life almost daily, and decisions are made for us over which we have no control.

Old age is full of challenges. But how you cope with them depends on more than just meeting each one as it comes. We can start preparing for the diminishments of old age long before we get there. We can get into training when we are young, especially learning how to deal with loss. If we sit lightly to our possessions, it will not matter so much when we have fewer of them. If we are not reliant on our work for our image of ourselves and our self-confidence, we will not feel that life is worthless when we can no longer earn our living. If we appreciate our friendships, we will remember them with gratitude when we no longer have them. Above all, if we learn early on to see life as a journey with God, old age will simply be the next stage in the journey, with new views to be seen, new things to be discovered, and a deeper understanding of our travelling companion.

Remember your creator in the days of your youth.

(part of verse 1)

So those of you reading these notes who are not yet old – start preparing now!

† Thank you, Lord, that our journey with you continues right up to the grave and beyond; it doesn't stop just because we grow old. Help me in old age still to travel hopefully and to enjoy your company.

Kate Hughes

Old age

Earning respect

'Respect' is the word today. Treat me with respect, or I will pull a knife on you. But respect has to be earned, it is not a right. I cannot demand respect simply because my hair is grey, and expect to go first, be spoken to politely, given a seat on the bus, just because I have managed to live for a long time.

In today's reading, Peter is addressing the leaders of the congregation, who were the older members. They are not to be autocratic: 'Do what I say, because I tell you to!' They are to be servants, willingly working for the good of the congregation. This does not mean that they will not sometimes need to give orders and make difficult decisions, but this will be accepted because others know that they have the good of the community at heart, that they are genuinely seeking what is best for all. The younger members will accept their authority and be grateful for their willingness to serve.

Do not lord it over those in your charge, but be examples to the flock . . . all of you must clothe yourselves in humility in your dealings with one another.

(verse 3, and part of verse 5)

Respect is not forced out of people at knifepoint. It is earned by willing work, humble appreciation of each other, and acceptance of responsibility. Peter is speaking to leaders, but often the greatest respect in a congregation is given to those who are always willing to help quietly in the background, cleaning, making tea, washing up, being there when they are needed.

September

† Lord, help us to respect each other, whether we are in positions of leadership or are the helpers without whom the local church could not survive.

Old age   Kate Hughes

Friday 24 September

2 Samuel 19:31-38

Knowing when to stop

One of the hardest things to do is to know when to stop. As you get older, you want to stay active, alert, involved. You may need to go on working well beyond retirement age. But there come times when you know that your physical energy is becoming less, and you have to decide what you can and can't do, and where your priorities lie. There come times when you gracefully have to let younger people take over tasks you have done all your life and still enjoy, or give help to others that you can no longer give. There come times when you have to accept help when you have always been independent – one of the hardest demands of old age.

Barzillai had to make one of these choices. King David wanted him to go with him to the royal court. Barzillai was wealthy, used to the best, and perhaps in his younger days he had enjoyed good food, drinking, social occasions, listening to singing, and all the pleasures of life. But now he was old, and he refused the king's invitation. Now was the time to stop, and hand over to a younger man:

Please let your servant return, so that I may die in my own town, near the graves of my father and my mother. But here is your servant Chimham; let him go over with my lord the king; and do for him whatever seems good to you.

(verse 37))

† Lord, it is good for me to remain active as long as possible, but please give me the wisdom to know when to stop, let go and accept help.

Kate Hughes

Old age

The gift of old age

No more shall there be in it
an infant that lives but a few days,
or an old person who does not live out a lifetime.

(part of verse 20)

There are still many parts of the world where infant mortality rates are high and most people die in their forties. In England, where I live, mortality rates have dropped dramatically in the last 150 years, thanks to advances in medicine and improved living conditions. When I first moved to Coventry I worshipped at a church that had been built in the nineteenth century. In the churchyard there were many graves of children, and most of the adults had died before they were sixty. Ironically, mortality rates are now beginning to rise again as people eat and drink too much.

Isaiah's vision of the 'new heavens and a new earth' (verse 17) includes old people, people who live to a good age, to their full span of life. Society needs both the joy of children who do not die at birth, and the wisdom and serenity of the old. And people need to live through the experience of growing old, to take its opportunities and learn its lessons, and share with others what it tells them about God.

Old age is a gift – not always, perhaps, the gift we would have chosen, but God's gift to us. He doesn't just give it to us and leave us to get on with it; he stays with us to show us how it works, and how to get the best out of it.

September

† Lord, thank you for the gift of old age. Help me to unwrap it, use it, enjoy it, appreciate it, and show me how to live through it to your glory.

Old age   Kate Hughes

Old age

2 Old age – lived with God

Notes based on the *New Jerusalem Bible* and
Grail Psalter by
Paula Fairlie OSB

For Sister Paula's biography, see p. 230.

Sunday 26 September: Preparing for the week

'Grow old along with me – the best is yet to be: the last of life for which
the first was made!' Robert Browning's lines seemed too optimistic when
I first read them at school. How could the end of life be the best part?
Old age, like ripe fruit, can be beautiful and firm – but it can also become
over-ripe and fall to the ground. Yet these lines have helped me now. The
readings for this week show that the promise made to Abraham and Moses
was fulfilled only when they had travelled far, endured much and resigned
themselves to the will of God. Peter, in John's Gospel, is warned of the
dependent helplessness of old age, and how he will glorify God through
his death. Luke shows how Jesus fulfilled a promise made to Simeon and
Anna, devout old people, who had been told that 'they would not see
death' until they had seen 'the Christ of the Lord'. Mark recounts how the
overwhelming generosity of the poor widow means far more to God than
the 'wealth' of youth. All these elderly people reveal both God's faithfulness
and their own constancy.

Text for the week: *Genesis 18:14*
'Nothing is impossible for Yahweh.'

For group discussion and personal thought

- Would you agree that old people do continue to trust, despite personal
failure and unfulfilled hopes?
- What do you really think of the poor widow?

September

The God of surprises

Many years ago a paper was written called 'The ABC of Religion'. A was for Altars, always a place for sacrifice; B was for the Blessings one hoped for, especially progeny; and C was the Cursing incurred through disobedience to the deity. By the time Abraham and Sarah emerged from the desert and reached Mamre, all these practices were well in place. Fertility was considered the prime blessing: being barren was a curse. Abraham had been meticulous in building altars and offering hospitality to strangers. Sarah, in a moment of generosity, allowed Abraham to have an 'issue from his own body' with a servant girl. This almost ended in disaster: Sarah was both jealous and vindictive.

Now Yahweh appeared as three men, and a promise was made. It seemed utterly ridiculous. How could a woman physically too old, with a husband lacking in virility, enjoy the pleasure and intimacy of procreation? There must have been good memories mixed with incredulity in the laughter of surprise. The promise was too good to be true. Afterwards Sarah said:

God has given me cause to laugh!
All who hear about this will laugh with me!. . .
Whoever would have told Abraham
that Sarah would nurse children!
Yet I have borne a son in his old age.

(part of verses 6-7)

Throughout the scriptures it is emphasised that only God is the giver of life. He makes barren women fertile: the sons they bear are children of promise. He is also the master of time, and can overturn the limitations of age.

September

† Let us pray for the gift of personal faithfulness.

Old age   Paula Fairlie

Tuesday 28 September

Deuteronomy 34:1-12

Faithful but firm

'I shall give [this country] to your descendants. I have allowed you to see it for yourself, but you will not cross into it.'

(part of verse 4)

From the beginning of recorded time human beings have moved across the world seeking a land of their own or a better place to live. Later, this resulted in territorial wars, when the original inhabitants were driven out, killed or maimed. A chain reaction resulted, and continues to this day. Moses is the supreme example of a man called by God to free his people from slavery. His example has inspired those in bondage to fight for emancipation, for equal rights.

But what about Moses, who had given his all to Yahweh and his people, growing old amid human disobedience, lack of response, doubt – including his own – being told that he would not enter the Promised Land? He was very old, too old to travel further, but was given a panoramic view of the Promised Land. Blood has been shed over it ever since. The people were still in the desert, the wrong side of the Jordan. Moses was to die in Moab: 'they buried him in the valley . . . but to this day no one has ever found his grave' (verse 6).

Despite the well-known name, the recorded deeds of power, his humility and faith, his need for an interpreter to communicate with the Hebrew slaves, and various, conflicting accounts, scholars are not sure if 'Moses' was one person or many different leaders. However, this 'person' was responsive to God and died in his service, having lived a very long life in heroic faith. He died in faith, trusting God still, and was satisfied.

---

† Grant, Lord, that we may always trust you.

Paula Fairlie

Old age

Honour your father and mother

Never speak sharply to a man older than yourself, but appeal to him as you would to your own father; treat . . . older women as mothers.

(part of verses 1-2)

This wise pastoral letter reminds us that we are all one family in Christ, and that all our relationships need to be based on mutual love and respect. The fourth of the Ten Commandments is: 'Honour your father and mother'. St Paul, in Ephesians, writes 'Children, be obedient to your parents in the Lord' because this commandment includes a promise, 'so that you may have long life and prosper in the land'.

The integrity of the family unit sustains society; families united in peace form a society at peace, and their disintegration has very wide repercussions. This is equally true of our Christian family – fragmented as it is throughout the world. The need for ecumenical dialogue requires the same courtesy and open heart.

There are other nuances that arise from today's text: 'Anyone who does not look after his own relations . . . has rejected the faith' (verse 8); and, 'a woman who is really widowed and left on her own has set her hope in God and perseveres night and day in petitions and prayer'. Such a woman is found in Luke 2:37 and became the image of the Christian community at prayer. Such consecrated women evolved into communities of nuns, dedicated to contemplative prayer, and into communities of sisters dedicated to caring for the poor, teaching and nursing. Without the bond of mutual respect, such communities cannot thrive.

September

† Let us pray for a loving and gentle heart.

Old age

Paula Fairlie

'Later you shall follow me'

The aspirations of youth, the heart's desire, are only partially fulfilled in life as it unfolds before us. We have to learn our dependency upon God, as we were dependent upon the adults who cared for us – or did not care for us – when we were children. We were not our own masters then, and we shall not be in enfeebled old age:

> 'when you grow old
> you will stretch out your hands,
> and somebody else will put a belt round you
> and take you where you would rather not go.'

(part of verse 18)

There is a spiritual counterpart. Our Lord told us that we must become like little children who still trust and believe, and who can live in the present moment either in sorrow or joy. In old age we may return to dependency both physically and, ideally, spiritually.

Peter was warned that later he would be taken captive and martyred. This message is still being fulfilled in many places in the world where there is religious persecution. We need to remember that our call has always been to follow Christ, and some of us may well be led through suffering before death opens the gates of life everlasting.

Peter had the chance to deny Christ definitively – after all, he had already denied him on several occasions – and so do we. It is not enough to say 'I am a Christian' and then not act like one. There are always consequences, and the whole of our life is a period of training; may we always say 'Not my will but Thine be done.'

† Let us reach out in love to all Christians.

Paula Fairlie

Old age

Prompted by the Spirit

We commemorate these verses every day in our monastic liturgy. As night falls we sing:

Now, Master, you are letting your servant go in peace
as you promised;
for my eyes have seen the salvation
which you have made ready in the sight of the nations.

(verses 29-31)

It is our song of fulfilment at the end of each day, and a wonderful hymn to hear or sing on our deathbeds. It is a song of deep faith and gratitude for a glimpse of what is in store, not yet fulfilled for Simeon, but both fulfilled and unfulfilled for us. Christ has been revealed to the gentiles (us) through the missionary work of his followers, and God's glory hovers over all the world. However, any form of goodness will meet with rejection. The child of promise and his mother will both suffer, and that is our mission, too. But our suffering will turn into joy as new life comes into the world. 'Young men will see visions and old men shall dream dreams' (Joel 3:1-3).

A vision is a glimpse of the future, or of a spiritual reality beyond our sight. Dreams tend to link us with the past, or to be prophetic. In the end, there is not a large gap between vision and dream, or between childhood and old age. The clutter and preoccupation of our active middle years are over, and the glow of grace may hover around us like a brilliant sunset.

We are all 'prompted' by the Spirit of God; when we act upon it, light increases in the world as God reveals himself in acts of kindness and of love.

October

† May we never cease to dream and to hope.

Old age   Paula Fairlie

277

Saturday 2 October

Mark 12:41-44

Everything

'She in her poverty has put in everything she possessed, all she had to live on.'

(part of verse 44)

When is love at its strongest? We tend to associate the reckless generosity of love with the young and untried, who pour out all they have and are before the beloved. In the account of the poor widow we see a totally reckless, hidden love, flowing from an old person. Perhaps we need to pause and reflect. By the time we are middle-aged (were the Magi middle-aged?) we may discover that we have not attained what we hoped for. We set out again, now seeing only dimly in the dark. The Magi returned to their own land to begin again. What else could they do?

The poor widow had no encounters, no vision, but her heart prompted her to put 'all she had to live on' into the treasury of the Temple. Was she mad? Her gift wouldn't be much use, would it? But it was given to God. He accepted this gift as a personal gift, and while she may have gone hungry that day, was she not filled with love? Who knows what happened to this nameless person? She can teach us that God does not value us according to our means but according to the unselfishness of our love. Old people can be very selfish and self-centred, while others are self-giving, emptying themselves as our Lord himself did for our salvation.

† May we be like the poor widow, and act with the same selfless love.

Paula Fairlie

Old Age

Consider a legacy

Help us to continue our work of providing Bible study notes for use by Christians in the UK and throughout the world. The need is as great as it was when IBRA was founded in 1882 by Charles Waters as part of the work of the Sunday School Union.

Please leave a legacy to the International Bible Reading Association.

An easy-to-use leaflet has been prepared to help you provide a legacy. Please write or telephone (details below) and we will send you this leaflet – and answer any questions you might have about a legacy or other donations. Please help us to strengthen this and the next generation of Christians.

Thank you very much.

International Bible Reading Association
1020 Bristol Road
Selly Oak
Birmingham
B29 6LB
UK

Tel. 0121 472 4242
Fax 0121 472 7575

Micah

1   What angers God?

Notes based on the *New Revised Standard Version* by
Sham Thomas

Sham P Thomas is an ordained priest of the Mar Thoma Church, serving
as Professor and Chairperson of the Department of Communication at
the United Theological College, Bangalore, India. He has served parishes
in both rural and urban India and continues to serve the church by
leading retreats and conferences. He lives in Bangalore with his wife Jolly and their daughter
Shyama.

Sunday 3 October: Preparing for the week

Understanding God's will and standing by it in all places and at all times is a
demanding task. This is specially so when the 'fence eats the crops'. Fences
are to protect the crops, but if they start devouring the crops, how will it
end? In this week's readings we see the prophet Micah proclaiming God's
judgement on nations and their leadership for breaching their covenant
relationship with God. When prosperity hides the plight of the ordinary
people and camouflages exploitation by the wealthy and established
leadership, God takes the side of the victims. The judgement and fury of
God should challenge us today to continue the prophetic ministry in our
apparently prosperous yet exploitative world.

Text for the week: *Micah 3:8*

*But, as for me, I am filled with power, with the spirit of the Lord, and
with justice and might, to declare to Jacob his transgression and to Israel
his sin.*

For group discussion and personal thought
• How do you understand the fury of God?
• What does it mean to regain the prophetic ministry of the Church?

Micah 1:1-7

Samaria found wanting

The book of Micah opens in a legal and courtroom setting where God pronounces judgement on the apostasy of the whole earth, especially on Samaria and Judah. These nations should have given priority and prominence to God but have compromised their faith by turning to un-gods. Worship of un-gods – idols like prosperity that attract ultimate devotion from people – hurts God and makes God angry.

> Then the mountains will melt under him
> and the valleys will burst open,
> like wax near the fire,
> like waters poured down a steep place.
> All this is for the transgression of Jacob
> and for the sins of the house of Israel.

(verse 4, and part of verse 5)

Micah portrays an angry God coming with wrath, with unbearable consequences.

God's fury reveals two truths. First, not everything that happens in this world is God's will, so we need to be cautious in accepting every happening as divinely ordained or destined. Jesus underlines this fact in teaching us to pray, 'thy will be done on earth as it is in heaven'. Second, God's fury reveals that God is not a dispassionate observer of sin and evil but is an intervening God. Often, when sin abounds and evil prevails, we may wonder whether God sees or cares. The furious intervention of God is, in this sense, a message of comfort and hope that in God's own time and ways, God will intervene in history to bring relief to people from their distress.

October

† God of justice and grace, help us to realise that the un-gods of prosperity may bring transitory fame and fortune but lead ultimately to doom, despair and desolation. Have mercy on us that you may not find us wanting in our devotion to you. Amen

Micah   Sham Thomas

Micah 1:8-16

Judah is no better

The prophet laments the fate of another nation, Judah. The impending political invasion is portrayed as God's judgement and the prophet uses a series of puns on the names of the twelve cities, contrasting their names and their coming downfall. For instance, Micah warns that the 'pleasant city' would go away in 'shameful nakedness' and the inhabitants of the 'going out' town would not get away.

Names of nations and peoples are very important in biblical tradition. Most of the time, a name symbolises a unique position in relation to God and others. Judah as a nation was commissioned to be God's people in the world. But when their conduct contradicts their commission, catastrophic consequences are inevitable. For the prophet it is only poetic justice that the nation and her cities get what they deserve. In other words, God will not always protect the people if they persist in brazen disobedience. God cannot be taken for granted or blamed for what happens to the nation and people.

For her wound is incurable.
It has come to Judah;
it has reached to the gate of my people,
to Jerusalem.

(verse 9)

God's anger is the result of being wounded by God's people.

Today, the Church is called to be in a covenant relationship with God in the world. As the body of Christ, it is our responsibility to represent Christ in our words and deeds. If we fail in this mission, God will be wounded and will not save us from the consequences. Can God be so angry with the Church?

† Wounded God, help us not to go on persecuting you. Guide us to be truthful to our calling. In the name of the one who was wounded for us, Jesus the Christ. Amen

Sham Thomas

Micah

Sharp words for the exploiters

Micah started his ministry as God's spokesperson at a time when Judah enjoyed comparative economic prosperity. He understood that the apparent prosperity brought privileges to the wealthy few and social injustice to the vast majority. In this sense, he helps us today to recognise the dynamics of material acquisition and exploitation getting camouflaged under beautiful words like 'development' and 'prosperity'. Why is it that the rich become richer and poor become poorer? Is it not the result of corporate sin?

They covet fields, and seize them;
houses, and take them away;
they oppress householder and house,
people and their inheritance.

(verse 2)

The wealthy and wicked exploiters in any society desire more land and property and they devise creative ways to grab them. The unholy alliance of money, muscle and media power breeds a culture of acquisition without any regard for the rights of people, especially the vulnerable. In the name of development, aboriginals and people of the land are evicted from their inheritance and birthplace. The result of such structural sins is that peace-loving people are threatened, women are driven out of their dwellings and young children are denied the promise of a future.

Micah declares in sharp words that God takes the side of the exploited; as the exploiters plan to rob people, God will also plan against them. When God bends their pride and shames them, their false sense of security and indulgent life will turn out to be a lament rather than a glamorous myth.

† Angry God, help us to understand, analyse and expose the social evils that are manifest in today's world and to take a stand on behalf of the victims of exploitation. Amen

October

Micah

Sham Thomas

Sharp words for bent rulers

In yesterday's reading, the prophet enumerated the reasons for divine judgement on the wealthy and exploitative; today he turns his focus on the rulers. Rulers and leaders are appointed to sustain and protect the people and work for their welfare. Instead, Micah observes that the political and judicial leaders collude with the exploiters and feed on the very people for whose sake they hold office.

> *And I said:*
> *Listen, you heads of Jacob*
> *and rulers of the house of Israel!*
> *Should you not know justice?*

(verse 1)

For the prophet – and for many today – it is a baffling question why many leaders think that, if people want justice, they should pay for it. It is not uncommon to see leaders, both political and ecclesiastical, enjoying power and perks as their birthright and getting fat, even intoxicated, on the blood of the people. In their pursuit of more and more power, they do not mind embracing evil and bent ways. Even more perplexing, they have scant regard for the people and their needs.

Micah had some sharp words for such leadership. God embraces the victims of injustice as God's people and judges the unjust rulers on the basis of their conduct towards them. As the leaders turned a deaf ear to the cries of the people, God will ignore them in their plight. Do we and our leaders hear this?

† Judging God, help us to understand that the way we lead is also a means of witnessing to your kingdom. Fashion our leadership in your mould. Amen

Sham Thomas

Micah

Prophets on sale

When nations and people deviate from the design of God, prophets are called to act as 'watchdogs', to warn of the dire consequences so that they will change their behaviour. But what could be more disastrous than the prophets themselves moving away from God and God's word of truth?

In today's reading, we face the irony of God's spokespersons becoming agents of Satan, the father of all lies. Instead of 'barking for God', false prophets of every age become 'lapdogs' of those who pay well. Of course, the poor are in no position to satisfy their greed and hence they may get only pronouncements of cursing and doom

Is it any different today? Preachers and prophets, perhaps more than ever, are increasingly becoming 'merchants of faith'. Some of the proponents of the 'prosperity' or 'health and wealth' gospel unashamedly proclaim that blessings will be bestowed upon people who give hefty donations to the preacher or their family run gospel enterprises.

Therefore it shall be night to you, without vision,
and darkness to you, without revelation. . .
the seers shall be disgraced,
and the diviners put to shame.

(part of verses 6-7)

In a stinging attack on the 'prophets on sale', Micah predicts their impending shame and disgrace. What else can a deeply hurt and pained God do except act in fury and judgement? When those supposed to stand for truth and justice crumble under the weight of material benefits, what might happen is beyond anybody's imagination. What could be more scandalous than the Church moving away from her prophetic vocation for a pittance?

† Lord, help us to speak truth in love and without fear or favour. Amen

Micah   Sham Thomas

Naming oppressors

Micah names all the oppressors in Jerusalem and suggests that the cumulative effect of the evil acts of the rulers, chiefs, prophets and priests will be nothing less than the total destruction and desolation of the privileged cities of God. What perhaps angers God and the prophet the most is the leaders' claim that God will be with them despite their unjust rule, bribe-taking and sale of the 'gospel'. What is built on aggressive seizure of property, forced labour, corruption and violence cannot be protected by 'faith'; it can only come to a violent end.

> *[Y]et they lean upon the LORD and say,*
> *'Surely the LORD is with us!*
> *No harm shall come upon us.'*
> *Therefore because of you*
> *Zion shall be ploughed as a field;*
> *Jerusalem shall become a heap of ruins.*

(part of verses 11-12)

'We have God with us' is the claim of tyrants and even terrorists. They use it to give false security to people and to protect their vested interests. They may be successful for some time, but the truth about where God stands and what God wants will not remain hidden for long. US President Abraham Lincoln was assured at a crucial juncture in his presidency that he would win the war to free the slaves because God was with him. To this he replied, 'I am sure God is with us. My only doubt is whether we are with God.' This is the question we need to ask continuously in our journey of faith.

† Judging God, do not deal with us according to our sins but according to your own grace and mercy. In Jesus' name. Amen

Sham Thomas

Micah

Micah

2   What does God require and promise?

Notes based on the *New American Standard Bible* by
Jules Gomes

The Revd Dr Jules Gomes is MA Course Leader and Lecturer in Biblical
Theology at the London School of Theology. He has served as Co-
ordinating Chaplain to the Old Royal Naval College Chapel, Trinity
College of Music and the University of Greenwich. Jules earned his
doctorate in Old Testament from the University of Cambridge and taught Old Testament in
India for a number of years. Before entering the ministry he was a journalist for a reputable
newspaper in Mumbai.

Sunday 10 October: Preparing for the week

This was Israel's golden age. Peace prevailed. Trade flourished. Wealth
multiplied. But the poor perished. For Micah, a crisis of economics was a
crisis of faith. His name said it all: Mi-ca-iah. Who is like Yahweh? Yahweh
was not a tribal but a global God. Yahweh was not a God of private
spirituality but a God of land, capital and labour. Yahweh was calling his
prophet of justice to challenge the profits of injustice.

Text for the week: *Micah 6:8*

He has told you, O man, what is good, and what does the Lord require
of you but to do justice, to love kindness, and to walk humbly with your
God?

For group discussion and personal thought
- Yahweh knows no distinction between the secular and sacred, between
  private and public morality. Why have we divided what God has united?
- Economics without ethics is disastrous. How does the Bible deal with
  issues of economic injustice?

October

Monday 11 October

Micah 4:1-7

Global peace is God's peace

[T]hen they will hammer their swords into ploughshares, and their spears into pruning hooks. Nation will not lift up sword against nation, and never again will they train for war.

(part of verse 3)

There can be no peace without justice, no justice without law, no law without a lawgiver. But human laws are limited. Human peace treaties are frail.

Micah paints a subversive picture of an incredible alternative. The coming of the new age will bring peace on earth and goodwill among people of every nation. The word of peace proceeding from the city of peace will bring about a world of peace and justice. The bad news of weapons of mass destruction will be replaced by the good news of mass salvation. God's peace is global peace. It begins with the worship of God; it is learned through the word of God and is ultimately the work of God. It is God's house that will attract the nations. Because their gods are idols, the nations do not have the necessary knowledge of justice and peace, and so must come to Jerusalem to receive guidance. The law is as pertinent to the nations as it is to Israel.

Micah broadens his canvas to include a pastoral picture of peace enjoyed by people sitting under their own vines and fig trees – a serene setting of economic and social *shalom*. But global peace is also gospel peace, inaugurated by Christ on Calvary, which has broken down the walls of hostility between peoples and nations.

† God of the nations, we pray for the day when your kingdom of peace and justice will come on earth as in heaven. May the nations find peace and the peoples find prosperity through Jesus Christ your Son. Amen

Jules Gomes

Micah

Micah 5:1-15

The God of small things

But as for you, Bethlehem Ephrathah, too little to be among the clans of Judah, from you One will go forth for me to be ruler in Israel.

(part of verse 2)

Kings had a bad reputation, so here Micah uses a more general Hebrew word for 'ruler', rather than 'king'. Like the other great prophets, Micah turns power on its head. Micah's God is the God of small things. When God is about to do something earth shaking, he summons someone small and powerless from an obscure place to accomplish his purposes. The promised ruler is from a small town called Bethlehem, also known as Ephrathah.

Both names make a double connection with David, Israel's best-known shepherd-king. David was a man after God's own heart, yet he, too, fell prey to the corrupting influence of power. But Micah does not lose heart or hope. He prophesies a new shepherd-king who will be 'peace' (verse 5).

The wise men of Matthew's Gospel, confronted by the power-crazy King Herod, quote Micah's prophecy to explain where the Messiah will be born. The new-born king Jesus will be forced to flee from Herod the tyrant. He will stand before Pilate, the powerful procurator, where 'with a rod they will smite the judge of Israel on the cheek' (verse 1). But the God of small things is also a God of great surprises who through the shepherd-king Jesus will turn the world upside down.

† Faithful God, we thank you for keeping your promise to Micah and sending us the Prince of Peace to be born in Bethlehem, the city of David. As we await his return as King of kings and Lord of lords we pray that you will watch over our rulers and keep them from the corruption of power.

October

Micah

Jules Gomes

Micah 6:1-5

Historical amnesia is a terminal illness

Indeed, I brought you up from the land of Egypt and ransomed you from the house of slavery.

(part of verse 4

Israel has failed because Israel has forgotten. She is now in the dock facing a lawsuit from Yahweh, who indicts her for breaking the covenant and summons the mountains and hills as his witnesses. Creation remembers Yahweh's mighty acts. But Israel has forgotten. A people who forget their past cannot hope for a future. Those who cannot remember the past are condemned to repeat it.

Once, the Israelites were slaves themselves. They are always to remember who they were so that they will never treat the less fortunate as slaves. But, tragically, Israel has forgotten. Oppression of the poor is rife in the land. It seems as if the only thing Israel has learned from history is that she has learned nothing from history. That is why God called prophets like Micah not only to foretell the future but to retell the past and remind God's people of their history.

Yahweh laments our forgetfulness. He saved Israel through the Exodus. How did she repay him? He has saved us from the slavery of sin through the new exodus of the death and resurrection of Christ. How do we repay him?

† God of the past and God of the future, we repent of our forgetfulness and our ingratitude, the way we treat those less fortunate, and our complicity with unjust structures that enslave others. Help us to read your word daily and to remember your saving acts in the history of salvation and your gracious acts in our own lives. Grant that we may never forget you, for you are the God who will never forget us. Amen

Jules Gomes

Micah

The God who cannot be bribed

The Israelites have perverted justice and auctioned it to the highest bidder. After a stinging reproach from Yahweh (verses 1-5), they now ask, 'Is it possible to buy God's favour and to grease his palm with ten thousand rivers of oil? Or burnt offerings? Or even one's firstborn child?' (verses 6-7). But exaggerated ritual, when justice is lacking, only serves to expose the nakedness of the worshipper who thinks he is dressed in his best. The Israelites are willing to offer the most comprehensive sacrifices, but are unwilling to comprehend the essence of true faith. Micah's answer boomerangs against them.

> He has told you, O man, what is good, and what does the LORD require of you but to do justice, to love kindness, and to walk humbly with your God?

(verse 8)

Justice for the Israelites meant fidelity to the demands of a covenant relationship. When people live in a right relationship with God and with one another, the life of the community is maintained in vigour and well-being and the needy and defenceless are cared for.

Loving-kindness is loyalty in the form of solidarity with those on the fringes of society. Humility is the antithesis of pride, which is sin in its most stubborn form. To walk humbly with God is to live in communion with him. Faith cannot dwell where a proud self-reliance seeks to usurp the place of God.

---

† Holy God, we repent if our majestic church buildings, our carefully constructed liturgies, our brilliantly written books, our attendance at conferences and our participation in our own Christian subcultures have isolated us from the widow, the orphan and the stranger. Help us to do justice, to love mercy and to walk humbly with you, our God. Amen

October

Micah

Jules Gomes

291

Micah 7:1-13

The rock of hope in a swamp of despair

But as for me, I will watch expectantly for the LORD; I will wait for the God of my salvation. My God will hear me.

(verse 7)

Micah's analysis of his society is astute. It is a cesspool of corruption, a culture of deceit and denial. Something is rotten in the state of Israel. The officials and judges demand bribes. Friends and family can no longer be trusted. Micah mourns the plight of his people. His heart is broken because God's heart is broken. But he does not wallow in despair. Despite the collapse and chaos around him he knows there is one who is faithful and unchanging.

But to arrive at the rock of hope, the prophet has to swim against the tide through the waters of lament and complaint, acceptance and praise. There is no shortcut from the swamp of despair to the rock of hope. That is why lament and praise must both be held together in the life of prayer. Unless believers plumb the depths of lament, they will never ascend to the mountain tops of praise. There is no shortcut to a quick-fix solution. The word 'watch' is paired with the word 'wait'. But it is not a waiting of resignation but a waiting of expectation. God, who has been our help in ages past, will be our hope for years to come.

† Loving God, we join Micah in lamenting the collapse of moral values in our own societies. Raise up prophets who will speak truth to power and pastors who will speak the truth with love. Grant us the patience to watch and wait, and lift us out of the swamp of despair onto the rock of hope. We pray this through Christ our Lord. Amen

October

Jules Gomes

Micah

God's faithfulness versus human fickleness

You will show faithfulness to Jacob and unswerving loyalty to Abraham, as you have sworn to our ancestors from the days of old.

(verse 20)

The only thing certain in life is the uncertainty of everything. Life is often one dizzying merry-go-round of uncertainty. This is because human beings are fickle and feeble. Politicians renege on their promises. God's chosen people fall prey to apostasy. But God's last word is not exile, punishment and abandonment of his people. The good news from Micah is that the faithfulness of God is immensely greater than the fickleness of humanity. Believers can surely say 'Amen' to that.

Indeed, the very word 'Amen', which means 'surely', is derived from the word 'emunah' which means 'faithful, dependable, or trustworthy'. In Hebrew, this word and its cognates are frequently used to describe the faithfulness of God. Micah affirms that God is faithful because God is merciful. But God is also faithful because God is forgetful! He does not remember our sins when we confess them.

It was Corrie ten Boom who said, 'God takes our sins and buries them in the deepest sea and puts up a notice saying – No Fishing Here.' One thing God does not forget is his promises. And all his promises are 'Yes' and 'Amen' to us in Christ Jesus his Son.

† God, you who answer prayer and keep your promise, we thank you for your faithfulness despite our fickleness. Keep us ever mindful of your promises and keep us faithful to you. Pardon our sins and forgive our transgressions. Heal our guilt and help us to forgive those who have sinned against us, through Jesus Christ our Lord. Amen

October

Micah

Jules Gomes

293

Reconciliation

1   Be reconciled to one another

Notes based on the *New International Version* by
Martin Hayward

Martin Hayward works within the Centre for Reconciliation at Coventry Cathedral and also ministers to the parish of St Francis of Assisi in the north of the city.

Sunday 17 October: Preparing for the week

The death of Jesus lies at the very centre of the Christian gospel as God's plan for reconciling sinful men and women to himself. His cross was made of two beams: one (the longer) firmly planted in the ground and pointing skywards as if to draw heaven and earth together. The second beam held Jesus' arms in a wide-open gesture that gathered people to himself. The vertical beam reminds us that the first commandment is to love God, whilst the second is to love each other: vertical reconciliation and horizontal reconciliation.

Jesus was let down and isolated by his disciples, friends, and the whole crowd who had welcomed him with palms and shouts just a few days earlier. But the one gesture of help he did receive was when Simon from Cyrene was forced to carry the cross beam for him. Vertical reconciliation with God was achieved for us by Jesus alone; horizontal reconciliation between men and women requires our involvement and co-operation.

Text for the week: *Luke 15:32*

'We had to celebrate and be glad, because this brother of yours was dead and is alive again; he was lost and is found.'

For group discussion and personal thought

- Is there an individual or group with whom you – or someone you know – need to be reconciled? How can you start the process, or help your friend to do so?

Reconciliation is a risky business

In every situation where communication has broken down one party has to take the initiative to break the deadlock and the other has to trust the integrity of the approach. Christianity declares that God has taken the initiative in Jesus Christ to deliver us from our sin. This is the main theme of the Bible. But we still have to take the risk of believing and following, of trusting God's purposes and obeying his commands with the help of his Spirit.

And so it is with human relationships. As we read the story of Jacob and Esau the thudding of their hearts can still be heard down through the centuries as they risked trusting each other again. Jacob dared to take the initiative and thereby risked not only his own life but those of his children and family too. Esau must have wondered if his brother was playing another trick and was trying to outwit him once again as he had when they were young men still living in their father Isaac's home.

But Esau ran to meet Jacob and embraced him; he threw his arms around his neck and kissed him. And they wept.

(verse 4)

Both men took a chance and risked everything for the sake of renewed brotherly relationships. And each one of us is called to do no less than that for the sake of the gospel.

† Lord, please give me courage to take the first step in reconciliation and to trust others when they reach out to me.

October

Reconciliation   Martin Hayward

Genesis 45:1-15

Learning the lessons of the past

For every dispute that leads to a breakdown in relationships there are three sides to the story: 'My side', 'Your side' and 'God's side'. Joseph's brothers were only too aware of the jealousy and malice that had led them to sell him into slavery for just 20 shekels of silver. For his part, Governor Joseph had every cause to look back over his younger life with mixed and bitter feelings. And yet, by the end of the story, he recognised that God intended it for good and would use the events of the past to save many lives.

'[D]o not be distressed and do not be angry with yourselves for selling me here, because it was to save lives that God sent me ahead of you.'

(verse 5)

Distorting the truth and rewriting history can only perpetuate animosity; facing up to the lessons of the past enables God to use all our experiences for good. If we human beings are to be reconciled to each other, then first we have to agree upon the events of the past and then leave them at the foot of the cross.

† Father, please forgive me for the sins of the past as I forgive those who once sinned against me.

Martin Hayward

Reconciliation

The great secret

Christians are instructed to love their neighbours, but not necessarily to like them! In such cases actions can speak louder than words. Abishai was all for killing Saul while they had the chance but, instead of murder, David took the opportunity to demonstrate his peaceful intentions, leading Saul to admit that his behaviour had been both unwise and ungodly.

C S Lewis summed it up perfectly: 'Do not waste your time bothering whether you "love" your neighbour; act as if you did. As soon as we do this we find one of the great secrets. When you are behaving as if you loved someone, you will presently come to love him. If you injure someone you dislike, you will find yourself disliking him more. If you do him a good turn, you will find yourself disliking him less' (*Mere Christianity*, ch. 9).

> *Then Saul said, 'I have sinned. Come back, David my son. Because you considered my life precious today, I will not try to harm you again. Surely I have acted like a fool and have erred greatly.'*

(verse 21)

Our enemies are not those who hate us but those whom we hate. Practical Christianity, love in action, is the first step to reconciliation.

---

† Lord, give me grace to be kind to someone this day not because I want to but because you want me to.

October

Reconciliation   Martin Hayward

Thursday 21 October

Psalm 85:8-13

Let them not return to folly

The psalmist reminds us that God will answer our prayers for a right relationship and peace with him but only if we stay away from trouble in the future. Reconciliation with God follows our repentance, and repentance follows confession. The Anglican *Book of Common Prayer* use a powerful prayer that includes the words: 'We have left undone those things which we ought to have done; and we have done those things which we ought not to have done; and there is no health in us.' It's significant that the prayer starts with our confession of those things by which we grieve God when we *omit* to do his will (for instance, *not* loving our brothers and sisters – which amounts to murder in God's eyes), before going on to those things that we *commit* (such as stealing, lying and swearing). Reconciliation with God only flows from active attitudes; for a healthy relationship with him we must practise being 'doers' rather than 'do-not-ers'.

[H]e promises peace to his people, his saints –
But let them not return to folly.

(part of verse 8)

---

† Lord, help me not to repeat the failures of the past but to be active in seeking your peace and reconciliation.

Martin Hayward   Reconciliation

Luke 19:1-10

Recompense not retribution

Dear Zacchaeus; he has gone down in history as one of the most eager and sincere converts of all time largely because he promised not only to give half of his possessions to the poor but that 'if I have cheated anybody out of anything, I will pay back four times the amount' (verse 8).

Jesus said to him, 'Today salvation has come to this house, because this man, too, is a son of Abraham.'

(verse 9)

'That old law about an eye for an eye leaves everybody blind', said Martin Luther King. He saw that law was designed as punishment; the victim remained uncompensated and the perpetrator was reduced to the same level as the person he or she had wronged. Christ's way is to restore wrongdoers by getting them to raise the victims back to the level they were at before they were wronged. Both sinner and sinned-against move forwards - hopefully together.

We can never turn back clocks or undo the past but we can compensate those we have wronged at our own expense: perhaps at the cost of our pride, our time, our energy and our love. Jesus declared Zacchaeus a 'true Jew', a son of Abraham, not because of his heritage but because of the way he treated those he had wronged. Recompense rather than retribution is the pathway to restored relationships.

† Father, may no one suffer loss because of my sin but may we walk together on the pathway towards life with you.

October

Reconciliation

Martin Hayward

True reconciliation

The parable of the lost son is about a young man who wastes his inheritance on wine, women and partying. Jesus told the story because he wanted to make a point about our relationship with our heavenly Father, but maybe the tale also has something to say about the broken and bitter relationship between the fictional brothers.

Clearly the older brother feels jealous and cheated; but if this was real life I wonder if his jealousy would be just confined to the clothes and the fatted calf? Could it be that he was secretly jealous of the 'good time' his brother had enjoyed on wild living until the money ran out? Perhaps he seemed to be disapproving because he's trying to hide his true feelings – even from his own self-righteous self?

'My son,' the father said, 'you are always with me, and everything I have is yours. But we had to celebrate and be glad, because this brother of yours was dead and is alive again; he was lost and is found.'

(verses 31-32)

Christians are often caricatured by others as being straitlaced and humourless, condemning rather than affirming. Could that be because we are constantly looking over our shoulders at the temptations that the world has to offer rather than keeping our gaze on Jesus? 'Joy does not simply happen to us. We have to choose joy and keep choosing it every day' (Henri Nouwen). True reconciliation with God, the knowledge that nothing – not even death – can separate us from him, is our one bottomless source of joy.

† Lord, please help me to keep my focus on you today and to rejoice in the relationship between us that Jesus earned for me on the cross at Calvary.

Martin Hayward

Reconciliation

Reconciliation

2 Called to be reconcilers

Notes based on the *New International Version* by
Gillian Kingston

Gillian Kingston is a Methodist Local Preacher, living in Shinrone, Co. Offaly, Ireland. For many years she has been involved in inter-church activity in Ireland, Britain and further afield. She is Director of the annual Glenstal Ecumenical Conference and a member of the chaplaincy team at University College, Dublin. She and Tom have three sons, three daughters-in-law, a daughter and a beautiful granddaughter.

Sunday 24 October: Preparing for the week

'Reconciliation' is one of the current 'buzz' words in Christian and other discourse. This is both helpful and unhelpful: helpful because individuals, society and the world at large need nothing quite as much as reconciliation in so many areas of relationship; unhelpful because, by using the term so much, we can be in danger of inoculating ourselves against its uncomfortable challenge. Let's be open to these readings and what they demand of us in our individual and community lives.

Text for the week: *2 Corinthians 5:20*

We are therefore Christ's ambassadors, as though God were making his appeal through us.

For group discussion and personal thought

• Where does reconciliation personally challenge you: in a person, a situation, or a group of people?

• Think of a situation where reconciliation is needed. How might you (singular or plural) try to bring this about? What is *your* ministry of reconciliation?

• God in Christ, reconciling the world to himself – just what *does* this mean?

October

2 Corinthians 5:16-21

A royal commission

This is a very special text for me. As Chair of the Program(me) Planning Committee, I was responsible for the organisation and running of the World Methodist Conference in Seoul, South Korea, in July 2006. It was from this text that the committee chose the theme of that conference, 'God, in Christ, reconciling'. There was much to be reconciled, in Korea as a country and among those attending the event – language, culture, history, race, gender, church issues, you name it! Yet, in spite of the difficulties, I really have only the most positive and grateful memories of the whole experience. In Korea, I met people from so many countries, such differing life circumstances, so many languages and cultures, yet all rejoicing in one Lord and Saviour and seeking to proclaim the gospel.

All this is from God, who reconciled us to himself through Christ and gave us the ministry of reconciliation.

(verse 18)

As Christians, we have each received a commission from the king. We are all his ambassadors in his world, bringing his message of love and reconciliation to those among whom we live and move and have our being. He has charged each of us with both a ministry and a message – that of reconciliation, of being one in Jesus Christ, despite the issues and circumstances that would otherwise divide us.

† God and Saviour of us all, give us grace to overcome that which divides us and enable us together to proclaim your message of reconciliation.

October

Gillian Kingston

Reconciliation

Matthew 5:21-26

Taking the initiative

Oh dear, this is a difficult one! We are challenged to take the first step and it's towards someone close to us and that alone is problematic. Little is more difficult than effecting reconciliation with those who are closest to us. The English poet, George Gordon, Lord Byron, once wrote, 'They have most power to hurt us, whom we love. / We lay our sleeping heads within their hands.'

If you are offering your gift at the altar and there remember that your brother has something against you, leave your gift there in front of the altar. First go and be reconciled to your brother; then come and offer your gift.

(verses 23-24)

This requires the utmost grace.

Perhaps Jesus had his own family in mind – it is clear that they didn't always understand him and his mission (look at Mark 3:21 and John 7:5, even Luke 4:14-30). It is clear too that Jesus saw his ultimate family as being those who did the will of God (Mark 3:31-35). Our families, our colleagues at work, those we have most to do with day by day are the very people, who, because they are closest to us, are the most difficult to forgive. We have to live with the consequences of whatever has happened – and mightn't it happen again? There are consequences to forgiveness – mightn't we be seen as weak? This is precisely where the challenge lies – are we *strong* enough to forgive?

† Loving Father, we are your children – help us truly to be brothers and sisters to each other.

Reconciliation

Gillian Kingston

A new relationship

Doesn't life throw up interesting challenges! And never more so than when we are required, one way or another, to enter into a new sort of relationship with someone we've known for a long time. Sometimes this is wonderful – like falling in love with the boy next door – you've known him for *ages*, and then something happens and it's all red roses and stars! But sometimes it's not so easy: it takes all we've got and a bit more. This is where God comes into the picture.

[You] have him back . . . no longer as a slave, but better than a slave, as a dear brother . . . even dearer to you, both as a man and as a brother in the Lord.

(part of verses 15-16)

Onesimus had run away and somehow he met Paul – and Jesus Christ. Paul knows that the proper thing to do is to return him to his master, Philemon – and yet . . . and yet . . .

However, Philemon and Paul are friends and Paul knows that, with the help of God, Philemon will be able take Onesimus back, even though he may, just may, be guilty of theft (verses 18-19). Onesimus is a new person in Jesus Christ and so everything is new, even the relationship between master and servant. They are now brothers in Jesus Christ. This is reconciliation of a very special and hard-won kind.

† Enabling God, help us with new and challenging relationships; may we see others as you see them.

Gillian Kingston

Reconciliation

Ephesians 2:11-22

Being built together

There is a beautiful house in Charleston, South Carolina, which has been rendered almost ugly by a wall built up the centre, dividing it in two. It had belonged to two brothers who disliked each other so much that they built this dividing wall so that neither need see nor have anything to do with the other.

[I]n him you too are being built together to become a dwelling in which God lives by his Spirit.

(verse 22)

The writer of the letter to the Ephesians, Paul or one of his disciples, uses the metaphor of a wall in two ways here. Walls divide and walls build up. A wall can keep people apart – walls have done this in Israel/Palestine, in Belfast, and, in former times, in China, England and many other places. Walls create 'us' and 'them' – those on one side and those on the other. But, suggests the writer, if we are both on the same side, then we can be built into something positive, a temple, a dwelling. It is in Christ that the barrier, the dividing wall of hostility (verse 14) can be pulled down; and in him too the temple, the dwelling place of God, can be built up. And, as Peter pointed out, *we* are the stones, the living stones (1 Peter 2:5) out of which such things may be built.

† Lord, we know that there is a time to tear down and a time to build – give us the courage to act at the right time.

Reconciliation   Gillian Kingston

Romans 14:7-19

Give over – for God's sake!

I wouldn't do things the way *she* does them – look at the mess she is in now! Just *who* does he think he is, behaving like that! What *I* do is *my* business and if you don't like it, too bad – keep away!

> *[N]one of us lives to himself alone and none of us dies to himself alone.*

(verse 7)

The community in Rome is obviously having problems of behaviour and attitude – some are judging others and some think they can behave any way they like regardless of how others may be affected, directly or indirectly. And aren't we rather like that too on occasions?

Paul is absolutely right – when we are part of a community, we can't live as if we are individuals in watertight capsules! The English poet, John Donne, put it this way, 'No man is an island, entire of itself. Every man is a piece of the continent, a part of the main.' So we need to be very careful how we regard each other, how we judge each other, how we act. It is tricky, because sometimes it is necessary to challenge someone's behaviour – other people may be hurt if we don't – and some people will act outrageously just as long as we let them! Living in community is about the reconciliation of rights and responsibilities – for God's sake!

---

† Caring God, grant us the gift of discernment in our relationships with others – when to speak and when to be silent, when to act and when not.

Gillian Kingston

Reconciliation

Reconciled by Christ

Recently there was media coverage of an unseemly brawl in the Church of the Holy Sepulchre in Jerusalem. Police had to intervene to separate the parties concerned. This was particularly sad because those concerned were Christians of different traditions. Both sides had a position, one way or another, that they could not concede to the other. Reconciliation, even in the name of Christ, seemed impossible.

God was pleased to have all his fullness dwell in him, and through him to reconcile to himself all things, whether things on earth or things in heaven, by making peace through his blood, shed on the cross.

(verses 19-20)

In Christ all things are possible – this is the message of today's text. In him, *all* things can be reconciled, whether on earth or in heaven. Paul affirms in the strongest possible terms the supremacy of Christ, the one sent by God to bring about that reconciliation. This was his mission and message, his work and his word, salvation and gospel. But look at the first verses of the reading too – we each have a responsibility to pray for each other in the Christian life, that we may be faithful to that mission and that message. Being reconciled to each other in God is a visible sign to the world of Christ's reconciling power. It shows forth the gospel.

† Loving God, keep us faithful in prayer for each other, and signs of your reconciling love in your world.

October

Reconciliation   Gillian Kingston

Women of the New Testament

1 Women disciples

Notes based on the *New International Version* by
Anne Roberts

Anne's previous life was divided between teaching – geography and religious studies – and church administration and teaching. Now almost retired, she works in college administration for part of the year and is a freelance writer, and preaches, and edits the magazine for her local church.

Sunday 31 October: Preparing for the week

Mary was called to offer her life in the service of God, Mary Magdalene became a close disciple, Martha realised what the men did not, and the woman of Samaria was told that Jesus was Messiah. A gentile woman received the blessings of the covenant and a woman who showed extravagant love was promised a place in history. Such examples reveal that Jesus was far ahead of his time in his attitude towards women. Part of his redemptive work was to restore them to their place in God's creation plan, to work alongside men in their stewardship of that creation. In these passages we come very close to the heart of Jesus.

Text for the week: *Mark 14:6-8*

'Leave her alone,' Jesus said. 'Why are you bothering her? She has done a beautiful thing to me. The poor you will always have with you, and you can help them any time you want. But you will not always have me. She did what she could.'

For group discussion and personal thought

- Do you work hard to understand who Jesus is and what he is willing to do in your life? What else could you do?
- Will you follow him at all costs?
- How have you shown or been shown extravagant love?

A woman blessed

Mary counts herself among those who need a saviour, those who are hungry and those who are at the lower end of the social scale. At the same time she is quietly self-assured, with an assurance firmly rooted in the goodness and mercy of God. In today's parlance, she knows she is 'worth it'.

'I am the Lord's servant . . . May it be to me as you have said' . . .
'From now on all generations shall call me blessed, for the Mighty One has done great things for me.'

(part of verses 38, 48 and 49)

Humility is not a popular virtue, being equated with allowing oneself to be trodden on and left at the bottom of the heap. It does not feature in many CVs! If a woman wants to succeed in today's world and take advantage of our equal opportunities culture, she must promote herself. This seems the opposite of humility. Yet Mary's story shows us that this is not the case. Without boasting, attributing all that she is and is to become to the mercy of God, she nevertheless feels able to accept the immense responsibility he is placing on her shoulders. She is confident that future generations will acknowledge her blessedness.

Humbly acknowledging that all we are, have and are to become is from God, women today can also offer themselves in the service of the world he came to save and know that he will be pleased – as he was with Mary.

---

† Women and men, we offer to you, Lord, all we have, are and are to become. May we be blessed, as Mary was, in believing what you have promised.

Women of the New Testament

Anne Roberts

Luke 8:1-3; 24:1-11

A woman transformed

Jesus travelled about . . . The Twelve were with him, and also some women who had been cured of evil spirits and diseases: Mary (called Magdalene) from whom seven demons had come out.

(part of verse 1, and verse 2)

We know nothing of the invasion of Mary's personality by seven demons. Dabbling in the occult was common in first-century Palestine. Perhaps she had wanted something more exciting than synagogue Judaism, even the power to heal that some of the possessed seemed to have. The reality of possession was nightmare – loneliness, perplexity, fear, and rejection by the community.

Luke tells us that the casting out of demons was a routine part of Jesus' ministry and one sabbath he cast an evil spirit out of a man at the synagogue in Capernaum. Magdala is five miles from Capernaum along the lake shore and perhaps Mary was one of those present that evening when he healed many and cast out demons. Along with several other women who had been healed or delivered, she became a part of Jesus' team, which was never exclusively male. The women's testimony and the respect shown them by Jesus would convince many other women that in Jesus' company there was room for all who wanted to be set free from the power of evil – gender was not an issue. Mary was sure enough of this to stay close to Jesus in his death and burial and so became a witness to the resurrection. We are invited to walk the same road.

† Lord, give me a humble heart to know my need of you, a faithful heart to stay with you to the end and to share your resurrection. Amen

Anne Roberts   Women of the New Testament

A woman affirmed

'Lord,' Martha said to Jesus, 'if you had been here, my brother would not have died. But I know that even now God will give you whatever you ask . . . I believe that you are the Christ, the Son of God, who was to come into the world.'

(verses 21-22, and part of verse 27)

Luke 10:39 portrays Martha as a woman of action and her sister as the woman who sits listening. True to her nature, Martha goes out to meet Jesus and to say what she feels needs to be said!

If Jesus seems to show a preference for Mary's nature over Martha's in Luke's story, this is certainly not the case here. Jesus seems to be leading Martha on, encouraging her to take a step forward in her understanding of who he is and what he can do. He first draws out of her her faith in the resurrection at the last day. He then makes the stupendous claim that he himself is the one in and through whom that resurrection will occur. In fact, those who believe in him can already experience that resurrection.

In asking her if she believes this, Jesus shows how important to him are the women of his acquaintance. They have intelligence and integrity and hearts that long for the true knowledge of God and he willingly shares it with them. Martha reveals that her understanding is equal to that of the apostle Peter, who made a similar confession at Caesarea Philippi.

† Lord, we acknowledge that you are our life. Draw us along in faith in your resurrection as we confess you as Lord.

Women of the New Testament

Anne Roberts

Thursday 4 November

John 4:1-30

A woman accepted

Only an outcast would come alone to draw water in the heat of the day. But Jesus had no problems with outcasts, including those who were women ('Come to me *all* you who are weary and burdened, and I will give you rest', Matthew 11:28). Yet when he tried to speak with her about her situation she opted for theology instead. How like us – looking for an easy answer, a justification, a prop for our self-esteem when we are offered wholeness.

Divorce was a one-way street in those days and this woman had been cast out by five husbands. It is easy to assume that she deserved it, but it is equally likely that she did not. Why would one man after another take her on if she was just a heap of trouble? But her reputation was decided by the society in which she lived and no one would sign a marriage contract with her now, so she had moved in with someone who would at least put a roof over her head.

Jesus knew all this and loved her, but he didn't force her into a confession. She wanted to merge into the background, to claim membership of the people for whom Messiah would come. So Jesus let her and declared himself her Saviour. He will do this for any of us, no matter how much we keep running for cover.

> *Jesus answered . . . 'the water I give . . . will become . . . a spring of water welling up to eternal life.' The woman said to him, 'Sir, give me this water.'*

(part of verses 13-15)

† Help me to trust you, Lord Jesus, with the truth about myself and to know you love me.

Anne Roberts   Women of the New Testament

Audacious faith

'First let the children eat all they want . . . for it is not right to take the children's bread and toss it to their dogs.'

(part of verse 27)

The woman of Syrian Phoenicia knew where she stood – outside the covenant God had made with Israel. She may have worshipped other gods but she had heard of Jesus' reputation and power and came to him with her need, claiming her share of blessing but not knowing if he would help her. Jesus' first words could have dashed any hopes she had, but she persisted – in faith and her faith was honoured; her child was delivered.

The lesson for us is one of humility. God owes us nothing. Those who took for granted their place within the covenant were soundly rebuked by Jesus. Whoever they were, they needed to acknowledge their utter dependence upon the mercy of God, or they would find themselves banished. And if those outside the covenant would acknowledge their need of the mercy of the God of Israel they could receive its blessings. The Syrian Phoenician woman was a forerunner of those gentiles who would eventually be included in the covenant through the atoning work of Jesus. Accounts such as this would settle arguments in the Early Church as to whether or not the gospel was in fact for gentiles.

So why did Jesus give this harsh answer? There were others – Jews – listening, perhaps with bated breath. In his answer Jesus stayed within the covenant but by his action clearly demonstrated that its benefits were open to all.

† Father, we come with that woman and acknowledge our need, with confidence in your mercy and our inclusion in your blessings.

Women of the New Testament

Anne Roberts

Extravagant love

While he was in Bethany, reclining at the table in the home of a man known as Simon the Leper, a woman came with an alabaster jar of very expensive perfume, made of pure nard. She broke the jar and poured the perfume on his head.

(verse 3)

What this unnamed woman did for Jesus is summed up in his own words as 'something beautiful' and has come down in history, as Jesus said it would, as an example to all those who want to honour him. We honour him by showing extravagant love, both to him and to the Father and in the way we live and act towards others. This does not come easily to mere mortals, but it is to be our aim as the Holy Spirit produces the fruit of love in our lives.

According to Matthew, those present were Jesus' disciples, but we need not suppose that their suggestion that the perfume could have been sold and the money given to the poor was out of an overflow of love for the poor. No – it was the Feast of Passover and the gift to the poor was an obligation of that feast. The woman's impetuosity was commended by Jesus because it indicated a heart that reflected the heart of the Father. All ceremonials, rituals and obligations outlined in scripture are pictures and reminders of the way we ought to live. If they become ends in themselves and we are satisfied once they have been carried out, we have missed the point. 'Love (and only love) is the fulfilment of the Law' (Romans 13:10).

† So fill us with your Spirit, Lord, that our lives may express your beauty.

Anne Roberts   Women of the New Testament

Women of the New Testament

2 Women in the Early Church

Notes based on the *New Jerusalem Bible* by
Joan Stott

Joan Stott is a Lay Preacher in the Uniting Church in Australia, and has
served the church and community in a variety of roles.

Sunday 7 November: Preparing for the week

Sharing in partnership in ministry and mission has been traditional since the
time of Jesus. Women's varying contributions to ministry and mission are
usually accepted, but not always valued or understood. In any era, culture
and tradition interpret differently the active involvement of women in the
Church; however, Jesus accepted and blessed women for their ministry to
him and his disciples.

Women were mostly not named in the Bible, but being named is a vital
part of recognising women's contribution to the kingdom. Partnerships in
ministry and mission are not dependent on location, status in the community,
gender, qualifications, or even equality in giving or receiving. The essential
ingredients are a common vision and purpose, and the commitment to
make it happen. Then, with the power and guidance of the Holy Spirit,
most obstacles become stepping stones in ministry. The 'Young Church'
was indeed blessed by God, as with 'one heart' they all joined in prayer.

Text for the week: *Acts 1:14*
With one heart all these joined constantly in prayer, together with some
women.

For group discussion and personal thought

- As the members of the 'Young Church' met united in prayer, what
  difference would the gift of the Holy Spirit have made to their combined
  worship?
- Jesus accepted the financial and physical support of women in his
  ministry, as did the members of the 'Young Church'. Why are those gifts
  acceptable, but limitations placed on other gifts offered by women?
- What is the difference between unity and equality?

November

Mary, the mother of Jesus

With one heart all these joined constantly in prayer, together with some women, including Mary the mother of Jesus, and with his brothers.

(verse 14)

Mary, the mother of Jesus, is only mentioned in Luke's Gospel when Jesus was at his most vulnerable: at his birth, being found in the Temple, at a stressful time in his ministry, and prior to his death when he arranged with his friend for her care. Mary often pondered on the events of her life, and recalled her Spirit-blessed pregnancy; Jesus' birth in crude surroundings that included many blessings, and some challenging, strange events; their journey into exile and return to Nazareth; Jesus becoming a carpenter like Joseph. She also recalled Jesus' ministry, and the way he redefined the meaning of family relationships, away from blood ties to the richer relationships of ties of the heart and spirit.

At the beginning of the Acts of the Apostles, they gathered together waiting for the gift of the indwelling Holy Spirit, which would be an especially personal gift to Mary from her son. Mary is mentioned as being one of Jesus' followers or disciples; however, her role as Jesus' mother gave her a unique position in history. Although the Apostle Peter exclaimed that 'God has no favourites' (Acts 10:34), Mary the mother of Jesus will always hold a special place in the hearts of believers.

The indwelling Spirit of God within us could be likened to a lifetime pregnancy, where each day we experience the life, movement and growth of God. We are all challenged to become pregnant with God throughout our lives, as we commit ourselves to being 'God-bearers'.

† God, help us all to be 'God-bearers' in your world. Amen

Joan Stott

Women of the New Testament

Acts 21:7-9

Four unnamed prophets

Many people are described as 'prophets'. The biblical expectations of 'prophets' were that they would be so blessed by God with spiritual insights that they could act as interpreters of God's will and purposes; or be advocates on God's behalf to bring about changes in attitudes and practices in society.

As was usual in biblical times, little is known of the family life of 'Philip the Evangelist', except that he had four daughters who were not married. Philip was one of the 'scattered' people who spread the gospel wherever he went, and led people to Christ through his personal witness and his evangelistic crusades. He was a deeply spiritual and yet practical man, and was appointed by the twelve apostles to be one of seven deacons responsible for the care of Hellenist widows in Jerusalem. Their job description required them to be men filled with the Spirit of God, and having wisdom.

Paul and his companions were on their way to Jerusalem, and visited Philip's home in Caesarea where he met Philip's four daughters, who were described as being 'prophets'.

[Philip] had four unmarried daughters who were prophets.

(verse 9)

These four women had shown extraordinary faithfulness and devotion to Jesus, causing even Paul to name them in an encouraging way in his greetings to the 'Young Church' leaders. With the cultural expectations of that time, four unmarried women would normally have had no status or influence, yet through their witness, they stood out as examples not only to women, but also to men. Are we limited in our ministry and service by others' expectations?

---

† God, help us all, regardless of expectation, to be faithful witnesses and interpreters of your love for all. Amen

November

Women of the New Testament

Joan Stott

Priscilla

When I visited Rome, I went to a site believed to be one of the original 'house churches' of the 'Young Church'. I experienced there an intense sense of connectedness to that 'house church', and a feeling of reverent awe, as if the very stones of that house and garden had soaked up the atmosphere and experiences of years of deep and sincere worship of God, so that the whole place had become permeated by the blessing and presence of God. The past and present became connected through the worship of God.

My greetings to Priscilla and Aquila, my fellow-workers in Christ Jesus.

(verse 3)

As partners in marriage and mission, Priscilla and Aquila not only offered home hospitality to Paul, but joined him as professional tent makers. They also travelled with him on his various missionary journeys. Priscilla overcame the cultural expectations of marriage relationships and the role of women, by being named by Paul as his 'co-worker'.

Wherever Priscilla and Aquila went, they invited people to join the 'church at their house' (Romans 16:5), which was dedicated to the worship of God. The believers came there to join in fellowship, to share their faith, to worship God, sing hymns, and celebrate the Lord's Supper. Paul thanks Priscilla and Aquila not only for himself but on behalf of 'all the churches among the gentiles' (Romans 16:4). The Greek words for 'church' has variously meant 'the called-out ones' or the 'gathered' ones who meet at a place 'dedicated to the Lord'. Later on, it also became known as a gathering of 'the Body of Christ', as described in Romans 12.

† God, help us to make our homes places dedicated to God's worship. Amen

Joan Stott

Women of the New Testament

Phoebe

The Apostle Paul recommended Phoebe to the church in Rome, calling her 'our sister', part of the wider family and community of faith, and he encouraged them to offer her all the help she required.

I commend to you our sister Phoebe . . . give her, in the Lord, a welcome worthy of God's holy people.

(part of verses 1-2)

It was an honour to be recommended by the Apostle Paul, but Phoebe's own life and actions spoke louder than any words of commendation.

Mrs Winifred Kiek was also a woman recommended by (British) church leaders to a faith community in another land. Winifred migrated to Australia with her husband in 1920, and later on was recommended as a suitable person to become ordained – becoming the first ordained woman in Australia. Winifred was born in Manchester, England, and raised as a Quaker, but married a minister in the Congregational/Independent Church. She and her husband moved to South Australia, where Winifred became the first woman to receive a Bachelor of Divinity degree from the Melbourne College of Divinity, and in 1929, she received a MA degree in philosophy at the University of Adelaide.

Winifred was a quietly spoken yet passionate woman, and throughout her ordained ministry she served in only two 'charges'. Her other great passion was for equality of opportunity for women in education and justice. She is especially remembered for her work in ecumenical circles within the Australian and World Council of Churches, where she served as a Liaison Officer for 'Women's Work'. The Winifred Kiek ecumenical scholarship was established to honour her name, vision and work, and it provides specialised training for Christian women from Asia and the Pacific.

† God, help us all to be worthy of recommendation as a follower of Jesus. Amen

November

Women of the New Testament

Joan Stott

2 Timothy 1:3-5

Lois and Eunice

Women are often required to do tasks for which they have no training. Parenting is one of those responsibilities that many women feel ill-prepared to carry out. Expert advice on parenting skills is available from books, videos, DVDs, TV and radio, but not everyone has access to those resources.

Women's education has always been one of my special interests. Whenever I visited developing countries during my regular world travels, I always sought opportunities to see firsthand the programmes designed especially for younger women. Usually, it was their mothers or the older women who taught the young women housekeeping skills, hygiene and health, and parenting skills. However, some young women chose not to learn these from their own mothers, because they did not want to repeat the mistakes they believed their mothers made.

In biblical times, learning skills from older women was also the way girls were taught. In Lois and Eunice, we have a great example of an older woman training a younger woman, but in this instance, it was matters of faith that were being taught. These lessons were then taught to Timothy, until he made his grandmother's and mother's faith his own. He then had a personal faith, rather than an inherited faith. As in Timothy's family, challenges abound where only one parent is a Christian. Lois and Eunice are often quoted as being fine guardians of the faith of the young Timothy, but Timothy would have had many faith and relationship issues to resolve.

I also remember your sincere faith, a faith which first dwelt in your grandmother Lois, and your mother Eunice.

(part of verse 5)

† God, help us all to take seriously the responsibility of teaching the faith to the next generation. Amen

Joan Stott   Women of the New Testament

The Lady

[M]y greetings to the Lady, the chosen one, and to her children, whom I love in truth . . . for so do all who have come to know the Truth.

(part of verse 1)

Do you like puzzles – struggling with issues until you reach a conclusion? Our reading for today could be seen as a puzzle.

• Is this letter written to a beloved woman and her family?

• Is it written to a church 'community of faith'?

• Does it matter to whom it is addressed?

Whether it is addressed to an individual or group, the comment about loving 'truth' is important. In one of Jesus' great 'I am' statements he said: 'I am the Way; I am Truth and Life' (John 14:6). Jesus the 'Truth' is the reality of 'God with us', and the full expression of God amongst us, showing us the way back to God.

John's second epistle challenges its readers to 'Watch yourselves' (verse 8), which is a reminder of how fragile we are in our journey of faith if we take our eyes off Jesus who is 'Truth' and 'Life' in all its fullness.

John also includes the words 'In our life of truth and love, we *shall* have grace, faithful love and peace from God the Father, and from Jesus Christ, the Son of the Father' (verse 3). These are promised gifts from God to the Church. If we ignore or belittle the role of women in the Church, are we acting differently to the way Jesus reacted to women, and to the gift of love and peace God gives the Church?

† God, help us all to be watchful as we live out our faith. Amen

Readings in Luke

8 Living in the kingdom

Notes based on the *New International Version* by
Elisa Gusmão

Born in Brazil, Elisa belonged to the Presbyterian and the Methodist
Churches, before moving to the UK with her Scottish husband in 1987.
From then on she has worked as a translator, while serving the United
Reformed Church as an elder and lay preacher. Between them, Eric and
Elisa have six grandchildren born in Switzerland, Canada, Mexico, and Brazil.

Sunday 14 November: Preparing for the week

The Gospel of Luke, a Greek physician, is the longest and most orderly
of the four Gospels. It presents Jesus to the world: the Son of Man is the
saviour of humankind, rich or poor, men, women and children. They are
all citizens of the kingdom. Luke emphasises Jesus' life of personal prayer
(Luke 5:16, 6:12, 9:18, 9:28-29) as well as corporate prayer (Luke 9:16;
22:17-19), giving special importance to the need for persistence in praying,
which is the focus of two parables. This week we are going to think about
the central place of Jesus Christ in our life, and examine passages that
teach us about life under his power, regarding human relations, prayer,
service and everything we possess.

Text for the week: *Luke 6:31*
'Do to others as you would have them do to you.'

For group discussion and personal thought

• What can you suggest that would improve the co-existence of different
racial groups in your country?

• What importance is given to prayer in your local church? In your life?

• In your personal experience, what have been the implications or
consequences of having 'seen the light'?

Luke 6:27-38

A world without conflict

'But I tell you who hear me: Love your enemies, do good to those who hate you, bless those who curse you, pray for those who ill-treat you. If someone strikes you on one cheek, turn him the other also. If someone takes your cloak, do not stop him from taking your tunic. Give to everyone who asks you, and if anyone takes what belongs to you, do not demand it back.'

(verses 27-30)

Today there is hardly a continent or island where there is not conflict and violent retaliation. These stem from centuries-old grudges and the deep hate that different populations have for each other, especially in occupied territories. The same happens on a smaller scale between classes, castes, institutions, families and individuals.

Nevertheless, 2000 years ago we were given a God-sent solution for all these problems in the person of Jesus, who lived all his teachings. Denying the old rule that said, 'Love your neighbour and hate your enemy', he inaugurated a life of fresh quality, energy and love, which is expressed in the Golden Rule: 'Do to others as you would have them do to you.' The Nazarene did not give us impossible rules to live by, but brought in a new spirit. 'Turning the other cheek', for example, means to be ready for further abuse, without the attitude of revenge that has kept the world at war. Why do we do as he told us? Simply to imitate God, the God of love he showed us, the God we believe in.

---

† Lord, may I be a channel of your peace, bringing your love where there is hatred, your pardon where there is injury, and your faith where there is doubt. Amen

Readings in Luke

Elisa Gusmão

Luke 6:39-49

Only one true master

Today's text brings us a series of imaginative pictures created by Jesus, in a traditional Jewish fashion, in order to teach. As happened sometimes in his preaching, they are pervaded with humour. First he tells us to be careful when choosing the master to follow, making sure he will not land us in the ditch. Then he gives us the story of the speck and the plank – a person who cannot see clearly cannot teach, let alone judge others. Here we can sense a warning against the dangers of false doctrines, or zealots who make a fuss about many petty things and forget about the very core of Christianity, which has to do with love and service. Faith in Jesus Christ brings a change of heart, and this shows in our deeds, just as good trees give good fruit. All these illustrations lead us to the main truth, which he then makes crystal clear: he is our teacher par excellence, the only way out of human disaster.

'Why do you call me, "Lord, Lord", and do not do what I say? I will show you what he is like who comes to me and hears my words and puts them into practice. He is like a man building a house, who dug deep and laid the foundation on rock. When a flood came, the torrent struck that house but could not shake it, because it was well built.'

(verses 46-48)

† Lord, help us not only to hear your word but to practise it, so that we may be grounded on you, our rock.

Elisa Gusmão

Readings in Luke

In contact with 'Abba'

Years ago, on Prince Charles's fiftieth birthday, the British Queen gave a reception for him at Buckingham Palace. There, in the presence of hundreds of guests and the media, he thanked her, saying, 'Thank you, Mum!' Everyone was touched by such a breach of protocol, a sign of intimacy between mother and son.

When the disciples asked Jesus to teach them how to pray, he began with the word 'Abba' – used by little children to their fathers in Palestine. By calling God 'Abba', Jesus inaugurated a previously unthinkable relationship of closeness with God, showing him – whose greatness is far beyond that of any earthly monarch – as our Father. A relationship we can understand, as it is part of our human experience.

There is no Christian life without prayer, but persistence in prayer is more difficult to learn. Jesus illustrated it with the story of the midnight visitor.

'I tell you, though he will not get up and give him the bread because he is his friend, yet because of the man's persistence he will get up and give him as much as he needs.'

(verse 8)

Our God is generous and willing to give. He doesn't mind being disturbed, nor will he be angry if we are shamelessly insistent.

'So I say to you: Ask and it will be given to you; seek and you will find; knock and the door will be open to you.'

(verse 9)

† O Lord my God, my only hope, hear me in your goodness; and do not let me stop seeking you when I am weary; but let me seek your presence ever more ardently.

(*Praying with Augustine*, translated by Paula Clifford , 1997)

November

Readings in Luke

Elisa Gusmão

Luke 11:29-36

Light of the world

My family has a house on top of a hill in the country. Years ago there was no electric light and I remember my father performing the daily ritual of lighting the gas lamp at dusk. In our world of electric light, we may forget the striking effect of a burning lamp in a dark room. In this passage once more, Jesus offers himself to a 'wicked generation' as the light that can illuminate their whole beings. But when Jesus' presence should be a sufficient sign, they ask for a miracle. Jonah proclaimed God's message to the gentile people of Nineveh – and they believed.

The heathen Queen of Sheba (modern Yemen) made a long journey to hear King Solomon's wisdom, which she fully acknowledged. These two Old Testament characters bring condemnation to Jesus' contemporaries, for they ignored his preaching (verse 32) and even when he came to life three days after being sacrificed, they were not convinced (Luke 16:31). It is by seeing the light in him, and letting it shine on us, that we become illuminated. For those who do this, splendid will be the day when he returns 'like lightning' (Luke 17:24).

'See to it, then, that the light within you is not darkness. Therefore, if your whole body is full of light, and no part of it dark, it will be completely lighted, as when the light of a lamp shines on you.'

(verses 35-36)

† Light of the minds that know you, Christ, be light to mine; may the light of your truth shine in my heart and my life.

Elisa Gusmão

Readings in Luke

Friday 19 November

Luke 12:35-53

Watchfulness

In August 2008 the whole world watched the sporting events of the Beijing Olympic Games. How well prepared the athletes were! Even their outfits had been carefully chosen to improve their performance. In Palestine, both sexes prepared for work by tucking their long robes into their belts.

'Be dressed ready for service and keep your lamps burning, like men waiting for their master to return from a wedding banquet, so that when he comes and knocks they can immediately open the door for him.'

(verses 35-36)

Jesus was engrossed in a battle with the powers of evil that would soon claim his life. If the disciples relaxed, they would be taken by surprise by terrible events. His illustrations of the servants, the house owner, and the manager, showed that serving the kingdom demands total dedication, and faults are punished with severity.

But was he also talking to us, his disciples two thousand years later? The answer to Peter's question in verse 41 is found in the Acts of the Apostles, also written by Luke: 'He said to them: "It is not for you to know the times or dates the Father has set by his own authority. But you will receive power when the Holy Spirit comes on you; and you will be my witnesses in Jerusalem, and in all Judea and Samaria, and to the ends of the earth"' (Acts 1:7-8).

† My Lord and my master, may the presence of the Spirit you sent us keep me prepared, serving you with dedication and faithfulness all my life.

November

Readings in Luke   Elisa Gusmão

Luke 18:18-30

Giving everything

'How hard it is for the rich to enter the kingdom of God! Indeed, it is easier for a camel to go through the eye of a needle than for a rich man to enter the kingdom of God.'

(part of verse 24, and verse 25)

Some scientists can only comprehend knowledge by excluding God. They cannot let God into their intellectual dominion, because science is their greatest passion and belief. The same can happen in other areas, like artists with their art, politicians and power, or the rich and their wealth. The rich ruler in today's reading could not serve God if this meant giving away his fortune. Possessions were what really mattered to him. He believed in acquiring things – including eternal life. He had kept the commandments as a negotiation with God, and now he wanted to know how much he still owed. But there is no hope of salvation through our own deeds; our only hope is in the divine way, that is, by grace.

Those who heard this asked, 'Who then can be saved?' Jesus replied, 'What is impossible with men is possible with God.'

(verses 26-27)

The rich man called Jesus *'Good* Master'; he had an idea of Jesus' sanctity, but did not recognise the overpowering presence he becomes in our lives. Christ touches the very core of our being, demanding our total surrender. We enter the kingdom by grace, but must be prepared to give him whatever he asks from us.

---

† Christ, may we no longer live for ourselves but for you and may we give ourselves as you give, so that we may be one with God, who became one with us to set us free.

Elisa Gusmão

Readings in Luke

Readings in Luke

9 Stories of the kingdom

Notes based on the *Contemporary English Version* by
Elizabeth Bruce Whitehorn

For Elizabeth's biography see p. 115.

Sunday 21 November: Preparing for the week

What does it mean to live as a Christian in today's world?
Jesus told many stories (parables) to help or challenge his hearers to think about how they could live under God's rule. God's kingdom (or 'new society' as some theologians have put it) is both a present reality and a hope for the future. The parables can help us to live consciously as members of this new society while also working to bring it about. Jesus based these stories on the everyday lives of his hearers. Even though the details of our lives may be very different, the stories can still speak to us today, turning the spotlight on our behaviour and challenging our priorities and underlying assumptions. You may feel that you know these stories very well. Do take time to read and reflect on them, asking God to speak to you through them in fresh ways. Then go and live out what you have discovered.

Text for the week: *Luke 10:28*

Jesus said, 'You have given the right answer. If you do this, you will have eternal life.'

For group discussion and personal thought

• What 'right answers' do you find in this week's readings and meditations? Plan how to put them into practice and then go and do so.

Monday 22 November
Luke 8:1-18

Open-handed love

A farmer went out to scatter seed in a field. While the farmer was doing it, some of the seeds fell along the road and were stepped on or eaten by birds.

(verse 5)

This farmer's sowing seems either careless or wasteful.
Could he afford to waste good seed?
Was he in such a hurry that he did not care about wastage?
Was he more concerned for the birds' welfare than his own?
Did he not care about the size and quality of the harvest?
God's giving is open-handed, generous, profligate even.
God's love is for all, giving everyone a chance, the benefit of the doubt.
What is my experience of God's open-handed love?
How do I live in the light of that experience?
Am I too concerned about results and returns for my efforts?
How do I balance wise stewardship and economy with open-hearted and open-handed generosity?
Do I miss enjoyment in the present because I am too concerned about the future?
Am I enthusiastic about God's kingdom?
How committed am I to bringing about God's new society?
Am I still growing and maturing in faith?

† Generous God, make me like the farmer – willing to sow freely and generously, with open hands, to make good use of what you have given me. Help me to live out my experience of you, to move beyond knowing the right answer so that I can grow in faith and extend your new society.

November

Elizabeth Bruce Whitehorn

Readings in Luke

Unexpected love

A man from Samaria . . . went over to [the man]. He treated his
wounds . . . and bandaged them. Then he put him on his own donkey
and took him to an inn, where he took care of him.

(parts of verses 33-34)

Did this Samaritan man not realise what dangers he might be exposing
himself to?
Perhaps this was a trap and the robbers were waiting to jump on him?
What if the victim died on him?
What if the innkeeper saw a good opportunity to boost his profits?
What if the victim and his family turned nasty later on?
How do I, a Christian, feel when I witness the loving actions of someone I
consider an outsider?
How easy is it to accept help from someone who is very different from
me?
What holds me back from expressing my love for God in compassionate
action?
What is my experience of God's unexpected love?
How do I live in the light of that experience?
How do I balance wise caution with loving charity and compassionate
service?
Who is my neighbour?
What kind of neighbour am I?

---

† Compassionate God, make me like the good Samaritan. Forgive me for passing by on
the other side, letting caution overcome charity, asking you to help someone when I am not
willing to do it myself. Help me to live out my experience of you, to move beyond knowing
the right answer so that I can put it into action for the sake of your new society.

November

Readings in Luke   Elizabeth Bruce Whitehorn

Generous love

[A rich man said to himself] 'You have stored up enough good things to last for years to come. Live it up! Eat, drink and enjoy yourself.'

(part of verse 19)

Knowing the end of the story, it's easy to criticise this 'rich fool'. I don't think like him – do I? I don't regard material possessions as purely for enjoyment and an easy life – do I? Whether I have a lot or a little, how important are material things to me? What other resources do I have (for example, family relationships, skills, time)? Do I value them and how do I use them?

What if the man had gone on to live for many years? Would he have learned to share his wealth? Or would his greed and selfishness have destroyed his ability to relate to others? If I had more, might I too fall victim to greed and selfishness?

The rich man died without warning. In what ways can I prepare to 'meet my Maker', starting now?

What is my experience of God's generous love? How do I live in the light of that experience? How do I balance wise provision for the future with being ready to die at any time?

---

† Challenging God, save me from being like this rich fool. Forgive me for attaching undue importance to material things. Replace my greed, selfishness and envy with delight in you. Help me to live out my experience of you, to move beyond knowing the right answer so that I can use the resources I have for the good of your new society.

Elizabeth Bruce Whitehorn

Readings in Luke

Uncompromising love

[T]he master became so angry that he said, 'Go as fast as you can to every street and alley in town! Bring in everyone who is poor or crippled or blind or lame . . . Not one of the guests I first invited will get even a bite of my food!'

(part of verse 21, and verse 24)

What role would I assign for myself in this story?
Perhaps Jesus' host, the Pharisee, listening to this story, assumed that he would be one of the guests invited to God's banquet.
Do I do the same?
But at the end the guests are all excluded without receiving so much as a crumb.
I don't want to find myself in that position,
yet how often do I refuse God's invitation or the Spirit's prompting?

Do I take God's love and patience for granted,
take advantage of God's mercy and willingness to forgive,
assume that God will wait for me rather than choose someone else?

Am I prepared to find myself alongside unlikely guests,
people I would naturally keep my distance from?
Am I prepared to find that others regard me as an unlikely guest?

What is my experience of God's uncompromising love?
How do I live in the light of that experience?
Am I putting off responding to God's invitation to do something now?
How do I balance wise reflection with prompt obedience?

† Merciful God, forgive me for making wrong assumptions about my own godliness, for making excuses and putting off what you want me to do. Help me live out experience of you, to move beyond knowing the right answer so that I can obey your promptings for the good of your new society.

November

Readings in Luke

Elizabeth Bruce Whitehorn

Luke 16:1-17

Practical love

The master praised his dishonest manager for looking out for himself so well. That's how it is! The people of this world look out for themselves better than the people who belong to the light.

(verse 8)

Why did Jesus tell this story and why did Luke record it?
Perhaps the focus is less on the manager's dishonesty and questionable methods than on his quick-wittedness and ingenuity.
He faces up to reality, the consequences of his behaviour.
He doesn't make excuses or protest his innocence
but takes steps to be ready for the crisis to come.
He makes provision for the future with the means at his disposal.
How do I measure up?

According to Matthew, Jesus told his disciples to be 'as wise as snakes and as innocent as doves'.
What is my attitude to money and how do I use it?
What do I think really important in life?
In a crisis, am I a practical person?

What potential crises in life could or should I be preparing for?
Is there a crisis of my own making that I need to face up to?
What is my experience of God's practical love?
How do I live in the light of that experience?
How do I balance being as wise as a snake with being as innocent as a dove?

---

† Down-to-earth God, forgive me for refusing to face reality and accept responsibility for my actions. Help me to live out my experience of you, to move beyond knowing the right answer so that I can take practical action for the sake of your new society.

November

Elizabeth Bruce Whitehorn

Readings in Luke

Unlimited love

[A] poor beggar named Lazarus was brought to the gate of the rich man's house. He was happy just to eat the scraps that fell from the rich man's table. His body was covered with sores.

(verse 20, and part of verse 21)

Did the rich man not notice the wretched state of the beggar at his gate? Did he not care?

Did he blame the man for bringing his troubles upon himself in some way?

Perhaps he thought he was being generous in letting the beggar have the scraps that fell from his table.

Was he afraid that helping the beggar would threaten his comfortable life?

Was the opportunity to help Lazarus God's way of inviting him to change, to join the new society?

Is my giving to others any better than the rich man's?

What wrong(s) do I tolerate or turn a blind eye to?

What should I question?

Am I prepared to have my standard of living questioned by God's love for others?

What is my experience of God's unlimited love?

How do I live in the light of that experience?

How do I balance wise concern for myself and my family with responding to others' needs?

† Inviting God, forgive me for being like this rich man: for turning a blind eye instead of acting, confusing generosity with giving what I don't need or want, limiting my love. Help me to live out my experience of you, to move beyond knowing the right answer so that I can be an active member of your new society, both here and now and for ever.

November

Readings in Luke

Elizabeth Bruce Whitehorn

Treasures of darkness

1 Are your wonders known in the darkness?

Notes based on the *New Revised Standard Version* by
Philip Wadham

Philip Wadham is a retired Anglican priest who has been extensively involved with the mission of the Church, working in Latin America and the Caribbean as well as England and Canada. As an executive officer with the Partnership Programme of the Anglican Church of Canada he travelled frequently to visit partner dioceses and churches. He and his wife currently live on Vancouver Island in western Canada.

Sunday 28 November (Advent Sunday): Preparing for the week

The title of this Advent theme comes from Isaiah 45:3, in which God promises to give 'his anointed, Cyrus' 'treasures of darkness and riches hidden in secret places, so that you may know that it is I, the Lord . . . who call you by your name.' This is an extraordinary, mysterious promise, rich with potential meanings. During the next four weeks we search out places in scripture where God is revealed in and through darkness. Jesus connected with his listeners by telling stories that drew on familiar incidents with which they could identify. In exploring the theme of darkness in this year's Advent season the stories are drawn from the present and from the writer's experiences. We live in a very different world but God's word, both written and expressed through our actions, still has the power to 'lighten our darkness'.

Text for the week: *Psalm 18:6,16*
In my distress I called upon the LORD . . . He drew me out of the mighty waters.

For group discussion and personal thought

- The question of human suffering and the will of God faces all religions. What are your thoughts about this?
- How are people with disability cared for in your community? You might start your thinking by asking someone who has a disability.

November

Together we can

The doctor had told Ian, 'You are suffering from clinical depression. I'll prescribe something that will help but it won't entirely cure you.' Ian knew the truth of this: all week, even on medication, his days had been a struggle. And now, on Friday night, he prayed for a restful, peace-filled sleep.

O LORD, God of my salvation,
when, at night, I cry out in your presence,
let my prayer come before you;
incline your ear to my cry.
For my soul is full of troubles

(verses 1-2, and part of verse 3)

An answer, of sorts, came. On the Saturday morning Ian joined a small group of people who faced struggles similar to his. He had resisted joining the group for some time, believing that sharing one's feelings with others similarly troubled could only make things worse. To his surprise, as he listened to their stories he began to feel some comfort. He described it to his doctor afterwards, 'It was as though we had a common bond. I realised that I am no longer alone; others face the same demon as me. As we all face this demon of depression, together we find some strength. We are like a presence of hope to each other, not that we will be cured but that we won't allow the sickness we face to overwhelm us. When it's particularly bad I have someone I can turn to, friends to go to who understand, and that's good news.'

† Lighten our darkness we beseech thee O Lord, and by your great mercy defend us from all perils and dangers of this night; for the love of your Son, our saviour, Jesus Christ. (Compline, *Book of Common Prayer*)

November

Treasures of darkness

Philip Wadham

Life and death at sea

Fishing off the west coast of Canada's Vancouver Island is a risky way to make a living. When Don had left the dock in Ucluelet the sea had been calm; now, eight hours later and far off shore, the waves were large and powerful and Don's small boat took on water and started to sink. As he abandoned ship, Don hoped that his radioed distress call had been heard.

In my distress I called upon the LORD;
to my God I cried for help.
From his temple he heard my voice,
and my cry to him reached his ears . . .
He reached down from on high, he took me;
he drew me out of mighty waters

(verses 6 and 16)

After two hours bouncing around in his small life raft, Don heard the sound of an engine. He recognised the approaching boat, larger than his and skippered by a neighbour. Pulled from the sea, he thanked his friend, and God, for his rescue.

Telling his story at church on Sunday he saw that Mary was weeping – her story was similar but with a different, tragic ending. Her brother Brian had perished when his boat had capsized in huge seas. Later, she explained: 'I too thank God for your rescue, Don, but I'm still grieving over my brother's death. I know that not even death can separate us from God's love (Romans 8:38-39) and I sincerely believe that, but I still feel pain at the loss of Brian.'

† Gracious God, may the light of Christ's abiding love shine through us as we reach out to those who grieve, and the lonely, the sick and the dying.

November

Philip Wadham

Treasures of darkness

Job 38:1-21

Grandmothers

Toronto, Canada. Stephen Lewis, for some years the United Nations Special Envoy for HIV/AIDS in Africa, was speaking to a large gathering of women. From his travels in Africa he described some of the suffering he had seen. 'In Africa as many as 13 million children have been orphaned by AIDS. Africa has become a continent of orphans. Grandmothers bury their own adult children and then step into the breach, caring for the orphaned children left behind. These courageous women, who have no time to grieve and limited financial resources, have become the heart of the response to AIDS in Africa.'

'Where is the way of the dwelling of light,
and where is the place of darkness?'

(verse 19)

Out of concern for these grandmothers, the 'Grandmother to Grandmother Campaign' was born. Grandmothers in Canada reach out to these grand-mothers in Africa, raising funds to support their immediate needs: food, transport, home visits, medical care, adequate housing, school fees and uniforms for orphans – and money to purchase coffins to give loved ones a dignified burial.

The story of Job examines the question of why people suffer. It rejects the view that suffering is the result of personal sin. Job rightly denies the accusation that he is the cause of his own misfortune. The Christian response to sickness must never be to lay blame or point accusing fingers, but to bring relief and comfort to the sufferer, to be a way of light in a dark place, exactly like these grandmothers in Africa and Canada.

---

† Pray today for all who are affected by AIDS, especially those known to you. Pray for the sick and the dying, for orphaned children and those who care for them. Lord in your compassion, hear my prayer.

Treasures of darkness

Philip Wadham

Thursday 2 December
Isaiah 45:1-7

God, who is One

This was the first time Ben had gone door to door asking for money, but he felt the cause was a good one: 'Christian Aid', a relief and development group based in England, funded a variety of projects in poor countries. Those who responded with a donation generally said very little. At one house the man commented, 'Christian Aid! Well, will you accept an offering from a Jew?' A question that of course required no response but thanks.

At another house Ben had a longer conversation. The man wanted to hear about some of the projects that the Christian group supported and whether any conditions were attached to the grants. Were they just a cover to get people to go to church? The man explained: 'I am a Muslim and in the country where I was born there is at times tension between Christians and non-Christians. Sometimes it's a tension that turns violent. That can't be right, can it?' Again the question needed no reply. The man continued, 'It sounds like the group you're collecting for is doing good work, with no strings attached. I'll support that, so please accept this donation, and may God, who is One, bless our work.'

> Thus says the LORD to his anointed, to Cyrus,
> whose right hand I have grasped . . .
> I call you by your name,
> I surname you though you do not know me.
> I am the LORD, and there is no other.

(part of verses 1 and 4)

† Lord, may I always have an open mind so that I may see your works and recognise your servants wherever and whoever they may be.

Philip Wadham

Treasures of darkness

December

Psalm 139:7-18

A mountain to climb

Ryan was born with cerebral palsy, a condition where the brain has been damaged and bodily movement is affected. Unable to walk any distance, he is confined to a wheelchair and unable to take part in school sports. But he had a dream.

[E]ven the darkness is not dark to you;
the night is as bright as the day,
for darkness is as light to you.'

(Psalm 139:12)

Each year members of the grade 11 class (aged 16 and 17) climbed Mount Albert Edward on Canada's Vancouver Island. It's an ambitious and difficult climb, so when Ryan asked, 'Is a trip like this ever possible for me?' the teacher in charge had to think long and hard. It might just be possible if the climbing group worked together and there was equipment to assist Ryan.

With help from various sources a sled was built for Ryan and the members of the group, both students and accompanying adults, hauled it up the mountain, still snow covered in early spring. It was a long, hard climb and not without some moments of danger when the sled almost tipped, but the group was persistent. Ryan had insisted that he reach the summit walking so, lifted out of his sled and supported by two teachers, he shuffled the final 20 metres to reach his goal. On reaching it he raised his arms high with the joy of success. Even difficult challenges can be conquered as people of all abilities work together for good.

† God of healing power, as your Son reached out to the disabled of his day may we too be a light to those who face the challenges of disability. Amen

Treasures of darkness

Philip Wadham

December

Mother and child

As long as she could remember she had been afraid of the dark. When she was very young, sleeping next to her mother had been a comfort in the darkness, but now she was five and in her own bed in her own bedroom and she cried in the dark.

Mum, always thoughtful, had a solution: she put a candle on a table next to Jenny, beside a small statue of a mother holding her child's hand, a girl just like her. As she drifted towards sleep her eyes, half open, sought the assurance of the lighted candle and she slept.

> *You who live in the shelter of the Most High,*
> *who abide in the shadow of the Almighty,*
> *will say to the LORD, 'My refuge and my fortress;*
> *my God, in whom I trust' . . .*
> *under his wings you will find refuge . . .*
> *You will not fear the terror on the night.*

(verses 1-2, and part of verses 4-5)

At church Jenny saw a much larger statue of a mother and her child; candles had been lit and placed in front of it. She asked her mother why the statue needed candles. 'They are lit by people who want to remember someone they love. They are a way of saying "Thank you" to God.' Jenny thought for a while. 'Do you think that the baby the lady is holding was afraid of the dark?' 'Perhaps he was,' said mum, 'but I'm sure the light from the candle would have comforted him, just as it comforts you.'

---

† Give us light in the night season, we beseech you, O Lord, and grant that our rest may be without sin, and our waking to your service. (Compline, *Book of Common Prayer*)

Philip Wadham   Treasures of darkness

Treasures of darkness

2   God leads the Israelites in darkness

Notes based on the *New Revised Standard Version* by
Philip Wadham

For Philip's biography see p. 336.

Sunday 5 December: Preparing for the week

Throughout Israel's wanderings, God leads the people at
night, through the dark; speaks to Abraham, Moses and many others at
night, often in dreams; and many of the most significant events of the
Hebrew scriptures – such as the crossing of the Red Sea and the giving of
the law on Sinai – take place at night, in mysterious darkness.

Text for the week: *Psalm 77:11*

*I will call to mind the deeds of the Lord; I will remember your deeds
of old.*

For group discussion and personal thought

• Think of a time when you have wrestled with a difficult decision.
What helped you in making your choice?
• Some Bible stories paint a cruel picture of God (e.g. 1 Samuel 15:2-3; 2
Samuel 6:1-7). How do you equate this with 'God who is love'?

Genesis 15:12-21

Child soldier

The story Alexander told shocked the group listening to him. He was just thirteen when he had been seized at night by men with guns in his village in Africa. Both his parents were killed that night. At the camp where these murderers took him he found other boys and learned over the next few days that he, like them, was expected to be a child soldier and kill as they killed. In the camp he was treated cruelly and he knew that if he didn't do as he was told he too would be killed. 'It was like being in hell,' he said.

As the sun was going down, a deep sleep fell upon Abram, and a deep and terrifying darkness descended upon him. Then the LORD said to Abram, 'Know this for certain, that your offspring shall be aliens in a land not theirs, and shall be slaves there.'

(verse 12, and part of verse 13)

Alexander was silent for a while, clearly reliving the horror of those times. One of the group broke the silence. 'But you escaped and you're here in Canada.'

Alexander told of how, one night, he and two other boys ran off and wandered in the bush for three days until, by chance, they met someone who directed them to a camp for refugees, where they would be safe. He arrived in Canada five years later, an orphan refugee sponsored by a Canadian Christian organisation. 'The darkness of those awful times is still very painful but I'm learning, with the help of friends, to build a new life.'

† Pray for all children who face terrible cruelty and give thanks for all who work to free them from it. Lord, hear my prayer.

Philip Wadham   Treasures of darkness

Genesis 32:22-32

Wrestling with God

Philip couldn't sleep. At first he tossed and turned in bed but then, realising he was disturbing his wife, he left the bedroom and sat at the kitchen table; but the thoughts he had been wrestling with earlier were still there. Recently retired from a parish in Ontario, Canada, he had learned that in Guyana, South America, there were few clergy and he wondered how he might help. There were many things to consider. If he worked there he would need to support himself and for two years he would be far from his children and grandchildren. In conversation with Adri, his wife, he found she was clearly not pleased with the idea. So here he was, wrestling with what to do.

> *A man wrestled with [Jacob] until daybreak. Then he said, 'Let me go for the day is breaking'. But Jacob said, 'I will not let you go unless you bless me. So he said to him, 'What is your name?' And he said, 'Jacob'. Then the man said, 'You shall no longer be called Jacob, but Israel, for you have striven with God and with humans, and have prevailed.'*

(part of verses 24, 26-28)

At an orientation programme they met with others considering work with a church outside Canada and learned about the countries they could go to and the people they would meet. At the end of the course Adri surprised Philip. 'Let's do it,' she said. 'The woman who had worked overseas spoke of the friends she had made and her sadness when it came to leaving. She talked of hardships but she experienced joy. Let's go.'

† As we wrestle with daily challenges, keep us always aware of your presence with us, Lord.

Treasures of darkness   Philip Wadham

A common interest

It was a poverty that Adri had not seen before. In Georgetown, Guyana, the local government sold small parcels of land at very low cost to poor families. Clem's house was no more than a shack, one room with a curtain dividing the living and sleeping areas. She shared this space with her two young children.

Adri and Clem met out running, they talked and became friends. Sitting at a table in her home, Clem shared her story with Adri. She had lived with a man, the father of her two children, but unemployment, drugs and alcohol had taken their toll. Returning home drunk late at night, he became violent. She feared for herself and her children and knew that this dark and dangerous situation had to change.

> [T]here was dense darkness in all the land of Egypt for three days. People could not see one another, and for three days they could not move from where they were; but all the Israelites had light where they lived.

> (part of verse 22, and verse 23)

One day she gathered a few belongings and, with her children in tow, left him, finding temporary shelter in a friend's already crowded home. A small deposit had secured her the land where she and Adri sat talking.

Adri asked, 'With two children, how do you support yourself?' 'The children go to school in the mornings and sometimes after lunch to a neighbour's. I work as a gardener, the running keeps me fit for my work and I earn enough for us to live on. It's not an easy life but I'll always do the best I can for my children.'

---

† Pray for the victims of addiction, for the addicted and for their families. Lord, hear my prayer

Philip Wadham   Treasures of darkness

Exodus 14:19-31

Sad story

Philip liked to tell the epic Old Testament stories; the crossing of the Red Sea was a favourite. On this Sunday morning in his Georgetown church he had a responsive audience – lots of children – and Philip was a good storyteller. He acted out Moses standing tall with outstretched arms as the waters parted, then walking across with the Israelites between walls of water. Fearful of being caught, his outstretched arms brought the waters back again to kill the pursuers. 'And the people were free!' shouted Philip.

> [T]he cloud was there with the darkness, and it lit up the night . . . The Israelites went into the sea on dry ground . . . The waters returned and covered . . . the entire army of Pharaoh that had followed them into the sea, not one of them remained . . . Thus the Lord saved Israel that day.

(parts of verses 20, 22, 28 and 30)

At the end of the story the congregation responded, 'Amen. Hallelujah!' All except one small girl, Anika, who was crying. 'No need to cry,' comforted Philip, 'the people were safe.' 'I know they were safe,' protested Anika, 'but that's not why I'm crying. I'm crying because all those Egyptian soldiers died. Didn't they matter, and what about their families, their wives and children? I'm crying because it's a sad story. Didn't God care about them?'

Philip was taken aback, not sure how to respond. And then, 'Thank you, Anika, it is a sad story, and you are right to cry about it. And you know what, I believe that God was crying too.'

---

† Impartial God, may we always remember that your love is for all people and help us to love even our enemies.

Treasures of darkness

Philip Wadham

Helping hand

Adri and Clem's common interest in running quickly grew into a valued friendship and Adri looked for ways to help. With Clem working long hours, Adri sometimes looked after the children and became like a grandmother to them. Clem never asked Adri for money but Adri looked for ways to make Clem's life easier.

As a gardener much of Clem's time was spent cutting grass and weeds. She did this by hand, using a machete. One evening, talking together, Adri made a suggestion: 'If you had a motorised grass trimmer your job would be easier, faster and you could have more customers.' 'I've thought of that,' replied Clem, 'but I can't afford to buy one and I won't borrow money. The money lenders here are crooks.' 'Then let me buy a machine. You can rent it from me and eventually you'll own it.' Clem, reluctant at first, agreed and a deal was struck.

Six months later and with increased custom, Clem had repaid Adri's 'loan'. She carefully guarded her new machine not just to prevent it being stolen but because it represented a valued friendship, a shared trust and life becoming easier, lighter.

These words the Lord spoke with a loud voice . . . out of the fire, the cloud and the thick darkness . . . He wrote them on two stone tablets, and gave them to [Moses].

(part of verse 22)

The Jewish rabbi (teacher) Hillel, who lived just before the time of Jesus, was a scholarly and wise man. When asked by a non-Jew to recite the Jewish law, which has 613 rules, whilst standing on one leg, he replied, 'Do not unto your neighbour what you would not have done to you; this is the whole Law, the rest is commentary.'

† Gracious God, may we always be aware that as we care for our neighbour we are loving you.

Philip Wadham   Treasures of darkness

Advent candles

St Albans, in Georgetown, Guyana, was a large building, 'modern' fifty years ago but now showing its age. Lack of funds had delayed repairs over the years and whatever former glory it had was now much faded. It looked uncared for and Philip was determined that this should change. He reminded the people that God's house should reflect the glory of God and challenged them: 'This Christmas Eve let's make this church shine.'

For the two weeks before Christmas, St Albans was a hive of activity: donated paint brightened up the walls, windows were washed and repaired, pews were varnished, floors swept and the banners and hangings cleaned. On Christmas Eve flowers were placed on window sills and the transformation was complete.

> Then Solomon said,
> 'The LORD has said that he would dwell in thick darkness.
> I have built you an exalted house,
> a place for you to dwell in for ever.'

(verses 12-13)

By 10pm the church was full and a grand procession signalled the start of the Eucharist for the birth of the Christ Child. Then, ten minutes into the service, complete darkness – a power cut, not uncommon in Georgetown. Candles were lit and placed around the church and within five minutes worship was resumed.

The effort made to clean and decorate St Albans was largely lost but in the candlelight something remarkable happened. As people's eyes grew accustomed to the candlelight, the church seemed to become brighter. Someone commented to Philip afterwards, 'It seemed as though there was a holy glow in the darkness' – as indeed there must have been in that stable in Bethlehem 2000 years ago.

† In the light of the Advent candle may we see the light of Christ.

Treasures of darkness   Philip Wadham

Treasures of darkness

3 Darkness in Jesus' life, death and resurrection

Notes based on the *New Revised Standard Version* by
Philip Wadham

For Philip's biography see p. 346.

Sunday 12 December: Preparing for the week

The psalms speak of God as one clothed in deep darkness,
and use the image of the 'shadow' of the Almighty to evoke the protective,
hidden place in which the disciple shelters under the divine providence.
The New Testament continues this tradition: the Holy Spirit 'overshadows'
Mary, and many of the most significant events associated with the birth
of Jesus take place at night. And of course, God submits himself to dwell
in Mary's womb – an utterly dark space, which is echoed at the crucifixion
when darkness covers the earth, and the dark space of the tomb in which
Jesus rests.

Text for the week: *Luke 1:38*

*Mary said, 'Here am I, the servant of the Lord; let it be with me according
to your word.'*

For group discussion and personal thought

• Cornelius (Acts 10:1-2) is described as a man who 'prayed constantly'.
  What do you think this means and what was Pedro saying about prayer
  (Wednesday)?

• Jesus' resurrection was a real event in history but how do we see
  the reality of resurrection around us today? (Friday may help.)

Opening night

The Church of the Holy Trinity in downtown Toronto, Canada, has presented 'The Christmas Story' every Advent since 1937. Choral music, scripture readings and mime combine to re-enact the beloved story of the birth of Jesus.

Over many years, Joanna had worked her way through the ranks – first as an angel, then a young shepherd, and now, this year, selected to play Mary. She was both pleased and fearful, so much depended on her. What if she was so nervous she let them down?

At rehearsals she was fine and Susan, the director, praised her, but this was the opening night and a large audience. How would she fare?

The angel said to her, 'Do not be afraid, Mary, for you have found favour with God . . . you will . . . bear a son, and you will name him Jesus . . . Mary said, 'Here am I, the servant of the Lord.'

(verse 30, and parts of verses 31 and 38)

It was dark as Joanna made her way onto the stage and there were objects she needed to avoid. In the darkness, she cautiously manoeuvred herself into position and, standing still, waited for the stage lights to be raised. Their brightness hid the audience so that all she was aware of was the light and the narrator's voice. 'Do not be afraid,' she heard, and she wasn't. Instead she was Mary hearing these words. She felt at ease and her performance shone.

Afterwards Susan praised her. 'Well done, Joanna. No first night nerves?' 'Well yes, a few,' she said, and added, 'but not as many as the real Mary must have felt on her opening night.'

† Always present God, in dark times help us to hear your voice saying, 'Do not be afraid.'

Treasures of darkness

Philip Wadham

Christ Child

Susan, the director of 'The Christmas Story', was insistent that a baby should be used to represent the Christ Child. One evening, 90 minutes before the pageant was due to begin, Susan received a phone call from a regretful mother. 'Sorry Susan, but baby Michael is sick.' With such short notice what could be done?

The Church of the Holy Trinity is next to a large shopping centre, a busy place at Christmas. 'Surely out there among the shoppers is a baby Jesus,' said Susan. 'Let's go look.' With Joanna, Mary in the pageant, they searched among the crowd for the 'baby Jesus'. They approached Alison and Mark, with Kylie, their eight-month-old firstborn. At first the parents hesitated but, assured that the request was legitimate and that Kylie would be safe, they agreed to Susan's request. Kylie would be the Christ Child.

[T]he shepherds said to one another, 'Let us go now to Bethlehem and see this thing that has taken place, which the Lord has made known to us.' So they went with haste and found Mary and Joseph, and the child lying in the manger.

(part of verse 15, and verse 16)

On stage, with Kylie on her knee, Mary welcomed the visitors. There were shepherds of all ages, with dirty faces and ragged clothes, staring down at Kylie. Alison, in the wings with Mark, was nervous about their daughter's reaction to these strangers, but there was no need for her anxiety. She squeezed Mark's hand. 'Look,' she whispered, 'Kylie is smiling and laughing.'

---

† Present God, in the face of a stranger give us eyes to recognise the Christ Child.

Philip Wadham   Treasures of darkness

Praying together

Bishop Adrian had told Andrew, a Canadian missionary newly arrived in Ecuador, South America, 'In your first month I want you to visit villages along the Napo river. I want a man from each to train as their pastor.'

In preparation for his first visit Andrew met with Pedro, an experienced priest who drew him a map of the six communities they would visit. On the first day of their trip, Andrew thought of the job ahead of him. 'Just how do I do this?' he asked himself. In late afternoon they arrived at Bella Vista, were warmly welcomed and shared a meal. Tomorrow there would be a meeting but now it was night and time to rest, except that Andrew needed to talk with Pedro. 'I am confused,' he confessed. 'How do I do what the bishop asks? I need some help, some guidance.'

Now during those days [Jesus] went out to the mountain to pray; and he spent the night in prayer to God. And when day came, he called his disciples and chose twelve of them, whom he also named apostles.

(verses 12-13)

For almost two hours Pedro and Andrew talked. Pedro described previous visits he and Bishop Adrian had made, the people they had met, their enthusiasm to have a school and church in their village. Pedro talked about the leaders in each community who might also be good pastors. Then he yawned. 'Andrew, I'm tired. Let's talk some more tomorrow. I need to sleep.' 'Of course,' replied Andrew, 'but shouldn't we say a prayer together first?' Pedro corrected him: 'Actually, Andrew, I think that's what we've been doing all the while we talked.'

† Listening God, accept all the prayers we offer to you – our thoughts, our concerns, our conversations, ourselves.

Treasures of darkness   Philip Wadham

Luke 23:33, 44-49

An innocent man

For five days each month six men, one from each village along the Napo river, came to the study centre in Tena, Ecuador. Training to be pastors in their community, they studied the gospel. In Luke they read the story of Jesus, his trial, torture and crucifixion.

When they came to the place that is called The Skull, they crucified Jesus . . . It was now about noon, and darkness came over the whole land . . . Then Jesus, crying with a loud voice, said, 'Father, into your hands I commend my spirit.' Having said this, he breathed his last.

(part of verses 33 and 44, and verse 46)

Andrew, leading the study, said, 'This is what happened to an innocent man 2000 years ago. Are innocent people killed today?'

Alcides, from Colonia Babaoyo, was the first to speak. 'I think of Archbishop Oscar Romero who was murdered in El Salvador in 1980 because he protested all the killing that was going on there. Each Sunday, on the radio, he read out the names of people killed that week, good people who were working to make life better for the poor in El Salvador. Those in power had them killed just like the powerful ones had Jesus killed. They were all innocent people.' He paused, then added, 'I wonder, do you think there was darkness when they were killed?'

Carlos spoke for many of them: 'Maybe there was darkness for a while. There's always darkness for a while when a good person dies. But the light of their lives still shines. The darkness can't kill that' (John 1:5).

---

† God of justice, we give thanks for all who in their lives have prayed 'Your kingdom come, on earth' and have worked to make this real.

Philip Wadham   Treasures of darkness

Luke 23:50-56

Lights in the darkness

Andrew commented, 'You're right, Carlos. Those days when Jesus was killed and Archbishop Romero was murdered were dark days. Was there any light at that time?' Pedro responded, 'On Holy Friday (Good Friday) there was Joseph.'

> Now there was a good and righteous man named Joseph, who, though a member of the council, had not agreed to their plan and action . . . This man went to Pilate and asked for the body of Jesus. Then he took it down [from the cross], wrapped it in a linen cloth, and laid it in a rock-hewn tomb.
>
> (verse 50, part of verse 51, verse 52, and part of verse 53)

'Joseph believed that what the powerful people had planned was wrong, but he wasn't able to stop them. He really cared for Jesus and that's like lighting a candle in the darkness, isn't it?'

Mariana, who worked at the centre and was sitting in the group, agreed. 'Those women too, who prepared Jesus' body. They were lighting candles in the darkness, weren't they?'

> The women who had come with [Jesus] from Galilee followed, and they saw the tomb and how his body was laid . . . and prepared spices and ointments.
>
> (verse 55, and part of verse 56)

Alcides spoke: 'I remember seeing a photo of Archbishop Romero's funeral. It was in the cathedral in San Salvador. All around the church there were candles, hundreds of them lighting up the place. It was a dark time for the people, but these candles were signs, signs from hundreds of people that the darkness wouldn't defeat them.'

† Ever present God, in times of deep darkness may our hope be in you and your love to light our way forward.

Treasures of darkness   Philip Wadham

Resurrection

At the centre there was a small library and, early next morning, Alcides was looking through the shelves. Today he was leading the worship that began each day. When they had gathered round a burning candle on a small table, he began. 'Yesterday we read about Jesus' death and burial and talked about it, but we know it's not the end of the story. Listen to this.'

> Jesus said to her, 'Woman, why are you weeping? For whom are you looking?' . . . [S]he said to him, 'Sir, if you have carried him away, tell me where you have laid him' . . . Jesus said to her, 'Mary!' She turned and said to him . . . 'Teacher!'

(parts of verses 15-16)

'That's what happened 2000 years ago and it's still true.'

Carlos said he didn't understand what Alcides meant. 'I took this book out of the library,' explained Alcides. 'It's about Archbishop Romero, the things he said. He knew that his life was in danger. He said so to a reporter two weeks before he was killed. Listen: "I have often been threatened with death. I have to say, as a Christian, I do not believe in death without resurrection. If they succeed in killing me they will be wasting their time. A bishop will die, but God's church, which is the people, will never perish." What that says to me is that Romero's struggle for a fairer, more caring world didn't end with his death. It continues to rise again as people share in that goal, which was Romero's and which was Jesus'.'

---

† Called by our Easter faith to be witnesses to the resurrected Christ, may our lives of love and service be a light to others.

Treasures of darkness

4   Riches hidden in secret places

Notes based on the *New Revised Standard Version* by
Philip Wadham

For Philip's biography see p. 336.

Sunday 19 December: Preparing for the week

Jesus' parables use images drawn from the natural world
– the darkness of the underground soil, the hiddenness of things being
buried and so on – to speak of the mystery of the kingdom. The notes for
these last days before Christmas focus on searching; on Christmas Day we
find again what we have been searching for – or perhaps God finds us.

Text for the week: *Matthew 13:45-46*

*[Jesus said] 'The kingdom of heaven is like a merchant in search of fine
pearls; on finding one pearl of great value, he went and sold all that he
had and bought it.'*

For group discussion and personal thought

• Jesus used illustrations familiar to people of his time to describe the
kingdom of heaven. Beginning 'The kingdom of heaven is like . . .', think
of an example that will help people in your community understand
the idea.

• What, for you, is the central message of Christmas and how do you
respond to it?

In the end, God

'But it's all such hard work', commented Gabriel as Alcides finished speaking. 'We all honour what Archbishop Romero did, and the way he inspires people. Alcides is right, he does live again in the people who work to make things better. But it would be so much easier if God simply came in and did it for us.'

Carlos nodded in agreement. 'I listened once to a missionary who visited our village. He told us that in the end God will change everything. He knew lots of Bible verses, he read them to us and said that the end was coming very soon.'

Nebuchadnezzar dreamed such dreams that his spirit was troubled . . . The king said to Daniel . . . 'Are you able to tell me the dream that I have seen and its interpretation?' Daniel answered the king . . . 'there is a God in heaven who reveals mysteries . . . what will happen at the end of days.'

(part of verses 1 and 26-28)

'And in the meantime, what did the missionary say you should be doing?' asked Alcides. 'He said that we shouldn't be worried,' replied Carlos, 'but I am worried. I have a family to care for and when my son is sick I worry because there is no one in our health clinic and the hospital is far away. That's wrong.' Others in the room agreed and added their own concerns.

It was left to Alcides to close the conversation. 'I'm content to leave the future in God's hands. Meanwhile we live in the present. We know some things are wrong but God can use our hands to change them.'

---

† Victorious God, use our hands in the present to help build the future that you intend.

Philip Wadham   Treasures of darkness

Fish pond

The main house at the centre was surrounded by a large garden, for which Mariana was responsible. Food grown in the garden was used in the kitchen to feed the students and staff. In one corner of the garden was a large pond and twelve months ago it had been stocked with small fish. It was Mariana's 'project' and she had fed them regularly, insisting that they needed good food in order to grow. Though a few had died, many of those left were now large enough to be harvested.

[Jesus said,] 'The kingdom of heaven is like a mustard seed that someone took and sowed in his field; it is the smallest of all the seeds, but when it has grown it is the greatest of shrubs and becomes a tree, so that the birds of the air come and make nests in its branches'.

(verses 31-32)

At dinner that evening, Carlos was asked to give the blessing over the meal. He looked at what had been prepared. There on the table were fresh tomatoes, beans and plantain, all from the garden. There was rice and, presented on a large dish, fried fish, more than sufficient for all. Carlos spoke: 'Mariana visited our village three months ago and spoke to us about her fish pond project. She said that with care and feeding the fish would grow and that they would be a reliable source of food. I wasn't convinced, but just look at this feast that's here. When I get back home I'll tell the others about this and we'll work together to follow Mariana's example. Let's pray.'

† For food, family and friends, and your word that helps us grow, we give thanks to God.

Treasures of darkness

Philip Wadham

A mixed bag

Sitting around the table eating the feast that Mariana had prepared, Andrew looked at the men. They were a diverse group.

Alcides was the eldest and not a native of the Napo region. He had been born and lived in southern Ecuador and had moved to Napo district when he and his neighbours were forced off their land. In Colonia Babaoyo, their village, they were more secure on their land but they remained as poor as before.

Carlos lived in Caspisapa, far down river. His wife, Teresita, and his two daughters tended their household and community garden while he earned some money by ferrying people and goods in a motorised canoe from villages to the larger towns.

Andrew wasn't sure how Gabriel earned money. He appeared to have a few small 'businesses', though Andrew had the wisdom not to enquire too closely what those were.

Pedro had been a pastor for a number of years and lived next to his church in Tena and received a small salary. He, like all those sitting around the table, was no saint, at least not in the conventional sense, but their commitment to Christ was genuine. 'A bit like those first disciples', thought Andrew.

[Jesus said,] 'Again, the kingdom of heaven is like a net that was thrown into the sea and caught fish of every kind; when it was full, they drew it ashore, sat down, and put the good into the baskets but threw out the bad.'

(verses 47-48)

† Ever present God, as Jesus called his first disciples to 'follow me' so you have called each one of us. As they responded we have responded. Help us to follow faithfully, in easy times and hard times, in light times and dark times.

Philip Wadham   Treasures of darkness

Searching

The fifth and final day of their course ended mid-morning with a Eucharist. With the group gathered around a table on which bread would be broken and wine shared, Pedro asked, 'When you lead worship on Sunday what will you say about these last five days?'

Carlos, always hungry, said, 'I'll tell them about the feast that we had yesterday, and I'll say that when Christmas is over we should all start digging that pond.'

Gabriel said, 'I'll light lots of candles on the altar and talk about the light of Christ that's coming into the world. That's what Christmas is about, isn't it!'

Alcides agreed. 'That's right' he said 'but there's some darkness too. Those shepherds, there in the darkness of the night when, all of a sudden there was light all around them. The angels said, "Jesus is born", so God broke through their darkness to bring light. God searched for these ordinary people to tell them good news, he found them and lit up their darkness.'

> *[Jesus said,] 'What woman having ten silver coins, if she loses one of them, does not light a lamp, sweep the house, and search carefully until she finds it?'*

(verse 8)

'That's right, Alcides', said Pedro. 'God searched out those shepherds, but the shepherds also had to do some searching. They chose to walk through the darkness searching for the Christ Child. That's what we do when come here. We're like those shepherds, seeking the Christ Child. This bread, this wine and this light tell us that he has found us.'

---

† O Lord, you have searched me and known me. You know when I sit down and when I rise up; you discern my thoughts from far away. Keep me ever faithful to you. (Psalm 139:1-2)

Treasures of darkness

Philip Wadham

December

Readings in Matthew 1–3

Emmanuel, God is with us

Notes based on the *New International Version* by
Corneliu Constantineanu

Corneliu Constantineanu is a Romanian Christian educator and pastor. He is Associate Professor and Academic Dean at the Evangelical Theological Seminary in Osijek, Croatia and the Executive Director of the Areopagus Centre for Christian Studies and Contemporary Culture in Timisoara, Romania. Corneliu is married to Ioana and they have two daughters, Anamaria and Carmen.

Preparing for the week

The biblical reflections for the Christmas season focus on one of the greatest and most hopeful truths for humankind. In the midst of our present circumstances of life, no matter how difficult they may appear, we receive the word of comfort and hope: God is with us! And it brings hope as God gives an unshakeable assurance that he is for us and with us, and desires to give us life: true, meaningful and abundant life.

Text for the week: *Matthew 1:22-23*

All this took place to fulfil what the Lord had said through the prophet: 'The virgin will be with child and will give birth to a son, and they will call him Immanuel' – which means, 'God with us.'

For group discussion and personal thought

- In a world that either rejects God or thinks of him as distant and uninvolved with his creation, how would you share the wonderful truth that 'God is with us' with others to give them a real sense of this most amazing and hopeful news?
- How does the reality of Jesus being 'with us' change the way you think, speak and act in your everyday life?

Matthew 1:1-17

God at work in history

The story of God's intervention in human history did not begin with Jesus; it began long before that in God's plan to redeem a fallen world. Probably no other text shows this as clearly as today's reading, which is,

> A record of the genealogy of Jesus Christ son of David, the son of Abraham.

(verse 1)

This genealogy has several interesting and revealing features. On the one hand it points to the important figures in the history of God's redemption, such as Abraham and King David, culminating in the centre around which the entire history revolves, Jesus Christ. This is indeed an important aspect of Matthew's retelling of his story: God was at work in human history; there were key events and people in this history; and its climax is the birth, life, death and resurrection of the Messiah. Matthew points to this truth again and again in his Gospel with the formula: 'and this is a fulfilment of'.

On the other hand, the genealogy reveals another significant and encouraging fact: in the history of God's redemption of the world it is not only great and unique heroes who have a role; ordinary people, men and women, also play a key role in the chain of events. This is extremely encouraging for all of us, especially in our age of celebrity idols who seem to be our only heroes. Matthew shows that anyone can be a channel of God's grace to the world, an instrument of God for the healing and salvation of our broken world.

† Lord, we thank you for all the simple and unimportant people you have used for your purposes throughout history, and we ask that we may also become your instruments to proclaim the good news to a needy world.

Readings in Matthew · Corneliu Constantineanu

December

Matthew 1:18-25

God with us

There can be no greater way to celebrate Christmas than to be reminded of the great truth this holiday represents, that God is with us! That we are saved from our sins and that Jesus, God incarnate, is the absolute proof of God's presence with us:

All this took place to fulfil what the Lord had said through the prophet: 'The virgin will be with child and will give birth to a son, and they will call him Immanuel' – which means, 'God with us.'

(verses 22-23)

We are left in no doubt that the birth of Jesus among us, this remarkable intervention in human history, was totally an act of God. God's decision to be 'with us' was nothing to do with us or our merits. It was God's sole decision and intention to rescue us and come to our aide. God surprised us with his grace, with his coming and living among us, as the apostle John puts it: 'the Word became flesh and made his dwelling among us . . . full of grace and truth' (John 1:14).

Today is Christmas and we have a glimpse into the nature and beauty of our God, into his grace and love – a God who renounces his own prerogatives and becomes a human person in order to save. Praise the Lord! God is with us!

† Dear God, we are so grateful for your amazing love and the wonderful display of your grace. We praise you and give you all the glory today when we celebrate your coming.

Matthew 2:1-12

The appropriate response: worship

The visit of the Magi from the east, their gifts of gold, incense and myrrh, and, especially, their bowing down in worship before the newborn Jesus, represent the most appropriate response to God's offer of salvation. Such a response may appear obvious to us, but clearly this was not the case: 'When King Herod heard this he was disturbed, and all Jerusalem with him' (verse 3). However, this did not hinder the Magi in their search for the newborn king and their worship of him as the only true God:

> *On coming to the house, they saw the child with his mother Mary, and they bowed down and worshipped him. Then they opened their treasures and presented him with gifts of gold and of incense and of myrrh.*

(verse 11)

When someone finds the true God, nothing can stand in the way. No amount of difficulties, scares, or even 'diabolic' plans, can deter someone from the worship of God. Yes, there may be, and most probably are, various attempts at intimidation by the powers that be, but ultimately nothing and no one can change the decision to do the right thing. And this is the wonderful lesson we learn from the Magi: the determination and persistence to respond appropriately to God's coming in this world by worship and adoration.

† Our heavenly Father, we worship and adore you for who you are and for what you have done. And we thank you that you make it possible for us to continue our worship despite the difficult circumstances of our life.

Readings in Matthew   Corneliu Constantineanu

Matthew 2:13-18

Rejection and rebellion at God's coming

Of course, not everyone bowed down and worshipped the true God. King Herod perfectly illustrated a common response to God's coming: rejection and rebellion. As a king, he had become so used to his great power and authority that, when confronted with a greater reality, he refused to accept it. Not only did he personally reject God but he planned an act of rebellion that would frustrate God's plan.

When Herod realised that he had been outwitted by the Magi, he was furious, and he gave orders to kill all the boys in Bethlehem and its vicinity who were two years old and under, in accordance with the time he had learned from the Magi. Then what was said through the prophet Jeremiah was fulfilled:
'A voice is heard in Ramah,
weeping and great mourning,
Rachel weeping for her children
and refusing to be comforted,
because they are no more.'

(verses 16-18)

Two things are clear from today's reading. First, no one can ultimately frustrate God's plan to save the world and put it to right. But a second, more painful lesson is that, through our rejection and rebellion against God, we can spread much suffering and pain. As Christians, as those who recognise the lordship of Christ, we have a duty to discern, unmask and resist any form of totalitarianism and absolutism, and to preserve the fundamental values of human life, based on God's intention and purposes for the redemption of the entire creation.

---

† Dear Lord, we ask you today to enable us to respond properly to your call of salvation and to give us strength to be your instruments for bringing truth, justice and hope to this world.

Corneliu Constantineanu

Readings in Matthew

God's providence and interventions

It is remarkable to read these stories of God speaking so clearly and directly to people as he guides them through difficult times:

After Herod died, an angel of the Lord appeared in a dream to Joseph in Egypt and said, 'Get up, take the child and his mother and go to the land of Israel, for those who were trying to take the child's life are dead.'

(verses 19-20)

Most of the time, we do not share in such encounters with the divine, which makes it easy to reject them. Such things may have happened in the past – rarely and in exceptional circumstances.

But the truth is that he does intervene, even though, in our increasingly secularised world, it is more and more difficult to believe in God's direct intervention. And yet we know for a fact that, as the Lord of history, nothing escapes God's control. Moreover, we know that he is also preoccupied with our everyday lives and that, in critical situations, he is always present with us.

This is probably the most encouraging word for us today: that this world belongs to God and that ultimately he will bring his purposes to completion. And also, he will answer our prayers and is concerned with every single detail of our lives.

† Heavenly Father, we thank you that in your providence you lead the destiny of the world, of the nations, that you are the Lord of history and that you also pay attention and intervene in our everyday life and guide us in your truth.

Readings in Matthew

Corneliu Constantineanu

December

367

Thursday 30 December

Matthew 3:1-12

'Repent, for the kingdom of heaven is near'

Our readings so far this week have focused on what God has done, his initiatives in the plan of redemption. Everything is from God and redemption can only start with God. Today's text, however, is a clear message addressed to people who should respond in a particular way to God's grace, by producing the fruits of repentance:

> In those days John the Baptist came, preaching in the Desert of Judea and saying, 'Repent, for the kingdom of heaven is near.' . . . But when he saw many of the Pharisees and Sadducees coming to where he was baptising, he said to them: 'You brood of vipers! Who warned you to flee from the coming wrath? Produce fruit in keeping with repentance.'

(verses 1-2 and 7-8)

John's words to the Pharisees and Sadducees may have made them stop and consider carefully the implications of acceptance into the kingdom of God. While God is the author of salvation, the believer who accepts God's invitation and enters the kingdom of God should live a radically new and transformed life – not in his or her own power and strength but with the power that comes from and is guaranteed by God, the Holy Spirit. The appropriate response to God's invitation and offer of salvation is repentance followed by a radically new life. And it is God, through his Holy Spirit, who gives us the grace and the power to respond and live adequately in the kingdom of God.

---

† Lord, forgive us if our lives have not always shown the fruits of repentance, and help us to be sensitive to the prompting of your Spirit within us, who enables us to live a renewed and transformed life.

Corneliu Constantineanu

Readings in Matthew

'This is my son, whom I love'

Suddenly, from the crowd coming to be baptised for repentance, someone appears who makes John the Baptist feel unworthy of the task. At first, he declines to baptise him, saying: 'I need to be baptised by you, and do you come to me?' (verse 14). John's reaction is both an expression of genuine humility and a sign of understanding who Jesus really is.

On his side, by asking to be baptised just like everyone else, Jesus shows an important aspect of his nature and confirms the practice of baptism as a vital symbol of entering and belonging to the kingdom of God. Then there is another remarkable happening:

As soon as Jesus was baptised, he went up out of the water. At that moment heaven was opened, and he saw the Spirit of God descending like a dove and lighting on him. And a voice from heaven said, 'This is my Son, whom I love; with him I am well pleased.'

(verses 16-17)

The divine nature of Jesus is doubly confirmed: the Spirit of God descending on Jesus shows the divine indwelling; and as the climax of the entire scene, God himself declares that Jesus, the one born in Bethlehem, is the very Son of God, is God incarnate. God with us! There is the news the world needs to hear: Jesus, the son of God, has redeemed this world and God is with us. And what a privilege for us to be ambassadors of Christ and carry out into the world this extraordinary, saving news.

† Lord, help us realise again and again your true nature and enable us to follow you wholeheartedly as we proclaim and embody the good news of redemption to the world.

Readings in Matthew   Corneliu Constantineanu

International Bible Reading Association

A worldwide service of Christian Education at work in five continents

HEADQUARTERS
1020 Bristol Road
Selly Oak
Birmingham, B29 6LB
UK

www.christianeducation.org.uk
ibra@christianeducation.org.uk

and the following agencies:

AUSTRALIA
UniChurch Books
130 Little Collins Street
Melbourne
VIC 3001

GHANA
Asempa Publishers
Christian Council of Ghana
Box GP 919
Accra

ymyesitso@yahoo.com

INDIA
All India Sunday School Association
Plot No 8,
Threemurthy Colony
6th Cross, Mahendra Hills
PB no 2099
Secunderabad – 500 026
Andhra Pradesh

sundayschoolindia@yahoo.co.in

Fellowship of Professional Workers
Samanvay
Deepthi Chambers
Vijayapuri
Hyderabad – 500 017
Andhra Pradesh
fellowship2u@gmail.com

NEW ZEALAND
Epworth Bookshop
157B Karori Road
Marsden Village
Karori
Wellington 6012

Mailing address:
PO Box 17255
Karori
Wellington 6147

sales@epworthbooks.org.nz

NIGERIA
David Hinderer House
The Cathedral Church of St David
Kudeti
Ibadan
PMB 5298 Dugbe
Ibadan
Oyo State

SOUTH AND CENTRAL AFRICA
IBRA South Africa
6 Roosmaryn Street
Durbanville 7550
biblereading@evmot.com

If you would like to advertise in *Light for our Path* please contact our **Marketing Department** at:

IBRA, 1020 Bristol Road,
Birmingham B29 6LB

telephone: 0121 415 2978
email: marketing@christianeducation.org.uk

All about IBRA

IBRA readings

The list of readings for the whole year is available to download from www.christianeducation. org.uk/ibra. You are welcome to make as many copies as you like.

IBRA books

Both extraordinary value at £8.50 each in the UK, with writers from around the world and many different Christian traditions.

IBRA samplers

From time to time IBRA publishes samplers using notes from *Light for our Path* and *Words for Today*, suitable for introducing new readers or for use with Bible study groups. Please contact us at the address below for availability.

IBRA Rep discount

If you live in the UK and purchase 6 or more copies of IBRA books, you can sign up as an IBRA Rep which entitles you to 10% discount off all your IBRA purchases. Just tick the IBRA Rep box on your order form and we'll do the rest.

IBRA International Fund

The IBRA International Fund enables the translation, printing and distribution of IBRA Bible notes and readings. For more details, see page 158. You can make a donation when ordering your books.

IBRA, 1020 Bristol Road, Selly Oak, Birmingham, B29 6LB, UK

IBRA themes for 2011

God still speaks
God's word at work in the world
Pay attention!

Attitudes to suffering
From anger to trust
Your will be done

Readings in Galatians
One gospel for all God's people
Freedom with the Holy Spirit

Marks of a successful church
Five marks of a successful church

Readings in Matthew (4–10)
Proclaiming the kingdom
Kingdom living
Healings

Mercy for sinners
God wants sinners to come to him
God's forgiveness is for everyone

Conversion and change
Power to change
Life transformed

Readings from Colossians
Christ in you, the hope of glory
Do everything in the name of the Lord Jesus

Living with Easter

Questions Jesus asked
Questions Jesus asked: in Mark
Questions Jesus asked: in Luke
Questions Jesus asked: in John

Imagination and creativity
Imaging the divine and the human
With the eyes of the heart
Jesus' imaginative teachings

Readings in Matthew (13–19)
Parables of thekingdom
Signs of the kingdom
Teaching of the kingdom

Marriage
Marriages good and bad
Marriage as metaphor

Readings in 1 Kings
Solomon and the temple
The demise of the kings
The prophetic ministry of Elijah

Openings and closings in the New Testament
Greetings and blessings

Readings in Matthew (20–25)
Going up to Jerusalem
Conflict
Signs at the end

Angels
Angels in the Old Testament
Angels in the New Testament

Prophecy of Jeremiah
Prophetic words in action
A prophetic life: memoirs
Chanting down oppressive nations

Trade between the nations

Gratitude
How to give thanks
What to give thanks for

Readings in Matthew (26–28)
Arrest
Trial

Salvation history
Salvation belongs to God
Salvation with a difference
Singing salvation
Salvation beyond boundaries

The good news

INTERNATIONAL BIBLE READING ASSOCIATION

1020 Bristol Road, Selly Oak, Birmingham B29 6LB, United Kingdom

You can order using this form or through your local IBRA rep, or online at http://shop. christianeducation.org.uk, or by email to sales@christianeducation.org.uk or by phone on 0121 472 4242

Please return this form to
IBRA, 1020 Bristol Road, Selly Oak, Birmingham B29 6LB

Order form for 2011 books

Name: _____

Address: _____

_____

_____

_____ Postcode: _____

Telephone number: _____

Postage is free. Please allow 28 days for delivery. Your order will be dispatched when all books are available. Payments in pounds sterling, please.

Code		Quantity	Price	Total
UK customers				
AA1021	Light for our Path 2011		£8.50	
AA1022	Words for Today 2011		£8.50	
	I am an IBRA Rep (see page 215)		10% off	
	I am ordering 6+ books and would like to become an IBRA Rep			
Europe				
AA1021	Light for our Path 2011		£11.50	
AA1022	Words for Today 2011		£11.50	
Rest of the world				
AA1021	Light for our Path 2011		£13.50	
AA1022	Words for Today 2011		£13.50	
			Subtotal	
		Donation to the IBRA International Fund		
			Total	

Please, tell us about yourself...:

Age: ☐ Under 30   ☐ 30-49

       ☐ 50-64   ☐ 65-80   ☐ Over 80

Gender: ☐ M   ☐ F

Denomination_____

Do you attend church?   ☐ Every Sunday   ☐ Frequently

                             ☐ Occasionally   ☐ Rarely

How long have you read IBRA? _____ years

Do you read the IBRA notes:

     ☐ Every day   ☐ Frequently

     ☐ When feel the need / time allows   ☐ Very occasionally

Would you like to see:	More	Same	Less
Whole OT Books / Gospel / Epistle	☐	☐	☐
Weeks using poetry	☐	☐	☐
Wide variety of writers	☐	☐	☐
Commentary rooted in personal experience	☐	☐	☐
Critique based on academic study	☐	☐	☐

Other comments

What national Christian periodicals do you look at?

☐ Reform magazine   ☐ Woman Alive

☐ Methodist Recorder   ☐ Families First (Home and Family)

☐ Magnet   ☐ Christianity magazine

☐ Baptist Times   ☐ Universe

☐ Church Times   ☐ Third Way

Other _____

THANK YOU